The Chinese Cookbook

Books by Craig Claiborne

The Chinese Cookbook

Craig Claiborne
&
Virginia Lee

Drawings by Barbra and Roderick Wells

J. B. LIPPINCOTT COMPANY
Philadelphia and New York

Some of the recipes in this book have appeared in *The Christian Science Monitor, Harper's Bazaar, House and Garden, House Beautiful,* and the *Ladies' Home Journal.*

First printing 25,000 copies September 1972
Second printing 9,750 copies November 1972
Third printing 10,000 copies November 1972
Fourth printing 4,140 copies December 1974
Fifth printing 5,050 copies June 1975
Sixth printing 22,500 copies June 1976
Seventh printing 12,500 copies January 1977
Eighth printing 10,000 copies June 1977
Ninth printing 15,000 copies June 1978

U.S. Library of Congress Cataloging in Publication Data

Claiborne, Craig.
  The Chinese cookbook.

  Includes index.
  1. Cookery, Chinese.   I. Lee, Virginia, joint author.
II. Title.
TX724.5.C5C6   1976   641.5′951
ISBN–0–397–00787–6   72–2919
ISBN–0–397–01173–3 (pbk.)   76–10418 (pbk.)

For Juliana Koo, without whose enthusiasm and encouragement
this book would never have been written . . .

. . . and for Henry Creel,
who washed all those woks

Contents

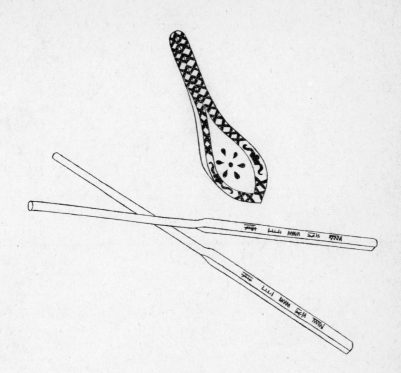

The Food of China

When I was seven or eight years old, my family took me to Birmingham to visit an aunt. I was born and raised in Mississippi during the Depression, and in that time and place anyone's idea of excitement or genuine adventure was a trip to a big town like Birmingham or Memphis. I remember—to tell the truth, it is the only thing I do remember about that trip—being taken to a Chinese restaurant. There were hanging Chinese lanterns and foreign waiters and real Chinese china and chopsticks and very hot and exotic tea. I cannot recall the menu in precise detail, but I did eat won ton soup and a dish that contained bean sprouts. I marveled over those bean sprouts. What an odd, enticing-looking vegetable! To this day I have not got over an inordinate fondness for won ton soup, and I have retained an all but insatiable appetite for any dish—even a mediocre dish— made with bean sprouts. It is reasonable to suppose that the food I ate then was quite spurious, adapted to the Southern palate, and dreadful. But it kindled a flame.

Yet while I am hopelessly infatuated with all forms of cookery, I never intended in a serious sense to "cook Chinese." My reasoning went something like this: I had trained in depth in French cookery in a Swiss hotel school, and it appealed to me from the beginning as a form of cookery that could be, let us say, wholly embraced. It is true that the French kitchen is without end in its variations, and yet the techniques are such that, with enough foundation, there is nothing that can't be mastered—be it brioche dough, puff pastry or the most elegant mousse, omelet or soufflé. It seems so logical.

On the other hand, the Chinese kitchen seemed, two years ago, as involved and interwoven as a bucket of boiling noodles. I love fried jao-tze (fried filled meat dumplings), for example, but who but a Chinese could master the technique of a simultaneous steaming-frying process? And who could master those myriad seasonings that blend so marvelously—ginger and garlic, scallions and chives, dark and light soy and the slightest trace of vinegar and sugar? Having heard so much over the years of the many "schools" of Chinese cooking and the seemingly endless nature of each, I was blindly in awe of Chinese cookery and therefore—with rare exceptions—avoided trying my hand at it. It seemed to me simply too vast to undertake. "If I cannot master the sum," I told myself, "I choose to ignore the parts."

Happily, I came around to "cooking Chinese" in a most felicitous and roundabout way.

There is probably no author on earth who has not, in the odious midst of finishing a book, sworn that he would never write another. That was my attitude two years or so ago while dotting i's and crossing t's for the final chapter of an international cookbook. "Never again," I vowed. Vehemently. And I meant it.

At that time I was also on the brink of leaving *The New York Times* after fourteen mostly happy, always hectic years as that newspaper's food news editor and restaurant critic. I had just returned from a long and somehow frustrating tour of the world. I was tired. I needed rest and a respite from cooking.

And then I met Virginia Lee.

Several letters had arrived on my desk extolling in a most laudatory fashion the lady's virtues and talents, and I reacted with the usual skepticism in the face of such high-flown praise. But why not pursue an interview? There was, after all, another column to fill.

I met Virginia in the autumn of 1970. When I arrived for that interview with the usual pad, pencil, and photographer, I was met by a strikingly handsome, smiling, and dignified Chinese lady who looked much too grand and refined ever to have handled a cleaver. I wondered if a lady with that style and elegance had ever washed a wok. Who, I wondered, really did the cooking behind those closed kitchen doors?

Ah, well, it was just another assignment and, if she wasn't doing the cooking, I could enjoy the company and never write about the meal. And then we sat at a table and a procession of foods of a most exceptional nature began—an incredibly good feather-light scallop dish on a bed of crisp fried greens; delicately spiced beef slices coated with rice powder and steamed until marvelously tender on a bed of dried lotus leaves; an elegant steamed flounder; a piping Hot and Sour Soup with its appealing, intriguing contrasts in flavor; the most gossamer of chicken dishes, called Chicken Velvet; and, as a vegetable, a delectable creation my hostess had labeled Cabbage Wellington. I learned later the genesis of that most admirable dish. It seems that when Mrs. Lee first came to this country, she remarked that wherever she went she heard someone speak of or was served beef Wellington. She decided to create a Chinese dish along the same lines and wrapped Chinese cabbage in pastry. She baked it. It was splendid—so good, in fact, that she named it after her long-time friends Dr. and Mrs. Wellington Koo.

I soon discovered, of course, that there was no hidden genie in Virginia Lee's kitchen turning out those miracles. It was Virginia herself.

On that morning Virginia decided to give cooking classes and allowed me to announce this in *The Times*. I did and listed her phone number. She was besieged with requests, and among them she found my own.

For the next few months, once a week, I took that long subway ride from Times Square to her simple kitchen above her daughter's thriving store in New York's Chinatown. And all my solemn vows about writing another book went by the board. I was hopelessly trapped. I agreed to join in writing with her *The Chinese Cookbook*, and together we worked for months testing recipes in my East Hampton kitchen.

I would not have traded my upbringing in Chinese cooking with

Virginia for all the tea in China, to coin a phrase. I learned an end-less number of things about seasonings and flavors and the countless virtues of the wok. I even learned to use a Chinese cleaver with a certain flair and expertise. But most important, I learned that Chi-nese cooking is by no means an impossible art. It can be done with ordinary Western cooking utensils, including skillets and kitchen scissors and quite ordinary knives. Although it is equally as sophisti-cated as the French, I find it to be far less complicated. The greatest French sauces at times take hours to prepare; a simple sauce like Hollandaise or Béarnaise can curdle at a most crucial moment; many French desserts—gateau St. Honoré comes to mind—require three or four distinct and involved preparations; and so on.

And by contrast, once you have mastered cutting, slicing, and chopping techniques, the vast majority of Chinese dishes are quite basic and simple. The advance preparation is at times tedious and time-consuming, but it is not difficult. Many dishes can be made in advance—the cold appetizers, steamed dishes, and casserole dishes; other dishes, such as soups, can be prepared earlier and fin-ished at the last moment; and even the stir-fry dishes can be—indeed, must be—cooked in seconds. Besides that, it is fun—more so, I have found, if you work in pairs, one person doing the stirring, the other handing him or her the ingredients.

I have spent many pleasant hours in the company of Dr. Welling-ton Koo, the distinguished Chinese statesman and scholar, who has a fine sense of humor about the Chinese table (he is also fond of Western wines, and I have always been amused that he serves a red Bordeaux with special dinners in his home). He told me once that there is a Chinese saying, "There are only two things we don't eat, a nine-headed bird in the sky and a Hupei man on the ground." And indeed, Chinese cooks are nothing if not frugal.

Dr. Koo remembered an enormous banquet given by Marshal Chang Tso-ling, the famous Manchurian war lord, and the soup turned out to be inordinately good.

"Do you know what you are eating?" his host asked.

"It is a bit unusual," Dr. Koo replied, "but delicious."

"It is the nose of the sturgeon." One nose had served the entire party of thirty guests.

Food has always been scarce in China, and hunger has been an ever-present threat throughout its history. A Chinese friend of mine avers that this is why the Chinese, under whatever dynasty or regime, have always treated food with such scrupulous respect and care. It is precious.

"Although my family in China," he said, "never suffered from want of food, I grew up to learn not to waste a single grain of rice. I have vivid childhood memories of my father, born as a peasant and worker in the rice fields, asking me at the end of a large meal to turn up my rice bowl to show him that not a grain was left uneaten."

That same acquaintance also associates the delicacy with which Chinese food is served to the peasant's reverence for his daily rice or wheat. "He knows that food is not to be gobbled, but savored; not to be chopped up in chunks, but sliced into delicate pieces; not to be haphazardly served to the tune of rattling metal, but ceremoniously presented." I count that a bit poetic and attribute the use of bite-size morsels to the practical but aesthetic nature of the Chinese in their ancient and honorable use of chopsticks. And I have never been more serious about the aesthetics and philosophy of eating in my life than when I say that to my mind Chinese food tastes better when eaten with chopsticks. Anyone who has tasted Chinese food only with a knife and fork has never really savored nor understood it. In this connection I once overheard someone ask a Chinese why his people used chopsticks. "We would prefer," was the reply, "not to butcher at table."

Of all the world's great cuisines the regional cookery of China is probably the most difficult to pinpoint or classify. One speaks of North and South Italian cookery, and immediate images come to mind: North Italy for the elegant, subtle, and refined dishes with rice as a staple; South Italy for the robust, earthy dishes frequently made with tomatoes and garlic and with noodle or pasta dishes as a staple. France is more complex, and its cooking has been admirably categorized by Waverley Root in his scholarly and admirable *The Food of France*, where he divides the nation into three domains: butter, oil, and fat. The cooking of the domain of butter (elegant sauces) is the most sophisticated, and that is what one usually has in mind when one speaks of "French cooking." It exists in the cities to the north and their surrounding areas and embraces both Burgundy and Bordeaux. The domain of oil (tomatoes and garlic) is where the olive trees grow in Provence and the south, while the domain of fat (sauerkraut, foie gras) is where pigs and geese are found in abundance.

In speaking of the regional cooking of China, one is forced to generalize, for the special dishes of one region have, over the centuries, been adopted and adapted in other regions. Chinese cooks are notably flexible and inventive, and new dishes and ingredients are constantly being incorporated into their menus. This process was hastened by the increase in trade and travel in modern times, and the Chinese cuisine is still changing and evolving. For obvious reasons, the best of Chinese cooking has been found in its great cities, where the art is nurtured and stimulated by wealthy merchants and travelers.

Some authorities state that the most logical way to categorize Chinese cooking is to divide it into three parts: Northern, Yangtze Valley, and Southern. Northern cooking finds its highest expression in Peking, which draws on the food of provinces as far south as Shantung and as far north as Manchuria. Peking has been the capital of China during much of the country's history, including the present. The most famous of all Peking dishes is the universally admired Peking Duck, accompanied by thin pancakes and a scallion garnish.

Northern cooking is strongly flavored. It uses dark soy sauce exclusively, and a great deal of bean paste and garlic. In the old days, at least, rickshaw coolies and the Northern poor in general often ate plain boiled noodles garnished with raw garlic cloves dipped in salt or bean paste. Northerners also have a passion for mutton, a meat which is somewhat disliked in the rest of China.

Although rice is eaten almost universally elsewhere in China, wheat is the staple of the North, and there are found the best dumplings—steamed, boiled, baked, and fried—and noodle dishes. This is where one would find baked flat breads, steamed buns, the dumplings called jao tze, and an infinite number of noodle dishes— with pork, fish, beef, chicken, duck, and vegetables in endless variations.

The second of the three major schools of cooking has grown up along the Yangtze River, which bisects China, running from west to east. Three great port cities—Ningpo, Yangchow, and Shanghai—have grown up at the eastern tip of the river, where it empties into the China Sea. The food of Ningpo, a historic port and trading center, tends to be salty, and many foods are preserved in salt. Ningpo also specializes in steamed dishes and dishes made with a fine variety of fresh fish. The salt-selling center of Yangchow was once the chief city of the region, but was gradually eclipsed by Shanghai after it became a treaty port. In its heyday Yangchow was known as the "Paris of China," and it was a center of fine dress, art, and food. Its specialties were little dumplings filled with meat and sauce, and other delicate snacks.

My friends from Shanghai claim that where variety of cuisine is concerned, it is traditionally the most cosmopolitan of Chinese cities. In years past, they say, it attracted the finest of cooks from all over China and was famous not only for Chinese but also foreign cuisine, including French, Italian, and Russian.

In general, the people of this region like their food to be somewhat more well done than that of their neighbors to the south; they excel at long-cooked casserole dishes, and even their stir-fry dishes are cooked somewhat longer than in the south. Both light and dark soy sauces are used, and as a rule the dishes are somewhat sweeter—with more sugar used in cooking—than is true elsewhere in China.

The Western region of the Yangtze Valley includes the cooking of Yunnan and Szechwan provinces. Where Chinese restaurants in New York are concerned, the wildest phenomenon of recent years has been the advent and proliferation of Szechwan restaurants from one end of Manhattan to the other. Szechwan food is notable for the sharpness of its flavors, the sting of its spices, achieved through the use of ginger and garlic but more pronouncedly through the use of Szechwan peppercorns and an assortment of fresh or dried hot red and green chilies or peppers, whichever term you prefer. Agronomists claim that these spiced dishes came about because of the isolated nature of Szechwan, a province in the Southwest with an uneven and mountainous topography. It is said to yield only one crop a year, and as a result the good people of Szechwan turned to preserving their foodstuffs in various hot spices, including the peppercorns and chili paste with garlic. The spiciness is also said to counteract the effects of the humid climate on the human body. As to Yunnan, it seems to be renowned only for its ham. That is distinction enough.

In America the best known of all Chinese "schools" of cookery is the Southern; the food of Canton or Kwangtung province in particular. The principal reason for the Canton influence in this country is that the first large migration of Chinese to America was from Canton (mostly from Toyshan, a mountainous region of Canton), brought to this country as laborers on the earliest railroads. My friend the cookbook writer Jim Lee, whose grandfather worked on the Transcontinental Railroad, once told me that these Chinese laborers were given the most menial jobs—the washing and the cooking. Once they left the railroad, they utilized these specialties —hence the proliferation of Chinese laundries and restaurants.

The Cantonese are blessed with a mild climate and nearby sea, and their cuisine is said to contain the greatest variety of dishes. Southerners in general believe that their food, in line with Taoist principles, should be eaten in as nearly the state as it was in nature as possible—that is to say, with as little cooking and seasoning as possible. Thus Cantonese chefs do a great deal of stir-fry—very quick—cooking. Hence we find Southerners developing and furthering the art of steaming, because they believe that steaming preserves more of the original flavor. The Southerner is outraged if his food is overcooked, but he is happy if the meat of his chicken close to the bone carries a tinge of pink. When he breaks the bone and finds that the marrow within is still red, he exclaims, "Beautiful! Beautiful! Well done!" The Cantonese use light soy sauce in their dishes rather than dark, and even frown on the use of monosodium glutamate because they say "it spoils the natural flavor."

Southerners eat five to seven small meals a day, and their men have made the teahouse world renowned: they get there at the crack of dawn to drink a cup of tea, to eat a dish or two of Dim Sum, or assorted steamed dumplings, and to read the newspaper; then they stay up as late as two or three in the morning for what they call the final "after midnight snack."

The Southerners who live in the province of Fukien enjoy dishes which the Chinese call "soupy" or laced with sauce, and, like their neighbors in Canton, they specialize in stir-fry, or quick-cooked, dishes. The seafood dishes of Fukien are noteworthy.

These are some of the facts I have gleaned during my two-year involvement with Chinese cooking. I am, of course, no scholar or historian, but I have been afforded a glimpse into China's culture and philosophy through its cuisine. This book is a tribute to the Chinese genius—and a testament to Virginia Lee, one of the great natural cooking experts of this age. It is a book that had to be written; I have been only the midwife.

CRAIG CLAIBORNE

East Hampton, New York
May, 1972

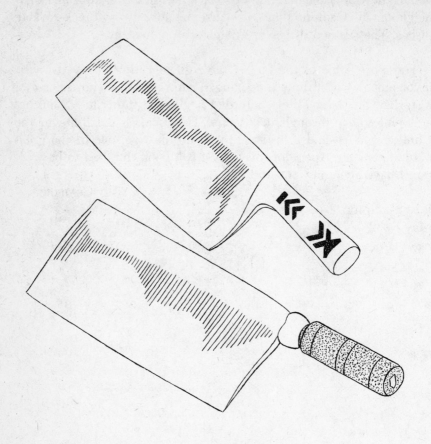

I

Chinese Cooking: Equipment, Methods, and Tips

If you have a desire to "cook Chinese," to cook well and yet not to needlessly complicate life, there are several things noted in this chapter that will speed you on your way.

PLANNING

To begin with, you should plan a menu and decide how many dishes you will serve. The basic Chinese family meal consists of four dishes and a soup plus, of course, rice. This assumes that there will be about four to six people at the table; another dish is added for every two additional persons. A Chinese cook will increase the number of dishes, rather than the quantity of each dish, when more people are expected at a meal. All the dishes are placed in the center of the table, and each person helps himself to a bit of every dish, which makes the Chinese meal a convivial one. There is of course nothing to prevent one from serving the dishes in this book Western-style, in individual portions, and the yields given at the end of each recipe have been planned with both alternatives in mind. The first and lower figure is calculated for individual Western-style servings, and the latter figure assumes that the dish is one of many, Chinese family-style.

If you are planning to serve more than one dish, some attention should be paid to diversity and contrast. If one dish is highly seasoned and flavored, another should be bland and smooth; if one dish contains meat, other dishes might consist predominantly of fish or vegetables.

Your own abilities should also be taken into consideration. Stir-fry dishes, for example, require last-minute cooking, and speed is of the essence. So if you are a beginner in Chinese cooking, it would be wise to limit yourself at first to only one stir-fry dish per meal. This does not mean that you need serve only one dish. A more elaborate meal, and one that a cook of normal ability should be able to cope with, might include Lemon Chicken or Aromatic Spiced Beef, either of which may be made in advance; a soup—either a simple one such as Egg Drop Soup, or the more complicated Hot and Sour Soup, which may be prepared in advance up to the final step; a casserole dish such as Lion's Head or Red-cooked Pork; and then a stir-fry dish—perhaps a vegetable or seafood to balance the meal—to be made at the last moment. And, of course, rice, which can be left to cook while the other dishes are being made ready.

One of the great dishes for entertaining a crowd without a lot of last-minute activity is the Mongolian Hot Pot. The Chrysanthemum Hot Pot is another. The hot pots are made with thinly sliced meat and other ingredients which each guest dips into a simmering broth, and both dishes will be found at the end of the chapter on Soups.

To simplify menu-planning, the recipes in this book are divided by category—Cold Dishes, Poultry, Beef, and so forth—and simpler recipes have been placed at the beginning of each category, leading up to the more complex ones at the end. Those dishes which do not require a lot of last-minute preparation and cooking—cold dishes, casseroles, and steamed dishes—have been marked with a symbol (✤) at the right of the recipe title.

PREPARATION

A Chinese cook spends a much larger proportion of his time in the kitchen on preparation than does a Western cook, and the most important part of his preparation is in the cutting of the ingredients. Cut is essential to the aesthetics of Chinese cooking: a properly shredded chicken or meat dish is a joy to behold, whereas an improperly shredded dish looks wounded, if not to say butchered.

Equipment

A well-equipped Western kitchen should already contain all the equipment needed for preparing Chinese food: a heavy, smooth chopping surface, and some sharp knives. A Chinese cook generally does all his cutting and chopping with one of two cleavers. The first cleaver is thinner, lighter, and sharper, and is used for slicing, shredding, and so on. An ordinary Western-style kitchen knife will suffice in its place; it should be sizable and sharp, the finer the quality the better. The other Chinese cleaver is heavier than the slicer, and it is used for chopping through bone. Any Western-style meat cleaver will do for this and *in extremis* you can get along without it.

A useful adjunct to the chopping cleaver is a hard rubber mallet obtainable in automobile supply stores. A Chinese chef can cut up a fowl freehand with dazzling speed and accuracy, but the rest of us will find the mallet useful in helping to pound the cleaver through the bone.

The Chinese use kitchen shears of a charming design in boning meats. However, an ordinary pair of kitchen shears will do just as well.

Cutting Methods

The major ingredients in a Chinese dish are generally cut to the same size and shape, so that they will cook in the same amount of time. In stir-fry dishes they are usually cut as thin as possible so that they will cook quickly. It is easier to slice meat thin and even if it is partially frozen so that the meat is firm and will not slip about under the knife. Meat should be sliced across the grain so that it will be tender. Always use a knife with the sharpest edge possible. Or, if you are fortunate enough to own one, use an electric slicing machine, which really gives uniformity in the slices.

Cutting for Chinese dishes is generally done in one of four ways. Although the dimensions of the pieces vary from one dish to another, the basic technique is the same:

Slicing

Most of the dishes in this book call for relatively uncomplicated slicing straight down through the meat or vegetable.

However, some ingredients—chicken breasts or pork kidneys, for example—are too thin to yield proper-sized slices unless they are sliced horizontally, with the knife held at an angle to the cutting board. To slice horizontally, first make a shallow cut downward into the meat or vegetable, cutting as deep as the finished slice is to be thick. Then with the left hand pressing down firmly on the meat, slice the meat across with a gentle sawing motion, with the blade of the knife pointed at an angle toward the cutting board.

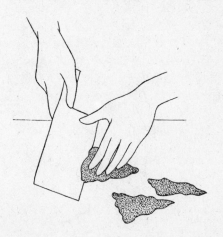

Shredding

Shreds should be as thin and fine as you can make them. To shred, first cut the meat or vegetable into the thinnest possible slices, then shred each slice, picking the side of the slice closest in length to the length of shred you want. After a little practice you will be able to stack several slices and shred them together.

Dicing or Cubing

First cut the food into slices as thick as the dice called for in a recipe; for instance, if ⅜-inch cubes are desired, make slices ⅜-inch thick. Cut the slices into ⅜-inch strips, then cut them into uniform ⅜-inch squares.

Scoring

Scoring is no doubt best known to American cooks in the preparation of baked ham, when the fat on top of the ham is cut at intervals, crosswise, usually to form a diamond pattern. The Chinese score their foods for two reasons: it makes a pattern to please the eye, and it helps make the food more tender. The size of the pattern and the depth of the cut vary from dish to dish, but it should always be done at an angle to the grain of the meat.

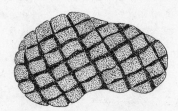

Other kinds of cutting of a more specialized nature—cutting up cooked fowl, for instance—will be discussed later on in the book as we come to them.

Aside from cutting, preparation of food in Chinese cooking is not difficult; it is a simple matter of following the directions. One process, however, deserves a further word of explanation. Many Chinese recipes in this book and elsewhere call for marinating various sliced, shredded, or cubed foods in a combination of egg white and cornstarch. This helps give a velvety texture to the foods and also makes them seem more tender. A secret of Chinese cooking is to refrigerate the foods for thirty minutes or longer after they are blended with the egg white and cornstarch. This prevents the egg white from puffing up when it is cooked and produces a better result.

COOKING

Organization is essential to the success of Chinese cooking. Prepare all the ingredients and have them ready before starting to cook. Seasonings such as garlic, ginger, and scallions, if they are called for, should be chopped and ready to be spooned into the wok or skillet on a second's notice. Similarly, have the wine, sugar, salt, or whatever is called for measured out and ready to add within seconds. Remember that the essence of almost all Chinese cooking, particularly stir-frying, is speed—not in the preliminaries, but in the cooking.

Almost all Chinese cooking, except for casserole dishes and soups, is done over high heat. The largest ring of a gas stove with a high flame is ideal, but I have eaten excellent Chinese meals cooked on an electric stove. The outdoor barbecue, if you have one, should not be overlooked; use the charcoal when it is flaming, not when it has died down. The hot fire generated by charcoal is probably the closest thing there is to the traditional Chinese stove.

Utensils

A wok is the traditional Chinese cooking utensil, but it, too, is not absolutely necessary in cooking Chinese. Any dish that can be cooked in a wok can be made in a skillet. In fact, it is our theory that skillets are preferable to woks when cooking over electric units, because the heat is generated more evenly over the entire bottom of the skillet.

A wok is, of course, a metal utensil with a round bottom. It comes in several sizes and several kinds of metal; we recommend the iron ones. Woks are widely available in department stores and specialty shops as well as in Chinese markets in any Chinatown. Woks are frequently sold as a set together with a cover and a wok ring. You will find the cover very useful and convenient although, again, you do not absolutely have to have one. A wok ring—a round metal ring to be placed over a burner, into which the wok is fitted—is sold along with the wok; it is supposedly a safety device.

We never use a wok ring for stir-frying, because we find that it lifts the wok too far off the flame on our stove. With proper caution it is not necessary, and without it cooking is simpler and more flexible. The ring is useful, however, when a wok is used for steaming

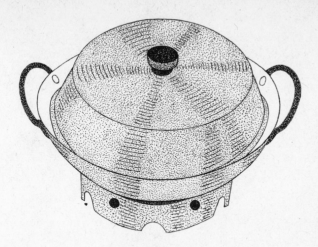

beneath a bamboo steamer, since the ring helps to hold everything steady.

We have experimented with electric woks, but we were not altogether pleased with the results for stir-frying, since the time lag in going from one heat to another was too long. Perhaps they will be more efficient in the future. In the meantime, they are useful for steamed and casserole dishes.

An iron wok should be seasoned when it is first purchased, and at intervals thereafter, by brushing unsalted oil or fat all over the inside surface and heating the wok over low heat until the whole wok is hot. After it is cooled and washed, it is ready for use.

Woks are easily cleaned with a scrub brush. Many people state that woks should never be cleaned with a soap or a detergent, but we find that it makes no difference so long as they are dried well after washing and are not allowed to rust.

There are two instruments traditionally used for cooking with a wok: a long-handled spoon and a long-handled perforated scoop with a slightly rounded edge. They are efficient for the purpose, but large kitchen spoons and spatulas may be used to replace them.

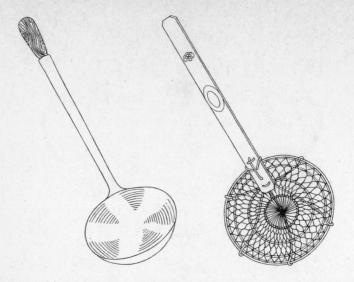

Many Chinese dishes require that an ingredient be scooped out of the fat and drained at some point during the cooking. There are special sieves designed for this purpose, and one of the best is a heavy round metal sieve with fairly large holes and a handle. This can be placed over a large bowl to catch the drippings when food such as shrimp or chicken is scooped into the sieve. However, any large Western-style sieve, or even a colander, can be adapted for the purpose.

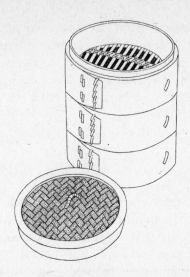

Steaming plays a large and important role in Chinese cooking, and bamboo steamers are ideal. These steamers, which come in many sizes, have no base and are made to be set onto a wok containing boiling water. They are convenient in that they come in layers, so that several dishes can be steamed at once. They are attractive enough that steamed dumplings, for instance, can be served directly out of their steaming vessel.

Western-style steamers can, of course, be substituted, and if you have none at all you can improvise by setting the dish to be steamed onto a bowl or some other kind of pedestal in a pot of boiling water. The pot should have a cover to keep the steam in, and enough room should be left around the dish so that the steam circulates freely.

Where rice is concerned, we offer the traditional recipe for rice in this book. On the other hand, we would like to add that there are some very good electric rice cookers on the market, most, if not all, made in the Orient and all of them designed to turn out quite acceptable rice for the Chinese table. They are simplicity itself to operate, and once the rice and water are added to the cooker it can be forgotten. They are wholly automatic, and cooking time is about 20 minutes.

Cooking Processes

While one Chinese writer has discerned about twenty separate cooking processes in the Chinese cuisine, there is actually nothing very complicated about Chinese cooking—again, it is simply a matter of following directions. There are, however, a couple of processes which could be explained in more detail than can be given in the individual recipes:

Stir-frying

The closest equivalent of this in Western cooking is sautéing, yet it is not the same. The point of stir-frying is to keep the food moving constantly so that all parts of the dish come in contact with the hottest part of the pan and cook quickly and evenly. This is accomplished by quickly and repeatedly sliding a spoon or spatula down between the food and the pan and turning the food over on itself with a digging and tossing motion. A wok is the best cooking vessel for stir-frying because the sloping sides and rounded bottom help keep the food in motion.

Deep Frying

In this book there is a technique special to Chinese cooking which might be translated as "pass through once" cooking. It involves dropping the shredded, sliced, or cubed foods into warm to slightly hot fat (about 280 degrees) and stirring it as an initial phase in cooking a dish. The food is only partially cooked, and the purpose of this technique is to prevent the pieces from sticking together during the final rapid cooking in hot fat, as they otherwise would.

We have avoided giving specific oil temperatures in most of our recipes because a great deal depends on the nature of your stove: whether it is gas or electric, how deep the fat is, and how long your stove takes to return it to the original heat after the food is dropped in. With these reservations in mind, here are the approximate temperatures we have in mind when we use certain phrases:

"Moderate" (200–300 degrees)—the temperature generally called for in cooking fish and shrimp.

"Very hot, almost smoking" (360–375 degrees)—the temperature used for the majority of dishes.

A temperature of 450 degrees is specifically called for in a few dishes such as Rice Cake and the noodles for Roof Brick Carp, where the heat is needed to make the dish fluff up properly.

The oil used in deep frying may be strained and reused up to five or six times if it is used half and half with fresh oil.

SERVING

As in all things, the style of dining Chinese fashion depends wholly on circumstances, including the resources and will of a host or hostess. In the days of strict tradition, and not infrequently for special occasions today, a Chinese banquet consisted of approximately ten courses and fifteen to eighteen dishes, but that would presume a staff of servants or dining in a restaurant. The courses progress from the light to the heavy, starting with at least four cold dishes (which could be called appetizers or hors d'oeuvres) and sometimes as many as six. These would be followed by two to four stir-fry dishes involving such things as pheasant, seafood, or meat. The real *pièce de résistance*, the greatest Chinese luxury, would be a shark's fin dish. Then the procession would continue with duck, either Szechwan or Peking style or in a casserole; a whole fish course; vegetable and soup; rice or noodle dishes (to fill a hunger hole, if any); and a sweet, usually in the form of a soup or pastry, or both. Although pork is one of the most frequently eaten dishes in China, it would rarely be used in a banquet dish. Too everyday.

As far as beverages are concerned, either shao hsing, the rice wine, or champagne would be served throughout the meal.

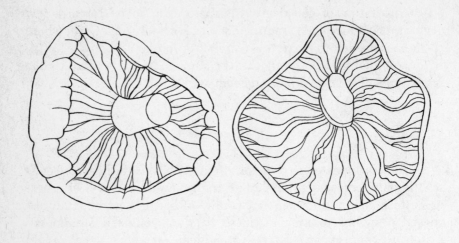

II

Cold Dishes
and Appetizers

The Chinese long ago realized that shin of beef is one of the juici-
est parts of the cow. This is a cold dish with a spicy sauce.

COLD SHIN OF BEEF WITH SPICY SAUCE ❖

  1   boneless, well-trimmed shin of beef (1½ pounds)
 10   cups cold water, approximately.
  1   small bunch fresh coriander * (about 7 plants with
        roots or about 30 to 40 sprigs)
2 to 4   cloves garlic, chopped (about 1 tablespoon)
  6   fresh green or red long hot peppers,* seeded and cut
        into fine dice
  3   tablespoons sesame oil *
  3   tablespoons light soy sauce *
  2   teaspoons sugar
  3   tablespoons red wine vinegar
      Salt to taste
  ¼   teaspoon monosodium glutamate (optional)

* Available in Chinese markets and by mail order. For more information see
Chapter XI.

1. Put the beef into a kettle and add 10 cups of cold water. Do
not add salt. Bring to a boil, then cover and simmer about 1½ hours.
Uncover.

2. Turn the heat to high and cook, uncovered, about 1 hour longer.

3. Test the meat with a fork. If it is tender, remove it. If it is not tender, let it cook a little longer before removing. When cool, cover with foil and refrigerate.

4. After the meat is taken from the kettle, continue cooking the broth over high heat to reduce to about 1 cup. This broth can then be strained and chilled and used as a garnish for the meat, or it can be used for another purpose, such as thickening soups.

5. Trim the root ends from the coriander and discard them. Drop the leaves into boiling water and stir quickly, then drain immediately without cooking. Run the leaves under cold water and squeeze them to remove most of the moisture, then chop them and set aside for garnish.

6. Combine the garlic, hot peppers, sesame oil, soy sauce, sugar, vinegar, salt, and monosodium glutamate. Stir to blend.

7. Slice the meat very thin and arrange it on a platter. Spoon the sauce over all and sprinkle with the coriander. If the chilled, thickened broth is to be used, unmold it and cut it into slices. Cut it into fancy shapes with a cutter and arrange them around the meat.

YIELD: 6 to 12 servings

There are many versions of Lemon Chicken, one of the most recent dishes to achieve a sudden—if not to say phenomenal—popularity in the Western world. The following is a cold version of Lemon Chicken made with fresh lemon juice and rind, which may be served as a cold first course or as a main dish.

LEMON CHICKEN ❖

1   whole chicken (4 to 5 pounds)
7   dried black mushrooms *
4   lemons
3   tablespoons peanut, vegetable, or corn oil
¼   cup finely shredded fresh ginger *

⅓ cup fresh green or red long hot peppers,* seeded and cut
   into very fine strips (julienne)
¼ cup sugar
½ teaspoon monosodium glutamate (optional)
   Salt to taste
2 teaspoons lemon extract

* Available in Chinese markets and by mail order. For more information see
Chapter XI.

1. Put the chicken into a small but deep heatproof casserole and
place in a steamer over boiling water. Steam about 1 hour, or until
tender.

2. Place the mushrooms in a mixing bowl and add boiling water
to cover. Let stand 15 to 30 minutes, then drain and squeeze to extract most of the moisture. Cut off and discard the tough stems. Set
the mushrooms aside.

3. Carefully peel one of the lemons in long strips (try to use the
yellow skin only, avoiding as much of the white part underneath as
possible). Carefully cut each strip into the finest possible shreds.
There should be about ¼ cup. Reserve the lemon shreds.

4. Grate the rest of the lemons to make about 1 tablespoon grated
rind. Reserve the lemon rind.

5. Squeeze enough lemons to make ½ cup of lemon juice. Save
any remaining lemons for another use.

6. When the chicken is cooked, let it cool in the cooking liquid.
As soon as the chicken is cool enough to handle, remove it. Strain
and reserve the broth.

7. Carefully remove the breast meat from the chicken and cut it
into bite-size morsels. Chop the wings, legs, and thighs into bite-size
pieces, leaving in the bone.

8. In a wok or saucepan, heat the oil over a high flame and add
the mushrooms and ginger. Cook about 30 seconds, then add the
slivered peppers and lemon shreds. Cook about 5 seconds, then add
the sugar and monosodium glutamate. Add 1 cup of the reserved
chicken broth, and when it comes to a boil add the lemon juice and

salt to taste. Add the chicken pieces and cook just to heat through, about 30 seconds. Transfer the pieces, one at a time, to a serving dish, arranging them neatly and symmetrically.

9. To the liquid, add the grated lemon and lemon extract. Pour the sauce over the chicken and let stand to room temperature.

YIELD: 6 to 8 servings

This is a cold, odd, easily made dish, jokingly referred to as "drunken chicken" because of the quantity of wine used in its preparation.

DRUNKEN CHICKEN ❖

1 plump fowl (5 to 6 pounds; preferably and traditionally
        with head left on, although this is not essential to the
        success of the dish)
    Salt, preferably kosher, to taste
1½ cups chicken broth, or more if needed
3   cups shao hsing wine,* or more if needed

* Available in Chinese markets and by mail order. For more information see Chapter XI.

1. Place the chicken in a fairly deep dish that will fit in the top of a steamer. Put the dish, uncovered, into the steamer top and place the whole over boiling water. Cover.

2. Steam until the chicken is thoroughly tender, 1¼ to 1½ hours. Let stand, with the steamer cover on, until cool.

3. Cut the chicken into 8 serving pieces. Spoon 4 or 5 tablespoons salt onto waxed paper and salt the chicken pieces, one by one, by hand. They should be fairly generously salted. Place the chicken in a bowl, layer by layer, until all the pieces are salted. Cover with waxed paper and then with a lid and let stand at least 6 hours.

4. Combine the chicken broth with the wine and pour enough of the mixture over the chicken to barely cover, reserving the remainder of the mixture, if any. Cover the chicken with foil and chill for 1 to 3 days.

5. Cut and chop the chicken pieces into bite-size morsels and arrange the pieces on a serving dish (see p. 42). Sprinkle with the reserved wine mixture, if any. If not, combine an additional ⅛ cup wine with ⅛ cup chicken broth and pour over the chicken. Serve.

YIELD: 6 to 8 servings

This is an original "Chinese" recipe. It came about one evening when there was an excess of chicken liver mixture otherwise destined for a chicken liver soup. It is a fine-textured dish, to be served as an appetizer, and is remarkably like a French chicken liver mousse, although it contains the juices of ginger and scallion.

LIVER MOUSSE

2 cups chicken or duck livers (about 1 pound)
2 tablespoons minced fresh ginger *
3 tablespoons chopped scallions, green part included
6 tablespoons water
1 egg plus 2 egg whites
1 tablespoon dry sherry or shao hsing wine *
1½ tablespoons melted lard
Salt and freshly ground pepper to taste
2 teaspoons rendered chicken fat (see Chapter XI)
1 coarsely chopped truffle (optional)

* Available in Chinese markets and by mail order. For more information see Chapter XI.

1. Carefully pick over and trim the livers to remove any veins or connective tissue. Place the livers in the container of an electric blender and blend on high speed 1 minute or longer. Pour the puree into a mixing bowl and rinse out the blender.

2. Place the ginger and scallions in the blender and add the water. Blend at high speed about 2 minutes. Strain the juices through cheesecloth and discard the solids.

3. Add 3½ teaspoons of the ginger-scallion liquid to the liver puree and stir in the egg and egg whites, wine, lard, salt, and pepper. Beat thoroughly.

4. Oil a 3-cup mold with the chicken fat and pour in the liver mixture. Place the mold in the top of a steamer over boiling water and cover. Reduce the heat so that the water below merely simmers and steam 20 to 30 minutes. Scatter the truffle pieces, if used, over the mousse after it has steamed exactly 5 minutes, then continue steaming.

5. Remove the mold from the steamer and cool, then chill. Unmold at serving time.

YIELD: 8 servings

There are hundreds of ways to make fried rice, some good, some bad or indifferent. The same is true of shrimp toast. This is a remarkably good recipe for shrimp toast with a sesame seed topping.

SHRIMP TOAST WITH SESAME SEED TOPPING

⅛   pound fresh, unsalted fatback
½   pound raw shrimps, shelled and deveined
2   egg whites
     Salt to taste
1   teaspoon dry sherry or shao hsing wine *
3   tablespoons cornstarch

    1   tablespoon chopped fresh coriander leaves * or parsley
    12 thin slices white bread
    ½   cup sesame seeds,* more or less
    1   egg yolk
        Peanut, vegetable, or corn oil for deep frying

* Available in Chinese markets and by mail order. For more information see Chapter XI.

1. Drop the fatback into boiling water and simmer about 5 minutes. Drain and chop enough to make 2 tablespoons.

2. Place the shrimps, 1 egg white, salt, wine, chopped fatback, and 2 teaspoons of the cornstarch into the container of an electric blender. Blend on low speed, stirring down as necessary. Continue blending and stirring down to make a spreadable paste. Spoon and scrape into a mixing bowl and stir in the chopped coriander or parsley.

3. Neatly trim away the crusts from the bread slices. Cut each slice into two 2-inch rounds or into triangles.

4. In a small bowl combine the remaining egg white with 2 tablespoons of the cornstarch and a little salt to taste. Brush one side of each round or triangle of bread with the cornstarch mixture.

5. Spoon equal portions of the shrimp mixture onto each round or triangle of bread on the cornstarch-brushed side, smoothing and rounding the top as the mixture is applied.

6. Pour the sesame seeds onto a piece of waxed paper and dip the top of each shrimp-covered round or triangle in the seeds to coat liberally.

7. Blend the egg yolk with the remaining teaspoon of cornstarch. Brush the bottom of the rounds or triangles with the egg-yolk mixture and set the pieces onto a rack. Cover lightly.

8. In a wok or deep-fryer heat the oil, and when it is just hotter than warm add the pieces with the shrimp side up. The oil must not be too hot when the pieces are added or the sesame seeds will scatter in the fat. Turn the heat to medium and let the pieces simmer quite gently in the oil. You will have to coax and encourage the pieces with a fork or a spoon to keep the shrimp side up, but try to.

After about 2 minutes the pieces will become easily manageable in the oil. Turn them shrimp side down and cook about 4 minutes. When nicely golden, increase the heat and cook 6 to 7 minutes longer. They should be cooked a total of about 12 to 14 minutes. Drain on paper toweling and serve hot.

YIELD: 24 pieces

The "gold coin" in the name of this recipe refers to the famed piece of metal currency in China. It is so called here because of the design on the top of the shrimp toast, which is served as an appetizer.

GOLD COIN SHRIMP TOAST

¼	pound raw shrimps, shelled and deveined
2	egg whites
2	tablespoons cornstarch
½	teaspoon sugar
¼	teaspoon monosodium glutamate (optional)
	Salt to taste
6 to 8	extra-thin slices white bread (such as Melba-thin or Diet-thin)
2 or 3	dried black mushrooms,* soaked in hot water to cover for 15 to 30 minutes
7 or 8	sprigs fresh coriander leaves *
¼	cup finely chopped, almost pulverized ham
	Peanut, vegetable, or corn oil for deep frying

* Available in Chinese markets and by mail order. For more information see Chapter XI.

1. Place the shrimps in the container of an electric blender and add 1 egg white and 1 tablespoon of the cornstarch. Blend thoroughly, then spoon into a bowl.
2. Add the sugar, monosodium glutamate, and salt to taste.

3. Blend the remaining egg white with the remaining cornstarch.

4. Place the bread slices on a flat surface and, using a 2- or 2½-inch biscuit cutter, cut out rounds from the bread. There should be 12 to 16 rounds.

5. Brush the top of each round with the egg-white mixture and spoon a mound of shrimp over each. Smooth over the tops.

6. Prepare the garnish. Cut off and discard the tough stems of the mushrooms and cut the mushroom caps into very thin shreds. Pull off small pieces of coriander leaves to add to the garnish, and have the ham ready. Decorate the shrimp toast rounds as illustrated.

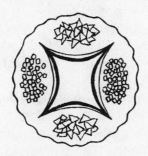

7. Heat oil for deep frying and when it is just hotter than warm add the pieces with the shrimp side up. Turn the heat to medium and let the pieces simmer quite gently in the oil. You will have to coax and encourage the pieces with a fork or a spoon to keep the shrimp side up, but try to. After about 2 minutes the pieces will become easily manageable in the oil. Turn them shrimp side down and cook about 4 minutes. When nicely golden, increase the heat and cook 6 to 7 minutes longer. They should be cooked a total of about 12 to 14 minutes. Drain on paper toweling and serve hot.

YIELD: 12 to 16 rounds

The following is an elegant tidbit that could serve both as an appetizer or as part of a banquet. It consists of seasoned ground shrimp sandwiched between thin rounds of pork fat. The sandwiches are then deep-fried, and come out crisp and melting.

SHRIMP BOXES

8 to 24   very thin slices unsalted pork fat
    2   tablespoons rose wine spirits * or imported Kirsch-
        wasser or cognac
  2½   teaspoons sugar
      Salt to taste
   ½   pound raw shrimps, shelled and deveined
   ¼   teaspoon monosodium glutamate (optional)
    2   egg whites
   ¼   cup chopped fresh coriander leaves * (optional)
    3   tablespoons plus ½ cup cornstarch
      Peanut, vegetable, or corn oil for deep frying

* Available in Chinese markets and by mail order. For more information see Chapter XI.

1. If the butcher is agreeable, ask him to slice the pork fat for you on his professional slicing machine. The thinner the slices, the better. A machine is all but essential for slicing.

2. After the fat is sliced, place one slice at a time on a flat surface. Using a cooky cutter or other cutter with a 2½-inch diameter, cut out rounds of pork fat. The number of rounds will depend, of course, on the size of the slices of pork fat. Chop the scraps and reserve ¼ cup.

3. Combine the liquor with 2 teaspoons of the sugar and salt to taste. Add the rounds and let stand briefly.

4. In the container of an electric blender, combine the shrimps, salt, remaining ½ teaspoon sugar, monosodium glutamate, 1 egg white, and the reserved ¼ cup unsalted pork fat. (If desired, the chopped coriander may be added for a change of flavor.) Cover and

blend, stirring down as necessary, to make a fine puree. Spoon the mixture into a mixing bowl and beat with a rotary motion, using a wooden spoon. Always beating in one direction, give it about 50 vigorous turns with the spoon.

5. Blend the remaining egg white with the 3 tablespoons cornstarch and stir in salt to taste. Blend well.

6. Spoon the ½ cup cornstarch onto a flat surface. Remove one round of pork fat from the marinade. Dip one side of it into the cornstarch. It should be lightly coated. Spoon about 1 tablespoon of the shrimp mixture into the center of the cornstarch-coated side and smooth the filling with moistened fingers, leaving a small border of pork fat.

7. Dip one side of another round lightly into cornstarch and place it, cornstarch side down, on top of the shrimp mixture, sandwich-fashion. Brush the sides of the "sandwich" all around to coat well with the cornstarch and egg-white mixture. This will seal the edges when the sandwich cooks. (The dish may be refrigerated overnight, or frozen at this point. Bring to room temperature before cooking.)

8. When all the "sandwiches" have been made, heat the oil in a wok or deep-fryer. Drop the sandwiches into the hot oil and cook over moderately low heat 4 to 6 minutes, turning once or twice, until they are golden brown and cooked through. Serve hot.

YIELD: 24 shrimp boxes

Among the curios of the Chinese kitchen are Tea Eggs or Spicy Eggs, as they are sometimes called in English. These are eggs that are hard-cooked, to say the least. They are simmered for about two and a half hours or longer, and when finished are beautifully perfumed with the flavors of cinnamon and star anise. The white flesh of the egg is mottled because after the eggs are cooked until hard in the traditional Western fashion, the shells are cracked all over, and the eggs are finally cooked in a boiling tea mixture with the spices. Not a bad idea for an Easter egg.

TEA EGGS ❖

(or Spicy Eggs)

2	dozen eggs
¾	cup ordinary black tea leaves
4	pieces stick cinnamon
6 to 8	pieces star anise *
7	tablespoons dark soy sauce *
1	teaspoon monosodium glutamate (optional)
2	tablespoons salt
½	tablespoon sugar

* Available in Chinese markets and by mail order. For more information see Chapter XI.

1. Place the eggs in a cooking utensil and let cold water run on them. Bring them to a boil slowly so that the shells will not break. When the water boils, reduce the heat and simmer about 15 minutes. Let cool, then drain.

2. Using the back of a heavy, large spoon, crack the eggs all over but do not peel.

3. Place the cracked eggs in a large kettle and add enough water to cover. Add the remaining ingredients and bring to a boil. Partially cover and cook the eggs 2½ hours, or longer. Drain, cool, and

either let stand at room temperature or refrigerate. Peel and cut into 6 wedges lengthwise before serving.

YIELD: 24 tea eggs

Steamed eggplant is an excellent dish, properly sauced, and the sauce for Cold Spiced Eggplant is a delicious sweet and sour concoction containing garlic, ginger, and sesame oil. The dish should be served cold as an appetizer.

COLD SPICED EGGPLANT *

2   medium young eggplant (about 1¾ pounds total)
3   tablespoons light soy sauce *
2   tablespoons red wine vinegar
2   tablespoons sugar
¼   teaspoon salt, or salt to taste
1½ teaspoons dry sherry or shao hsing wine *
1   tablespoon sesame oil *
1   tablespoon peanut, vegetable, or corn oil
1   tablespoon chopped garlic
1   tablespoon chopped fresh ginger *
1   tablespoon white sesame seeds *

* Available in Chinese markets and by mail order. For more information see Chapter XI.

1. Put the eggplant into the top of a steamer, cover, and place over boiling water. Steam about 30 minutes or longer, until the eggplant is tender to the core and in a "collapsed" condition. Let cool.

2. Meanwhile, combine the soy sauce, vinegar, sugar, salt, wine, and sesame oil.

3. Over a high flame, heat the tablespoon of oil in a saucepan and add the garlic and ginger. Cook about 10 seconds, then stir in the vinegar and soy sauce mixture. Bring just to a boil and remove from the heat. Let cool.

4. Empty the sesame seeds into a saucepan and "toast" over medium low heat, shaking the pan and stirring the seeds, until they are pale brown and have a nutty odor. Do not let them burn. Once they are toasted, remove them from the heat and continue shaking the pan and stirring because they keep cooking briefly from retained heat. Let cool.

5. Cut or pull the eggplant into shreds. If the seeds are tough (because the eggplant is too mature), discard them. Pour the cool sauce over, sprinkle with the toasted sesame seeds, and serve.

YIELD: 4 to 8 servings

There is a fascinating and altogether economical dish in Chinese cooking the principal ingredient of which is the skin of a boiled chicken. It is a chicken skin and cucumber salad, and it is served cold. It is not the kind of dish you would deliberately boil a chicken to make, but if you are going to prepare the chicken anyway, for a dish such as Pon Pon Chicken or Bean Curd Casserole Soup (see recipes) and have no other need for the skin, you can use the skin to good advantage as follows.

CHICKEN SKIN AND CUCUMBER SALAD

1   chicken (2½ to 3 pounds; this is on the assumption that the
        chicken after cooking has another good use)
⅓   cup tree ear mushrooms *
1   fairly large cucumber
1   tablespoon light soy sauce *
2   teaspoons sesame oil *

1 tablespoon dry sherry or shao hsing wine *
1 tablespoon red wine vinegar
4 teaspoons dry mustard
   Salt to taste
1 teaspoon sugar

* Available in Chinese markets and by mail order. For more information see Chapter XI.

1. Place the chicken in a saucepan and add cold water to cover. Cover the saucepan, bring to a boil, and simmer 15 to 20 minutes. Turn off the heat and let the chicken stand about 10 minutes, then remove and run it immediately under cold water to make the skin firmer. Pull off the skin, leaving it in as sizable pieces as possible, and reserve the chicken for another use. Cut the skin into bite-size morsels.

2. Put the tree ears into a saucepan and add about 2 cups of water. Bring to a boil and simmer 10 minutes, then drain and rinse under cold water. Pick over the tree ears to remove any tough centers. Set aside.

3. Trim off the ends of the cucumber. Peel or not as desired. Split it in half, then, using a melon ball cutter or a spoon, scoop out the seeds. Slice thin crosswise and pile the cucumber in the center of a serving platter. Garnish with the chicken skin and tree ears.

4. Combine the remaining ingredients and let stand 20 minutes. Stir to blend and pour the sauce over the contents of the platter.

YIELD: 6 to 8 servings

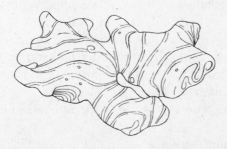

CORIANDER AND BEAN CURD
WITH SESAME SAUCE

The coriander and bean curd:

1   square dried brown bean curd *
1   cup peanut, vegetable, or corn oil
½   cup raw shelled and hulled fresh unsalted peanuts,*
    blanched
¾   pound fresh coriander leaves,* trimmed and washed

The sauce:

3   tablespoons light soy sauce *
3   tablespoons sesame oil *
2   teaspoons sugar
¼   teaspoon monosodium glutamate
½   teaspoon salt

  * Available in Chinese markets and by mail order. For more information see Chapter XI.

1. Place the bean curd in a small saucepan and add water to cover. Simmer about 15 minutes, then drain and cool. When it is cool, slice and shred it, then cut into very fine dice, as uniform as possible. Place in a bowl.

2. Heat the oil, and when it is almost smoking turn off the heat and add the peanuts. Cook, stirring with a wooden spoon, until the peanuts are golden brown, 30 to 40 seconds. Take care that they do not become dark brown. Drain and reserve the oil for another use. Pour the peanuts onto paper toweling to remove excess oil.

3. Drop the coriander into 2 quarts boiling water, then drain immediately. Chill under cold running water and squeeze with the hands to extract as much water as possible. Tear off and discard any really tough stems. Chop the remainder fine and add it to the bean curd. Toss to blend. Spoon the mixture onto a serving dish and scatter the peanuts over all.

4. Blend the ingredients for the sauce and pour over all.

YIELD: 8 or more servings

COLD CHRYSANTHEMUM LEAVES
WITH SESAME OIL ❖

1 large or 2 small bunches chrysanthemum leaves * (about
   2 pounds)
1 piece dried brown bean curd *
¼ cup light soy sauce *
1 tablespoon dry sherry or shao hsing wine *
2 tablespoons sesame oil *
½ teaspoon monosodium glutamate (optional)
1 teaspoon sugar
   Salt to taste

* Available in Chinese markets and by mail order. For more information see Chapter XI.

1. Cut off and discard the tough ends of the chrysanthemum leaves. Normally the leaves have a great deal of sand, which must be washed away, so drop the whole leaves into cold water and wash well. Rinse each leaf individually, and when thoroughly clean drain in a colander.

2. Bring enough water to a boil in a saucepan to cover the leaves. Add the leaves and turn off the heat. Stir with chopsticks for about 1 minute, then turn the heat on high and cook 2 minutes longer, stirring. Drain and run under cold water immediately. Squeeze between the hands to extract as much moisture as possible. Chop the greens fine and put into a mixing bowl.

3. Bring more water to a boil, drop the bean curd in, and let simmer about 10 minutes. Let stand until thoroughly cool. Slice the bean curd very thin, then stack the slices and cut into very fine dice (about ⅛-inch cubes). Add the bean curd to the chrysanthemum leaves.

4. Combine the remaining ingredients and pour over the chrysanthemum–bean curd mixture. Serve cold.

YIELD: 6 to 8 servings

SZECHWAN CABBAGE PICKLE ❖

      1   quart water
          Salt to taste
      1   teaspoon Szechwan peppercorns *
      1   pound very fresh cabbage (about three-quarters of a
          firm head)
 2 to 4   hot dried red peppers *
      4   cloves garlic, peeled and crushed but not chopped (op-
          tional)

 * Available in Chinese markets and by mail order. For more information see
Chapter XI.

1. In a saucepan, bring the water to a boil. Add salt to taste and
remove from the heat. Pour the water into a very clean 2-quart jar
and let cool.

2. Place the peppercorns in a skillet and cook over moderate heat,
shaking the skillet, until roasted. Add to the water.

3. Cut the cabbage into pieces about 2 inches square. Rinse well
and shake to remove excess water. Add the cabbage to the water,
then add the hot peppers and the garlic. Cover closely and let stand
in a cool place overnight. The cabbage should be ready to eat after
24 hours. It will keep for about 2 weeks in the refrigerator, and fresh
cabbage (celery cabbage may also be used, as well as strips of fresh
cucumber) may be added to replace that which is eaten.

YIELD: About 2 quarts

There is an unusual appetizer in Chinese cookery that blends cold, thinly sliced, cooked kidneys with thin slivers of celery. This is chilled, then served with a savory, spicy sauce containing sesame oil and soy sauce.

COLD KIDNEY AND CELERY ❖

The kidneys and celery:

    ¾   pound pork kidneys (4 to 6, depending on size)
8 or 10   ribs tender celery

The sauce:

  2½   tablespoons light soy sauce *
   2   teaspoons dry sherry or shao hsing wine *
   2   teaspoons sesame oil *
      Salt to taste
   ¼   teaspoon monosodium glutamate (optional)
   2   teaspoons hot oil,* homemade or purchased
   2   teaspoons sugar
   1   tablespoon red wine vinegar

* Available in Chinese markets and by mail order. For more information see Chapter XI.

1. The most important step in this recipe is the proper preparation of the kidneys. The thin transparent membrane surrounding each kidney must be pulled off, the center core must be totally and neatly trimmed away, and the kidneys must be sliced as thin as possible, always holding the knife at an angle.

2. Place the raw kidneys flat on a cutting surface and split them neatly in half. Place the two halves cut side up. Holding the knife parallel to the cutting surface, carefully cut away and discard the core. Have a basin of cold water ready for the kidney slices.

3. Now, hold the knife almost parallel but at a slight angle to the cutting surface and slice the kidney very thin, ⅛ inch or less, the

more uniform the slices the better. There will be irregular slices, of course, and some will be thinner than others. No matter. Continue until all the kidneys have been sliced, always dropping the pieces as they are sliced into the cold water. (Some of the less thin slices, incidentally, may be butterflied.) Let stand in cold water, changing the water several times to bleed the slices. Finally, drain and rinse well.

4. Meanwhile, rinse and pat dry the celery ribs. Pare the outside, if necessary, to remove bruised spots, using a swivel-bladed vegetable cutter. Cut each rib into 2-inch lengths, then flatten each piece lightly with the flat side of a knife. Cut the pieces lengthwise into very fine matchlike strips. There should be about 3½ to 4 cups.

5. Bring 2 quarts of water to a rolling boil and turn off the heat. Immediately add the kidney slices and let stand, stirring, about 1 minute. To test for doneness, pull one slice in two. If it is not bloody inside, it is done. Drain immediately and run under cold water.

6. Bring 2 more quarts of water to a boil and turn off the heat. Immediately add the celery and let stand, stirring, 45 seconds—no longer, or the celery will become limp. Drain immediately and run under cold running water. Pat the celery dry.

7. Arrange the celery on a serving dish and place the kidneys on top. Cover with clear plastic wrap and chill.

8. When ready to serve, combine all the ingredients for the sauce, blend well, and pour over the kidneys and celery.

YIELD: 8 or more servings

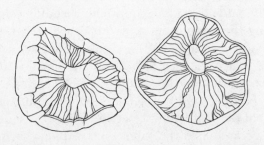

There is a fascinating cold dish in Chinese cookery made with squid and celery. It is served with a sweet and pungent light sauce flavored with sesame oil, one of the world's most seductively flavored oils.

SQUID AND CELERY ❖
(A Cold Dish)

The squid and celery:

2 pounds very fresh squid
1 teaspoon baking soda
¾ cup tree ear mushrooms *
4 or more ribs celery, trimmed, thinly sliced lengthwise, then cut into 1½-inch lengths (about 3½ cups when shredded)

The sauce:

6 tablespoons light soy sauce *
1 tablespoon sugar
Salt to taste
1 tablespoon red wine vinegar
2 tablespoons sesame oil *
2 teaspoons hot Chinese mustard (see Chapter XI)

* Available in Chinese markets and by mail order. For more information see Chapter XI.

1. Hold one squid at a time under cold running water, rub the mottled, purplish outer skin with the fingers, and pull the layer away. Discard it. Cut off the tentacles, then pull away and discard the center bone, ink sac, jaw, and eyes, leaving only the triangular body of white firm meat. Rinse thoroughly. Continue until all the squid are cleaned.

2. Cut the bodies of the squid into rectangles, measuring roughly 1½ by 4 inches. Place the pieces of squid, inner-skin side up, on a flat surface.

3. Using a sharp knife or Chinese cleaver, score the squid pieces as you would score the fat of a ham, but at ⅛-inch intervals. Score lightly, making sure that the skin is not cut through. This technique is important, because the squid will curl nicely when it is cooked.

4. Place the squid in cold water to cover and dissolve the soda in the water. Let stand one hour, then drain and rinse thoroughly in cold running water.

5. Bring 6 cups of water to a boil and add the squid pieces. Blanch no more than 30 seconds. The pieces will curl. Drain quickly in a colander and run under very cold water.

6. Meanwhile, place the tree ears in a small bowl and add ¾ cup cold water. Work with the fingers to wash the sand out. Drop into boiling water to cover and simmer 2 minutes when the water returns to a boil. Remove with a slotted spoon and drop into cold water. Drain well.

7. Bring another 6 cups of water to a boil and add the celery. Let stand 30 seconds and drain immediately, then run under cold running water. Drain well.

8. Combine all the ingredients for the sauce and stir to blend.

9. Arrange the celery on a platter, cover with the squid, and garnish with tree ears. Cover and refrigerate.

10. When ready to serve, spoon the sauce over all.

YIELD: 8 or more servings

III

Poultry

HOW TO CUT COOKED POULTRY FOR SERVING, CHINESE STYLE:

1. Cut off the head, if any, and reserve or discard. Cut off the neck and reserve.
2. Cut off the wings close to the body and reserve.
3. Lay the fowl on its back, breast side up, and cut it in two down the center of the breast. A rubber mallet to pound the cleaver through the bone, and a pair of kitchen shears, are helpful.

4. Cut off the backbone section along the length of each half of the fowl.

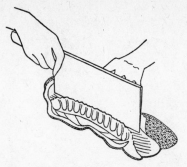

Cut the backbone into bite-size pieces and re-form in the center of a serving platter.

5. Cut the reserved wings into 2 or 3 serving pieces and arrange on the platter on each side of the cut-up backbone.

6. Cut the reserved neck into sections and arrange on one end of the platter. If the head is to be served, split it in half lengthwise and put at the top of the platter above the neck bones.

7. Take the remaining 2 halves of the body and chop crosswise into pieces 1 inch wide, one half at a time. Re-form each half into its original shape on the platter, on top of the bones, with the tail at the opposite end of the platter from the head or neck.

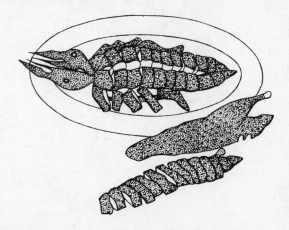

Garnish with fresh coriander or parsley and serve.

HOW TO SKIN AND BONE A FOWL

Place the fowl, back side down, on a flat surface and cut off the wing tips and the second wing bone. Leave the main wing bone intact. Using a sharp boning knife, work carefully from the neck down, separating the skin from the bones by cutting the fibers holding them together.

It is important to work as carefully as possible so as not to puncture the skin of the fowl. Always cut toward the flesh—it doesn't matter if the flesh becomes a bit mangled. As you separate the skin from the carcass, pull the skin downward as if you were peeling off a sweater.

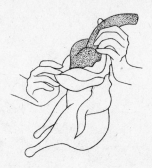

As you go past the wing just below the "shoulder" of the fowl, detach the lower part of the main wing bone with kitchen shears so the lower end of the bone goes along with the skin. Keep on peeling the skin down, detaching the fibers as you go.

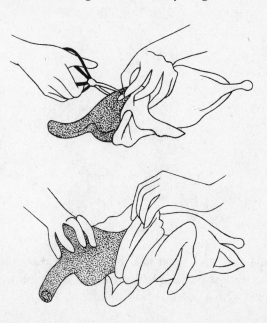

When you come to the middle of the leg below the meaty part of the drumstick, sever the bone so the lower portion of the leg bone comes off with the skin. The ends of the wing and leg bones will keep the stuffing from leaking out of the bird.

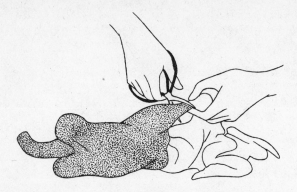

The tail should come off with the skin as a whole. Detach it by snipping all around the tail with kitchen shears.

Pull off the skin and lay it flat. If you have made any holes in the skin (and it's almost inevitable around the wing joint, where the skin is thin), mend with a needle and thread.

Chinese cooks, like European cooks, have a penchant for sauces. But whereas most European sauces are cream or brown sauces, Chinese sauces are frequently made with a base of soy sauce and oil, with the spice of ginger and the delicate flavor of scallions.

POACHED CHICKEN WITH GINGER
AND SCALLION SAUCE ❖

1 whole chicken (2½ to 3 pounds)
  Sesame oil *
6 tablespoons of peanut, vegetable, or corn oil
¼ cup finely shredded fresh ginger *
3 scallions, green part included, trimmed and cut into 4-inch
  lengths, then cut into fine strips
2 tablespoons light soy sauce *
2 teaspoons sugar
  Salt to taste
1 tablespoon dry sherry or shao hsing wine *
½ teaspoon monosodium glutamate (optional)

* Available in Chinese markets and by mail order. For more information see Chapter XI.

1. Place the chicken in a kettle and add water to cover. Bring to a boil and simmer about 20 minutes. Turn off the heat and let the chicken stand in the cooking liquid just until warm. Drain, reserving the broth for another use. Run the chicken under cold water, drain, pat dry, and rub lightly with sesame oil.

2. Cut the chicken into serving pieces, then chop into bite-size morsels. Arrange neatly on a platter.

3. Heat the peanut, vegetable, or corn oil in a saucepan, and when it is hot add the ginger and scallions. Cook about 30 seconds. Drain, but reserve the oil.

4. Scatter the ginger and scallions over the chicken.

5. To the oil add the remaining ingredients. Bring to a boil and pour over the chicken. Serve at room temperature.

YIELD: 4 to 8 servings

The following dish seems especially well adapted to very small chickens or Cornish game hens weighing about one pound.

DEEP-FRIED CUT CHICKEN
IN SCALLION MARINADE

1   chicken (1 pound), cut into serving pieces
2   tablespoons light soy sauce *
1   tablespoon dry sherry or shao hsing wine *
¼   teaspoon monosodium glutamate (optional)
1   1-inch piece fresh ginger,* crushed
1   teaspoon sugar
    Salt to taste
1   scallion, green part included, trimmed and cut into 1-inch
       lengths
    Cornstarch for dredging
    Peanut, vegetable, or corn oil for deep frying

* Available in Chinese markets and by mail order. For more information see Chapter XI.

1. Place the chicken in a mixing bowl.

2. Blend the soy sauce, wine, monosodium glutamate, ginger, sugar, salt, and scallion. Pour this mixture onto the chicken and let stand about 10 minutes.

3. Remove the chicken pieces and dredge generously in cornstarch, massaging briefly.

4. In a wok or skillet heat the oil, and when it is hot add the chicken pieces, one at a time. Cook, turning the pieces in the oil, about 5 minutes. Remove the chicken pieces but leave the oil in the pan.

5. Let the chicken stand 5 minutes or longer. Just before serving, return the chicken to the pan and cook over high heat until crisp, 2 minutes or less.

YIELD: 2 to 4 servings

Does anybody remember—or not remember—those porcupine meat balls that were so popular in America and perhaps elsewhere in the 1930s? They were made with ground beef and raw rice, and when they were steamed the balls did look a little prickly. We'd be willing to wager they had their origin in China. Here is a similar, infinitely more sophisticated recipe made with chicken and glutinous rice.

SNOW-WHITE CHICKEN ❖

1   cup glutinous rice *
2   whole chicken breasts, split in half and boned but with
      skin left on
1   tablespoon dry sherry or shao hsing wine *
1   tablespoon rendered chicken fat (see Chapter XI) or oil
      Salt to taste
½   teaspoon sugar
¼   teaspoon monosodium glutamate (optional)
1   egg white
2½ tablespoons cornstarch

* Available in Chinese markets and by mail order. For more information see Chapter XI.

1. Place the rice in a bowl and add 3 cups water. Soak overnight or at least 6 hours.

2. Place each breast half on a flat surface and cut into 6 or 8 more or less uniform pieces, leaving the skin attached. Turn each piece over, skin side down, and score lightly, crisscross fashion. As each piece is scored, put it into a bowl.

3. Add the wine, chicken fat or oil, salt, sugar, and monosodium glutamate. Mix with the fingers and let stand 10 minutes or longer.

4. Drain the rice, pour it onto a flat surface, and pat dry.

5. Lightly oil 3 plates that will fit inside a steamer and set aside.

6. Blend the egg white, cornstarch, and salt to taste. Dip each piece of chicken into the cornstarch mixture, then into the glutinous rice. The pieces should be well coated with the rice. Arrange the pieces on the oiled plates.

7. Place the plates inside a steamer top (in steamers with two or three tiers all the plates can steam together; otherwise, steam the plates one at a time). In any event, cover and steam 30 minutes. Pour off any fat that might accumulate around the chicken pieces and serve.

YIELD: 4 to 8 servings

Chicken has the most remarkable facility for bringing out and complementing the flavors of other foods. Broccoli is a case in point. This is an inexpensive dish, inasmuch as it is made with chicken wings.

CHICKEN WITH BROCCOLI

8	chicken wings
2	teaspoons plus 1 tablespoon cornstarch
	Salt
1¼	teaspoons sugar
3	branches broccoli taken from 1 large stalk
1	tablespoon dry sherry or shao hsing wine *
¼	teaspoon monosodium glutamate
1	cup peanut, vegetable, or corn oil
½	cup chicken broth
2	tablespoons water

* Available in Chinese markets and by mail order. For more information see Chapter XI.

1. Cut the chicken wings at the joints. Discard the small wing tips or use them for soup.
2. Using a sharp knife, split the main wing bone and second wing bone lengthwise to facilitate boning. Use the fingers and scrape with the knife to remove the flesh and skin of the wings. Cut the meat

from each joint in half to make bite-size pieces and put these into a mixing bowl. Discard the bones or use them for soup.

3. To the chicken in the mixing bowl add the 2 teaspoons cornstarch, 1 teaspoon salt, and ¼ teaspoon of the sugar. Set aside.

4. Cut or break the tops of the broccoli into "flowerets." If necessary, scrape the stems of the flowerets with a swivel-bladed potato peeler to make them tender. Scrape the main broccoli stalks with the peeler. Cut the stalks diagonally into bite-size morsels.

5. Blend together the wine, salt to taste, the remaining sugar, and monosodium glutamate. Set aside.

6. In a wok or skillet heat the oil and add the chicken pieces. Cook, stirring, about 90 seconds, then spoon out the chicken, leaving the oil.

7. Add the broccoli to the pan and cook in the oil, stirring, about 60 seconds, or until crisp-tender. Spoon out and drain. Pour all but 1 tablespoon of oil from the pan.

8. Return the broccoli and chicken to the pan and cook, stirring, about 20 seconds. Add the wine mixture and cook about 1 minute, stirring. Add the chicken broth, and when it boils, about 15 seconds, add the 1 tablespoon cornstarch blended with the water. Serve hot.

YIELD: 4 to 8 servings

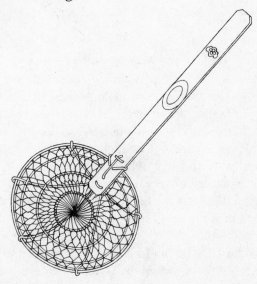

Chicken with Walnuts is another dish that was all but unknown to Westerners a few short years ago. Within the past decade, however, it has had a remarkable but understandable surge of popularity.

CHICKEN WITH WALNUTS

1 cup whole walnut halves
2 whole chicken breasts, boned and skinned (about 1 pound)
½ egg white (beat the egg white lightly, then divide in half)
1 tablespoon cornstarch
  Salt to taste
½ teaspoon sugar
¼ teaspoon monosodium glutamate
1 cup peanut, vegetable, or corn oil
3 thin slices fresh ginger,* peeled
4 cloves garlic, flattened but left whole
8 pieces hot dried red peppers * (optional)
1 tablespoon dark soy sauce *
1 tablespoon dry sherry or shao hsing wine *

* Available in Chinese markets and by mail order. For more information see Chapter XI.

1. Aesthetically, both to the palate and to the eye, it is preferable to peel the walnut halves, but it is time-consuming and tedious and rarely done in restaurants. If you want to peel them, place the halves in a bowl and pour boiling water over them to cover. Let stand about 2 minutes, then take out the walnuts one by one and pull off the skin.
2. Cut the chicken breasts into ½-inch cubes. Put the cubes into a mixing bowl and add the egg white, cornstarch, salt, sugar, and monosodium glutamate. Refrigerate for at least ½ hour.
3. In a wok or skillet heat the oil and add the chicken cubes. Cook, stirring, over high heat about 45 seconds, then spoon out the chicken, leaving the oil in the pan.
4. Add the walnut halves and cook, watching carefully and stirring, until they are golden brown. Take care that they do not burn.

Drain well into a sieve-lined bowl to catch the drippings, discarding all but 1 tablespoon of oil.

5. Heat the 1 tablespoon of oil in the pan and add the ginger, garlic, and hot peppers. Remove and discard the seasonings, but leave the oil.

6. Add the soy sauce and the chicken and toss and stir quickly over high heat about 10 seconds.

7. Add the wine and stir over high heat about 10 seconds. Add salt to taste, then spoon the chicken onto half of a serving dish. Spoon the walnuts onto the other half and serve immediately.

YIELD: 3 to 8 servings

What can anyone say about snow peas except that they are one of the most luxurious of vegetables? They're a marvelous foil for chicken.

STIR-FRY CHICKEN WITH SNOW PEAS

24	snow peas *
1	chicken (2½ to 3 pounds), cut into serving pieces
2	tablespoons cornstarch
3	tablespoons dry sherry or shao hsing wine *
8 to 10	large dried black mushrooms *
1	tablespoon light soy sauce *
1	tablespoon dark soy sauce *
2	teaspoons sugar
	Salt to taste
	Peanut, vegetable, or corn oil
2	teaspoons water

* Available in Chinese markets and by mail order. For more information see Chapter XI.

1. Pinch or pull off the stem ends of the snow peas and, if necessary, "string" the peas.

2. Run a knife along the bone structure of each piece of chicken, cutting through to the bone. Run the knife around the bone and remove it. Discard the bones or use them for stock.

3. Do not skin the chicken pieces, but carefully cut away and discard the stringy white fibers and membranes where they occur. Cut the boned meat into bite-size morsels.

4. Put the pieces into a mixing bowl and add 1 tablespoon of cornstarch and 1 tablespoon of wine. Stir to coat the pieces.

5. Place the mushrooms in a bowl and add boiling water to cover. Let stand 15 to 30 minutes, then drain and squeeze to remove excess liquid. Cut off and discard the stems. Set the mushrooms aside.

6. Blend the soy sauces, sugar, salt, and remaining 2 tablespoons of wine. Blend and stir in the remaining tablespoon of cornstarch. Stir to blend. Set aside.

7. Heat about 2 cups of oil in a wok or saucepan, and when it is hot and almost smoking add the chicken. Cook over high heat, stirring, 3 to 4 minutes. Remove the chicken pieces with a slotted spoon or strainer, but leave the oil in the pan.

8. To the hot oil add the mushrooms and snow peas and cook, stirring, about 30 seconds.

9. In a clean wok or skillet add 2 tablespoons of oil, and when hot stir in the soy sauce mixture. Stir about 5 seconds and turn off the heat. Add the chicken and water and turn the heat to high.

10. Add the snow peas and mushrooms and cook, stirring, about 30 seconds. Serve immediately.

YIELD: 3 to 6 servings

Although whole or quartered tomatoes are used on occasion in Chinese cookery, they are not common. Tomato sauces, on the other hand, play a fairly important role. The following is an excellent dish of chicken in a light tomato sauce.

CHICKEN BREASTS IN TOMATO SAUCE

2   whole chicken breasts, split in half, skinned, and boned
1   tablespoon egg white (beat the egg white lightly, then measure)
2   teaspoons cornstarch
    Salt to taste
    Peanut, vegetable, or corn oil
¾   pound tomatoes, cored, peeled, and quartered
8   water chestnuts,* cut in half
6   thin slices fresh ginger,* peeled
6   cloves garlic, flattened but not chopped
¼   teaspoon monosodium glutamate (optional)
3   teaspoons sugar
⅓   cup frozen green peas, partially defrosted

* Available in Chinese markets and by mail order. For more information see Chapter XI.

1. Place the chicken pieces on a flat surface, skinned side down. Cut each piece into rectangles or squares ¾ inch long, more or less.

2. Turn each piece boned side up and lightly score in a crosswise fashion, making a diamond pattern. Place the pieces in a mixing bowl and add the egg white, cornstarch, and salt. Blend well. Refrigerate at least 30 minutes.

3. Heat 2 tablespoons of oil in a wok or skillet and add the tomatoes. Cook, stirring, over high heat about 5 minutes. Stir in another tablespoon of oil and set aside.

4. Heat about 3 cups of oil in another wok or a kettle and add the chicken. Cook, stirring, about 45 seconds, then drain by removing the chicken into a large strainer set over a bowl.

5. Pour off all but about ¼ cup of the oil from this pan and add the water chestnuts. Cook about 10 seconds, then add the tomatoes. Add salt to taste, the ginger, garlic, monosodium glutamate, and sugar. Cook about 3 minutes, stirring, then add the peas and cook quickly. Add the chicken and cook, stirring, just until the chicken is heated through. Serve hot.

YIELD: 4 to 6 servings

There is an expression in Chinese recipes that seems odd to Western ears, although it is logical to the Chinese. It occurs when a certain nonfish dish is labeled "with fish flavor." It does not mean that the dish will taste of fish, but that it will be served in a sauce that is also used for fish.

CHICKEN WITH FISH FLAVOR

2 whole chicken breasts, boned and skinned (about 1 pound), and finely shredded
1 tablespoon egg white (beat the egg white lightly, then measure)
   Salt to taste
2 teaspoons sugar
3½ teaspoons cornstarch
6 dried black mushrooms *
2 tablespoons chili paste with garlic (Szechwan paste) *
2 tablespoons light soy sauce *
¼ teaspoon monosodium glutamate (optional)
1 tablespoon dry sherry or shao hsing wine *
1 cup shredded bamboo shoots *
8 small fresh green long hot peppers * (optional), cut into thin strips (julienne)
3 tablespoons peeled, thinly sliced fresh ginger *

½   cup thinly sliced carrot rounds
4   cloves garlic, flattened but left whole
    Peanut, vegetable, or corn oil
⅓   cup plus 3 tablespoons water
1   teaspoon sesame oil *

* Available in Chinese markets and by mail order. For more information see Chapter XI.

1. Prepare the chicken and put it into a mixing bowl. Add the egg white, salt, ½ teaspoon sugar and 1½ teaspoons of the cornstarch and blend. Refrigerate for at least 30 minutes.

2. Place the mushrooms in a bowl and add boiling water to cover. Let stand 15 to 30 minutes. Drain, cut off and discard the tough stems, and cut the caps into shreds. Set aside in a bowl.

3. Combine the chili paste with garlic, the soy sauce, 1½ teaspoons sugar, monosodium glutamate, wine, and salt to taste. Set aside.

4. Add the bamboo shoots, fresh hot peppers, ginger, and carrots to the mushrooms. Set aside.

5. Prepare the garlic and set aside.

6. In a wok or skillet heat 1 cup of oil and add the chicken shreds, stirring to separate the shreds. Cook about 30 seconds, stirring over high heat. Drain immediately.

7. To the same pan add 2 tablespoons of fresh oil and the garlic. Cook, stirring, over high heat 30 seconds. Add the mushroom mixture and cook, stirring, over high heat about 50 seconds.

8. Add the chili paste mixture and the ⅓ cup water. Stir and cook over high heat about 2 minutes, then add the chicken and cook, stirring, about 30 seconds.

9. Blend the remaining 2 teaspoons of cornstarch with the 3 tablespoons water and stir it in to thicken. Cook about 1 minute, stirring, and pour into a serving dish. Dribble the sesame oil over all and serve.

YIELD: 3 to 8 servings

Fermented, salted black beans have an almost winy flavor, and they give an intriguing flavor to almost any dish in which they are cooked. Here they are used with chicken and shallots, a not too common ingredient in Chinese cookery.

CHICKEN WITH BLACK BEANS AND SHALLOTS

      1   chicken (2 to 2½ pounds), cut into serving pieces,
               plus liver, heart, and gizzard
      2   tablespoons cornstarch
      4   tablespoons fermented, salted black beans *
      3   tablespoons dry sherry or shao hsing wine *
      2   tablespoons chopped fresh ginger *
      4   cloves garlic, crushed but left whole
10 to 14   shallots, peeled and left whole
      ¼   cup rendered chicken fat (see Chapter XI) or pea-
               nut, vegetable, or corn oil
      1   tablespoon light soy sauce *
      1   tablespoon dark soy sauce *
      1   teaspoon sugar
           Salt to taste

* Available in Chinese markets and by mail order. For more information see Chapter XI.

1. Using the fingers and a small knife, bone the chicken pieces but leave the skin on. Discard the bones or use them for soup.

2. Cut the chicken flesh into 1- or 1½-inch cubes and put into a mixing bowl with the liver and heart. Cut away and discard the tough membrane or muscle from the gizzard, then add the gizzard. Add the cornstarch and blend.

3. Blend the black beans with 2 tablespoons of the wine and let stand.

4. Combine the ginger, garlic, and shallots.

5. Heat the fat or oil in a wok or skillet and add the chicken. Cook about 4 minutes, stirring, over high heat, then add the ginger mix-

ture. Cook, stirring, about 1 minute and turn off the heat. Scoop out the chicken mixture, leaving the oil in the pan.

6. Turn on the heat and add the black bean mixture, mashing down with a spoon. Add the soy sauces and sugar. Cook about 30 seconds and add the chicken mixture. Add the remaining tablespoon of wine and salt to taste. Stir over high heat about 1½ minutes and serve hot.

YIELD: 4 to 8 servings

It is not apocryphal to say that there are certain sauces in Chinese cookery that last for twenty years or longer—that is to say, a basic sauce is prepared, it is added to over the years, and thus the original sauce is perpetuated for twenty years. The sauce for the following chicken dish could be in that category. The sauce would be saved after the chicken is cooked, and when it is reused the same ingredients would be added, but in lesser quantities and according to taste.

SOY SAUCE CHICKEN ❖

1   chicken (3½ to 4 pounds), freshly killed and preferably with
      head on
    Salt
1   cup dark soy sauce *
½ cup light soy sauce *
3   cups cold water
1   cup sugar
½ cup dry sherry or shao hsing wine *
1   tablespoon rendered chicken fat (see Chapter XI)
    Sesame oil *

* Available in Chinese markets and by mail order. For more information see Chapter XI.

1. Remove and reserve the fat, if there is any, from the cavity of the chicken for use at another time. Rub the cavity with about 1 tablespoon of salt.

2. Tie a string around the chicken neck to facilitate maneuvering the chicken in the sauce as it cooks.

3. In a wok or flameproof casserole large enough to hold the chicken, add the soy sauces, water, sugar, and salt to taste. Bring to a boil.

4. Put the chicken into the sauce, breast side down, letting the string hang out of the utensil. Pour the wine over the chicken, bring the liquid to a boil, and immediately turn down to a simmer. Cook uncovered, turning the chicken in the sauce every 10 minutes or so to cook evenly. Add more water if the liquid cooks down too much.

5. When the chicken is thoroughly coated with the liquid, add the chicken fat to the sauce and continue cooking until the chicken is tender, about 1 to 1½ hours depending on the size and age of the chicken. Turn the chicken as necessary.

6. Remove the chicken and brush it all over with sesame oil. The cooking liquid may be saved and reused, if desired.

7. Let the chicken stand to room temperature, then cut it into chopstick-size morsels, bone and all, and serve.

YIELD: 4 to 8 servings

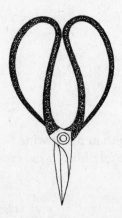

There is a traditional legend about the dish that is known in Chinese cookery as Beggar's Chicken, and it has to do with a rogue who many years ago made off with a fine, fat fowl from a rich man's coop. He took his feathered loot in a bag to the river's edge and made a roaring fire preparatory to roasting. Just when the ashes were right he glanced up the hill and spied the law approaching. He hastily scooped up mud from the river's bank, enclosed the chicken, feathers and all, to disguise it, and dropped the chicken in the smoldering ashes. The police arrived and bided their time for an hour or so. On their departure the beggar cracked the clay which, when removed, took the feathers with it. His prize, thus roasted, was, or so the legend has it, delicious. This is the modern version of that dish, with the chicken cleaned and defeathered to be sure—and baked in a clay utensil designed for fowl.

BEGGAR'S CHICKEN ❖

1   chicken (3½ to 4 pounds), left whole (see Note)
     Salt
2   tablespoons dark soy sauce *
3   tablespoons dry sherry or shao hsing wine *
6   dried black mushrooms *
½   cup shredded Szechwan preserved vegetable * (or use an
        equal amount of sauerkraut that has been well rinsed)
⅓   cup peanut, corn, or vegetable oil
¼   pound ground pork
1   cup thinly sliced bamboo shoots *
½   teaspoon sugar
½   teaspoon monosodium glutamate (optional)
1   large piece of caul fat (lace fat) *

* Available in Chinese markets and by mail order. For more information see Chapter XI.

1. Rub the chicken inside and out with salt, 1½ tablespoons of the soy sauce, and half the wine. Set aside for an hour or so.

2. Meanwhile, place the mushrooms in a small bowl and add boiling water to cover. Let stand 15 to 30 minutes, then drain and squeeze to extract much of their moisture. Cut off and discard the tough stems. Slice the caps thin and set aside.

3. Preheat the oven to 450 degrees.

4. Rinse the preserved vegetable well and slice thin. Cut each slice into thin strips and set aside.

5. Heat the oil in a wok or skillet, and when it is hot add the pork. Cook quickly, stirring, until lightly browned. Add the mushrooms, preserved vegetable, and bamboo shoots, then add the remaining soy sauce and wine, salt to taste, sugar, and monosodium glutamate. Cook 1 minute, stirring, then set aside to cool.

6. Stuff the mixture inside the chicken and sew up or skewer the cavity. Wrap the chicken in a single layer of the caul fat. The chicken should be totally enclosed in the caul, but use a minimum amount of it. Cut off excess pieces of the fat.

7. Rub the inside of a clay mold with caul fat and line the bottom with a small piece of caul. Place the chicken in the mold and cover. Bake 1 hour at 450 degrees, then reduce the heat to 350 degrees and continue cooking 30 to 45 minutes longer. Serve the chicken from the mold.

YIELD: 4 to 6 servings

Note: Traditionally (though it is not necessary) the head is left on the chicken. Chickens with head and feet left on are available in poultry markets in any Chinatown.

This is one of the most elegant of Chinese dishes, preferably made with blanched walnuts from which the skin has been peeled from the meat. Directions for peeling walnuts will be found in the Chicken with Walnuts recipe. On the other hand, peeling the walnut meats is a tedious, laborious task, and few people will have the necessary patience. Thus, Brazil nuts are recommended as a substitute.

CHINESE CHICKEN WITH NUTS

2 whole chicken breasts, split in half, skinned, and boned (4 separate pieces when ready)
¼ cup cornstarch
2 teaspoons salt
¼ teaspoon monosodium glutamate (optional)
1 teaspoon sugar
1½ tablespoons dry sherry or shao hsing wine *
2 egg whites
1¼ cups finely chopped fresh walnuts, or use an equal amount of skinned, chopped Brazil nuts
Peanut, vegetable, or corn oil for deep frying
Fresh coriander * or parsley sprigs for garnish

* Available in Chinese markets and by mail order. For more information see Chapter XI.

1. Slice the chicken breasts at an angle into paper-thin slices (about ⅛-inch thick). (This is easier to do if the meat is partially frozen.) Set aside on waxed paper.

2. Place the cornstarch, salt, monosodium glutamate, and sugar in a bowl. Add the wine and blend. Beat the egg whites lightly but not until frothy, and gradually stir them into the cornstarch mixture. Stir until smooth.

3. Arrange the chopped nuts in a pie plate or other plate.

4. Dip the chicken fillet first into the cornstarch mixture on both sides, then into the chopped nut mixture. Place on waxed paper and let stand until all the fillets are coated.

5. In a wok or deep-fryer, heat the oil almost to the smoking point. Turn off the heat and add the chicken pieces, a few at a time, without crowding. Cook, stirring and turning the pieces in the oil, until golden brown, no longer than 2 or 3 minutes. Turn on the heat if necessary for the last pieces, but do not overcook. Drain on paper toweling. Garnish with fresh coriander or parsley sprigs and serve immediately.

YIELD: 8 or more servings

Chinese sausages—those red and white, cigar-shaped morsels that hang by the hundreds in Chinese groceries—have a sweet-spice flavor that is altogether admirable. They give a fine aroma and flavor to chicken when steamed together. An excellent casserole dish.

CHICKEN STEAMED WITH CHINESE SAUSAGE ❖

1   chicken (3 pounds), cut and chopped into bite-size pieces (bone included)
2   tablespoons cornstarch
2   tablespoons dark soy sauce *
2   tablespoons dry sherry or shao hsing wine *
2   teaspoons sugar
   Salt to taste
2   tablespoons peanut, vegetable, or corn oil
¼   teaspoon monosodium glutamate (optional)
4   Chinese pork sausages *

* Available in Chinese markets and by mail order. For more information see Chapter XI.

1. Place the chicken in a mixing bowl and add the cornstarch, soy sauce, wine, sugar, salt, oil, and monosodium glutamate. Mix well with the hands.
2. Arrange the pieces in a soufflé dish or similar heatproof utensil about 8½ inches in diameter. Start with the neck and back pieces as

a base and continue making layers until all the chicken is arranged.

3. Rinse and pat the Chinese sausages dry. Slice them diagonally, into ¼-inch-thick slices. Arrange these slices neatly and close together over the chicken.

4. Place the dish, uncovered, in the top of a steamer, cover, and steam over boiling water 1½ hours.

YIELD: 6 to 8 servings

The following dish was named for a high-ranking Chinese official, Ting Kung Pao, who fled to Szechwan as a political refugee a few hundred years ago during the Ching Dynasty. It became popular in many provinces where the inhabitants dote on hot foods, such as Hunan and Kweichow. An interesting spiced dish, it is redolent with garlic and chili paste, hot peppers, and bean sauce.

KUNG PAO CHICKEN

1	large whole chicken breast, boned but not skinned
½	egg white (beat the egg white lightly, then divide in half)
2	teaspoons cornstarch
	Salt to taste
2	tablespoons bean sauce *
1	tablespoon hoi sin sauce *
1	tablespoon chili paste with garlic (Szechwan paste)*
1½	teaspoons sugar
1	tablespoon dry sherry or shao hsing wine *
¼	teaspoon monosodium glutamate (optional)
1	tablespoon red wine vinegar
4	cloves garlic, peeled and flattened but not chopped
2	cups peanut, vegetable, or corn oil
12 to 16	hot dried red peppers,* cut in half
1	cup raw shelled and hulled fresh unsalted peanuts *

* Available in Chinese markets and by mail order. For more information see Chapter XI.

1. Cut the chicken into ¾-inch cubes. Combine with the egg white, cornstarch, and salt. Refrigerate for 30 minutes.

2. Combine the bean sauce, hoi sin sauce, chili paste with garlic, sugar, wine, monosodium glutamate, vinegar, and garlic and set aside.

3. Heat the 2 cups of oil in a wok or skillet, and when it is almost boiling hot but not smoking turn the heat off and add the peanuts. The peanuts should turn light golden brown from retained heat, but if they don't, turn the heat on and cook briefly, watching carefully—they cook very fast and will continue to cook after being removed from the heat. Drain and reserve the oil.

4. Heat 1 cup of the reserved oil in the pan (save the rest for another use). When the oil is hot, add the chicken mixture. Cook quickly, only about 45 seconds, stirring, until the chicken becomes translucent. Do not brown. Remove the chicken and drain well. Pour off all but about 2 tablespoons of the oil from the wok.

5. Add the peppers and cook until dark—about 15 seconds longer. Add the sauce and the chicken and cook about 1 minute. Serve sprinkled with the peanuts.

YIELD: 4 to 8 servings

The chicken and spinach in the following recipe have a most remarkable affinity for each other. As an added conceit the whole dish may be sprinkled with toasted pine nuts, sometimes called pignolia nuts.

SHREDDED CHICKEN WITH SPINACH

1   whole chicken breast, skinned and boned
2   teaspoons egg white (beat the egg white lightly, then measure)
2   teaspoons cornstarch
    Salt to taste
1   teaspoon sugar

½ teaspoon monosodium glutamate (optional)
2 cups peanut, vegetable, or corn oil, approximately
¼ cup pine nuts (optional)
1 pound fresh spinach in bulk or 1 10-ounce package fresh spinach, washed well and picked over to remove any tough stems
2 tablespoons dry sherry or shao hsing wine *
¼ cup water

* Available in Chinese markets and by mail order. For more information see Chapter XI.

1. Place the chicken breast on a flat surface and slice it thin on the bias with a sharp knife. Then cut the slices into very thin shreds. (This is easier to do if the meat is partially frozen before slicing and the slices stacked before shredding.) There should be about 1 cup lightly packed.

2. Place the chicken in a bowl and add the egg white, half the cornstarch, salt to taste, half the sugar, and half the monosodium glutamate. Stir to blend with the fingers, then refrigerate 30 minutes.

3. If the pine nuts are going to be used (they are not essential), heat 2 cups of oil in a wok or saucepan until almost smoking. Add the pine nuts and immediately turn off the heat. Let stand without adding more heat, but stir them. They should brown fairly quickly. If not, turn on the heat again and cook until they are golden brown, taking care that they do not become too brown. Drain and reserve the oil. Drain the pine nuts well and set aside.

4. Put 1½ cups of the reserved oil (or fresh oil, if you are not using the pine nuts) into the pan and heat it moderately. Add the chicken and cook, stirring, until the pieces separate and start to turn white, about 15 seconds. Do not overcook. Drain in a sieve-lined bowl and save the oil. Set the drained chicken aside.

5. Add 3 tablespoons of the reserved oil to the pan and heat until almost smoking. Add the spinach and cook, stirring briskly, about 45 seconds. Add the remaining sugar and monosodium glutamate. Add salt to taste, and after about 45 seconds add the wine. Cook, stirring, briefly, taking care not to overcook. Drain and place the spinach on one end of a serving platter.

6. Mix the remaining cornstarch with the water.

7. Quickly wipe out the pan. Heat it and add about 2 tablespoons of the reserved oil from the chicken. Heat the oil until almost smoking, add the chicken, and cook briskly, stirring. Stir in the water and cornstarch mixture and cook, stirring, about 30 seconds. Spoon the chicken onto the other end of the platter, next to the spinach. Scatter the pine nuts, if used, over all and serve.

YIELD: 4 to 8 servings

What follows is a most incredibly delicate chicken dish, a genuine banquet dish. Despite its delicate nature, however, it isn't difficult to make.

CHICKEN VELVET

 1 whole chicken breast, skinned and boned
1½ tablespoons plus 2 teaspoons cornstarch
     Salt to taste
 ½ teaspoon sugar
 ¼ teaspoon monosodium glutamate (optional)
1½ cups chicken broth
 1 tablespoon dry sherry or shao hsing wine *
 8 egg whites
 ¼ cup water
 2 cups peanut, vegetable, or corn oil
 ½ cup frozen peas, slightly thawed to separate
 2 tablespoons rendered chicken fat * (see Chapter XI)
 ½ cup very finely chopped ham (preferably salt cured, or
        Smithfield boiled ham), about the consistency of coarse
        salt

* Available in Chinese markets and by mail order. For more information see Chapter XI.

1. Using a sharp knife, cut away and discard the slender, silvery sinew that may be found on each chicken breast half. Cut the chicken breast halves into small cubes and place in the container of an electric blender.

2. Add the 1½ tablespoons cornstarch, salt to taste, sugar, monosodium glutamate, 1 cup of the broth, and the wine. Blend, stirring down as necessary with a rubber spatula.

3. Place the egg whites in a mixing bowl and stir in the blended mixture with chopsticks until smooth and combined. But stir—do not beat.

4. Combine and have ready the remaining 2 teaspoons cornstarch and the ¼ cup water. Set aside.

5. Heat the oil in a wok or skillet, and when it is hot but not smoking turn off the heat and immediately add the liquid chicken mixture. Turn on the heat and cook, stirring very gently with a flattish round spoon (the traditional wok spoon is ideal for this, but, if the dish is cooked in a skillet, a pancake turner might be best). This must be delicately done. Cook about 1 minute in all or until set, and gently transfer the preparation to drain in a colander with large holes, set over a bowl.

6. Pour off all but 2 tablespoons of oil from the pan. Heat the oil, and when it is hot add the frozen peas. Toss them quickly in the oil and return the chicken to the pan. Stir by gently bringing the mixture from the bottom of the pan to the top in a folding motion. Pour the remaining ½ cup of broth over all and stir to bring it down to the bottom. Stir up the reserved cornstarch and water mixture and gradually stir it in until thickened. Add salt to taste. When the dish is cooked, sprinkle with the 2 tablespoons of chicken fat. Transfer to a serving dish and garnish with the finely chopped ham.

YIELD: 6 to 8 servings

Over the past hundred years or so the Chinese have adopted—for better or for worse—numerous ingredients that seem more or less typically Western. Among them are tomatoes and corn. The English made a slight mark in the Chinese kitchen with Worcestershire sauce. The following very good, very inexpensive dish employs both tomatoes and Worcestershire sauce.

CHICKEN WINGS WITH TOMATO SAUCE ❖

> 2 pounds chicken wings (about 10 to 12)
> ¼ cup peanut, vegetable, or corn oil
> 1 tablespoon chopped fresh ginger *
> 1½ tablespoons chopped garlic
> 2 cups fresh or canned drained, peeled tomatoes
> 2 tablespoons Worcestershire sauce
> 2 tablespoons light soy sauce *
> 1 tablespoon red wine vinegar
> Salt to taste
> 2 teaspoons sugar
> ¼ teaspoon monosodium glutamate

* Available in Chinese markets and by mail order. For more information see Chapter XI.

1. Rinse and drain the chicken wings.

2. Cut off and discard the small wing tips. Cut between the main and second wing joints and set aside.

3. Heat the oil in a wok or skillet, and when it is hot add the chicken pieces. Cook over high heat, stirring, about 3 minutes.

4. Add the ginger and garlic and cook, stirring, about 1 minute. Then add the remaining ingredients, cover partially, and cook, turning the chicken pieces occasionally until the sauce is concentrated. This should take about 25 minutes. If the sauce is not sufficiently reduced, turn the heat to very high and cook briefly. Spoon out and serve hot or at room temperature.

YIELD: 6 to 8 servings

There are wide variations in the nomenclature of Chinese dishes. Some of the names are largely poetic—Eight Precious Jewel Pudding (see recipe), for example, or "golden scallops in green meadows." Some of them bear the names of people, such as Kung Pao Chicken (see recipe), which, as we have pointed out, was named for a high official. And some of them are simply descriptive of the principal ingredients. Moo Goo Gai Pin is a case in point. *Goo* is the Chinese word for mushroom; *moo goo* is the Chinese name for button mushroom. *Gai* means chicken and *pin* (sometimes spelled "pan") means slices.

MOO GOO GAI PIN

1 chicken breast (about ¾ pound before skinning and boning)
5 teaspoons cornstarch
1 teaspoon plus 2 tablespoons water
   Salt to taste
1 teaspoon dry sherry or shao hsing wine *
¼ teaspoon ground white pepper
1 pound button mushrooms or ¾ to 1 cup drained, canned
      mushrooms (see Note)
   Chicken broth
1 cup peanut, vegetable, or corn oil
⅓ cup thinly sliced bamboo shoots *
¾ cup celery cabbage,* stalk part only, cut into 3-inch lengths
½ teaspoon sugar
¼ teaspoon monosodium glutamate (optional)
1 tablespoon rendered chicken fat (see Chapter XI)
1 15-ounce can straw mushrooms * (optional; see Note)

* Available in Chinese markets and by mail order. For more information see Chapter XI.

1. Have the chicken breast skinned and boned or skin and bone it yourself.
2. Cut the chicken into the thinnest possible slices. (This is easier if the meat is partially frozen.) Put the slices into a mixing bowl and

add 1 teaspoon of the cornstarch blended with 1 teaspoon of the water, salt, wine, and pepper. Blend to coat the chicken pieces.

3. If fresh button mushrooms are used, cut off the stems and rinse well. Add chicken broth to cover and simmer 5 minutes. Drain. There should be about ¾ to 1 cup.

4. In a wok or skillet, heat the oil over a high flame and add the sliced chicken. Cook, stirring, just to separate the pieces and until the meat has lost its pink color, about 15 seconds. Drain into a sieve-lined bowl to catch the drippings, leaving 2 tablespoons of oil in the pan.

5. To the oil in the pan, add the mushrooms, bamboo shoots, and cabbage. Cook, stirring, about 2 minutes. Add 1 cup of chicken broth and bring to a rapid boil. Add the sugar and monosodium glutamate. Cook about 30 seconds.

6. Blend the remaining cornstarch with the remaining water and stir it in. When thickened, add the chicken. Cook, stirring, until the chicken is piping hot. Dribble the chicken fat over all and serve immediately.

YIELD: 2 to 6 servings

Note: Imported canned straw mushrooms give added elegance to this dish. (The 15-ounce can specifies that it offers 8 ounces drained weight.)

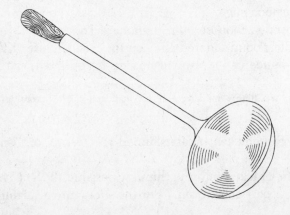

This is a fascinating dish, so named because it is traditionally garnished with chrysanthemum flower petals, although they are not essential to the success of the dish. The filling for the chicken is shrimp and crab.

CHRYSANTHEMUM CHICKEN

The chicken and filling:

1	whole chicken (3 to 3½ pounds; traditionally the chicken for this dish has the head on and must be purchased at a poultry farm; it can be made successfully, however, with supermarket chickens)
8	raw shrimps, peeled and deveined
	Salt to taste
1	teaspoon sugar
½	teaspoon monosodium glutamate (optional)
3½	tablespoons dry sherry or shao hsing wine *
2½	tablespoons cornstarch
2 to 3	ounces fresh pork fat
¾	pound additional shrimps, in the shell
1	cup lump crab meat, picked over to remove all traces of shell and cartilage
	Fresh chrysanthemum petals (optional)

The sauce:

2	cups chicken broth
1½	tablespoons cornstarch
3	tablespoons water
1	tablespoon dry sherry or shao hsing wine *
	Salt to taste
¼	teaspoon monosodium glutamate
3 to 4	tablespoons milk
2	tablespoons rendered chicken fat (see Chapter XI)

* Available in Chinese markets and by mail order. For more information see Chapter XI.

1. The chicken must be boned entirely except for four bones, which are left intact: the leg bones and the main wing bones. Follow the instructions on p. 44.

2. Lay the chicken, opened up, on a flat surface with the skin side down.

3. Drop the 8 peeled and deveined shrimps into boiling water and cook until just pink. Drain immediately. When they are cool enough to handle, chop them coarse-fine. There should be about ⅓ cup. Put them into a small mixing bowl and add salt, the sugar, monosodium glutamate, 1½ tablespoons of the wine, and 1½ teaspoons of the cornstarch.

4. Drop the pork fat into boiling water and cook until tender, then drain and cut into fine cubes. Add to the shrimp mixture, blend, and set aside.

5. Peel the remaining shrimps and devein under cold running water. Split the shrimps in half and put them into the blender. Blend, stirring down as necessary, until coarsely blended. Do not over-blend, or the mixture will become a puree. Mix with the cooked shrimp and pork fat mixture.

6. Dust the opened-up chicken with the remaining 2 tablespoons of cornstarch and spread the chicken flesh with the shrimp mixture.

7. Combine the crab meat with salt to taste and the remaining 2 tablespoons of wine. Stir lightly and spread this over the shrimp filling.

8. Bring the outside edges of the chicken (where it was split in the first place) together and sew up the opening, or fold one edge firmly over the other. Place the chicken in a Pyrex dish or another plate that may be fitted inside the top of a steamer. Cover the top of the steamer, place the whole over boiling water, and steam 45 minutes to 1 hour, depending on the size of the chicken. Let cool slightly before carving.

9. Meanwhile, prepare the sauce. Put the chicken broth into a saucepan and, when it boils, stir in the cornstarch blended with the 3 tablespoons of water. Add the wine, salt, monosodium glutamate, milk, and chicken fat. Slice the chicken, removing the sewing thread, if any, and arrange on a serving dish. Pour the boiling sauce over

all and, if available, sprinkle with chrysanthemum petals that have been rinsed in cold water and patted dry.

YIELD: 6 to 8 servings

One of the specialties of the province of Fukien (one of the provinces closest to Hong Kong) is a fermented red paste made with rice and frequently called "red wine rice sauce." It has a beguiling flavor and is a principal ingredient in the dish below. The paste is available in Chinese markets but is by no means so common as soy sauce. Dark soy sauce can be substituted for the red wine sauce.

RED WINE SAUCE CHICKEN

2 cups boneless, skinless, finely shredded chicken breast
2 tablespoons red wine rice paste * or dark soy sauce *
1 tablespoon dry sherry or shao hsing wine *
1 tablespoon rendered chicken fat (see Chapter XI)
½ egg white (beat the egg white lightly, then divide in half)
1 tablespoon plus 2 teaspoons cornstarch
2 teaspoons sugar
Salt to taste
1 tablespoon chicken broth
¼ teaspoon monosodium glutamate
Peanut, vegetable, or corn oil
10 ounces (1 cellophane package) fresh spinach, rinsed and patted dry
6 tablespoons water
½ cup pine nuts, deep fried until golden (optional)

* Available in Chinese markets and by mail order. For more information see Chapter XI.

1. Place the shredded chicken in a mixing bowl and add the red wine rice paste, wine, chicken fat, egg white, and the 1 tablespoon cornstarch. Knead briefly, then add the sugar, salt to taste, chicken broth, and monosodium glutamate. Knead just enough to blend. Refrigerate for 30 minutes.

2. In a wok or skillet heat 2 tablespoons of oil, and when it is hot add the spinach. Cook, stirring, about 15 seconds. Add salt to taste and cook, stirring and tossing over high heat, about 1 minute. Drain and press down to remove excess moisture. Arrange the spinach in a circular or oval border on a plate. Keep warm.

3. Heat 1½ cups of oil in a wok and turn off the heat. Add the chicken, quickly stirring to separate the shreds. Immediately turn on the heat and cook over high heat, stirring, about 1 to 2 minutes. Drain in a sieve-lined bowl, pressing down to remove excess oil. Discard the oil.

4. Return the chicken to the pan and add ¼ cup of the water and toss about 1 minute over high heat. Blend the 2 teaspoons cornstarch with the remaining 2 tablespoons of water and stir it in to thicken.

5. Spoon the chicken into the center of the spinach ring and garnish with the nuts, if desired.

YIELD: 4 to 8 servings

It is fascinating, if not unfortunate, how many people are not pre-disposed to liking a certain food if it is uncommon to their diet or if they hear of eating something that they have known only in another context. Dried jellyfish when soaked and cooked with other foods is delicious, and the texture is interesting. One of the best dishes with jellyfish is this one, in which it is stir-fried with chicken shreds.

STIR-FRY CHICKEN SHREDS WITH JELLYFISH

1 1-pound package dried jellyfish *
1 whole chicken breast (about ½ pound), skinned and boned
1 tablespoon plus 1 teaspoon cornstarch
1 tablespoon egg white (beat the egg white lightly, then measure)
   Salt to taste
¾ teaspoon monosodium glutamate (optional)
1½ teaspoons sugar
2 cups plus 6 tablespoons peanut, vegetable, or corn oil
1 tablespoon water

* Available in Chinese markets and by mail order. For more information see Chapter XI.

1. Wash the salt from the dried jellyfish and place it in a bowl. Add water to cover to a depth of about 1 inch above the jellyfish. Let stand for several hours or overnight, changing the water several times.

2. Drain the jellyfish and cut it into fine shreds. Put it into a mixing bowl. Pour boiling water to cover over the jellyfish and let stand about 30 seconds. Drain well and immediately run under cold running water. Drain thoroughly.

3. Cut the chicken into very thin slices, then cut the slices into very thin shreds. (This is easier to do if the meat is partially frozen before slicing and the slices are stacked before shredding.) Put the shreds into a mixing bowl and add the 1 tablespoon cornstarch and the egg white, salt to taste, ¼ teaspoon of the monosodium glutamate, and ½ teaspoon of the sugar. Blend with the fingers and refrigerate for at least 30 minutes.

4. In a wok or skillet heat 3 tablespoons of the oil. Add the jelly-fish and cook over high heat, stirring, about 10 seconds. Add salt to taste, ¼ teaspoon of the monosodium glutamate, and ½ teaspoon of the sugar. Cook, stirring, over high heat about 1½ minutes. Drain. You will note that the jellyfish gives up a great deal of water as it cooks.

5. In another wok or skillet warm the 2 cups of oil and add the chicken. Cook briefly until the shreds are separated and the meat turns white, no longer. Drain in a sieve-lined bowl to catch the drippings. Wipe out the pan.

6. Heat 3 tablespoons of the oil to almost smoking and add the chicken. Stir quickly and add salt to taste, the remaining ¼ teaspoon of monosodium glutamate, and the remaining ½ teaspoon of sugar. Add the jellyfish and cook over high heat, stirring and tossing, about 30 seconds.

7. Blend the 1 teaspoon cornstarch and the water, stir in quickly, and serve hot.

YIELD: 4 to 8 servings

The Coconut Chicken below is in truth not basically Chinese but a recipe adapted to the Chinese cuisine from some of the curries of the Portuguese colonies. It is an excellent curry made with a curry paste and coconut cream available from Kalustyan's Orient Export Trading Corporation, 123 Lexington Avenue, New York, N.Y. 10016.

COCONUT CHICKEN ❖

1   chicken (3 pounds), cut into serving pieces, plus the
       liver, gizzard, and heart
1½ pounds potatoes (3 or 4, depending on size)
¾   pound onions (4 or 5, depending on size)
5   tablespoons peanut, vegetable, or corn oil
4   tablespoons hot Indian Vindaloo paste (Jawahir brand,
       available in tins from Kalustyan's)

¼ teaspoon monosodium glutamate (optional)
10 small whole cloves garlic, peeled and flattened with a knife
2 tablespoons dry sherry or shao hsing wine *
   Salt to taste
2 tablespoons sugar
5 to 10 hot dried red peppers * (optional)
3 cups plus 3 tablespoons water
½ cup Philippine coconut cream (Jawahir brand, available in tins from Kalustyan's), more or less
1 cup milk
4 teaspoons dark soy sauce *
1½ tablespoons cornstarch
2 tablespoons fresh bread crumbs

* Available in Chinese markets and by mail order. For more information see Chapter XI.

1. Cut the pieces of chicken into bite-size morsels, 1 or 2 inches in length. Place the pieces in a mixing bowl with the liver, gizzard, and heart.

2. Peel the potatoes into 2-inch cubes and drop the pieces into cold water to prevent discoloration. There should be about 3 cups.

3. Peel the onions. Slice in half, then cut each half into ½-inch-thick slices.

4. Preheat the oven to 350 degrees.

5. In a wok or large skillet heat 3 tablespoons of the oil, and when it is hot add the onions. Cook, stirring, until they are wilted, about 2 minutes. Add the chicken pieces, including the liver, gizzard, and heart, and cook, stirring, about 5 minutes. Drain and add the potatoes.

6. In another pan heat the remaining 2 tablespoons of oil and add the Vindaloo paste. Cook, stirring, about 1 minute without browning, then add to the chicken. Cook about 5 minutes.

7. Add the monosodium glutamate, garlic, wine, salt, sugar, red peppers, and the 3 cups water. Bring to a boil and cover. Cook about 10 minutes over medium heat, then uncover and stir.

8. Add the coconut cream and milk and cook 5 minutes, then add

the soy sauce. Blend the cornstarch with the 3 tablespoons water and add it while stirring. Cook 3 minutes, then transfer the curry to a large heatproof casserole. Sprinkle with the bread crumbs.

9. Bring to a boil on top of the stove, then place the uncovered casserole in the oven and bake 20 minutes. Serve piping hot.

YIELD: 8 to 10 servings

Chinese cooking in many respects is one of the most economical cuisines of the world. The Chinese prefer for most recipes the lesser cuts of beef and poultry, and they make much of chicken wings.

SPICED CHICKEN WINGS ❖

12	chicken wings
3	tablespoons dry sherry or shao hsing wine *
	Water
2	whole star anise,* or the equivalent thereof in broken pieces
2	small sticks cinnamon (each about 1 inch long)
2	tablespoons dark soy sauce *
1	tablespoon sugar
	Salt to taste

* Available in Chinese markets and by mail order. For more information see Chapter XI.

1. Place the chicken wings in an ungreased wok or heatproof casserole and add the wine. Cook until almost all the wine has evaporated.

2. Add 1 cup water, cover, and cook over medium heat about 10 minutes. Add the star anise and cinnamon and cook, covered, about 5 minutes, then add the soy sauce, sugar, and salt. Cover and let simmer about 30 minutes. As the dish cooks, uncover occasionally to stir the chicken wings around in the sauce. If it seems as if the wings are becoming too dry, it may be necessary to add a little

water, 3 to 4 tablespoons. When cooked, the wings should be tender and nicely coated in the sauce. The total cooking time for the chicken wings should be about 45 minutes.

YIELD: 4 to 6 servings

When almost anyone is asked what frogs' legs taste like, the answer is almost invariably, "Like chicken more than anything else." The Chinese cook takes advantage of this and combines the two in this stir-fried dish.

STIR-FRY CHICKEN WINGS WITH FROGS' LEGS

6	chicken wings
8	pairs frogs' legs
½	egg white (beat the egg white lightly, then divide in half)
2	teaspoons plus 1 tablespoon cornstarch
5	dried black mushrooms *
	Peanut, vegetable, or corn oil for deep frying
3	cloves garlic, crushed
3	scallions, white part only, trimmed and cut into 1-inch lengths
1 or 2	sweet or long hot green or red peppers,* cored, seeded, and cut into 8 or 10 rectangles
8	very thin slices fresh ginger,* peeled
½	cup chicken broth
1	tablespoon dry sherry or shao hsing wine *
¼	teaspoon ground pepper
1	teaspoon sesame oil *
2	tablespoons water
1	tablespoon rendered chicken fat (see Chapter XI)

* Available in Chinese markets and by mail order. For more information see Chapter XI.

1. With a knife or cleaver, cut the wings into 3 parts at the joints. Discard the wing tips.

2. Using a boning knife or sharp paring knife, bone the remaining chicken pieces. To do this, use the knife to follow the bone line of each piece and slit the flesh. Work the knife around the bone and remove the flesh in one piece, including the skin. Place the boned flesh on a flat surface and pound lightly on the boned side. Score each piece lightly with a knife.

3. Cut each pair of frogs' legs in half, then cut each leg to separate the pieces at the joints. Bone the frogs' leg pieces just as the chicken was boned. Combine the meat of the frogs' legs with the chicken meat. Blend the egg white and the 2 teaspoons cornstarch and stir into the chicken and frogs' leg mixture. Refrigerate for at least 30 minutes.

4. Put the mushrooms into a mixing bowl and add boiling water to cover. Let stand 15 to 30 minutes. Drain and squeeze the mushrooms to extract most of the moisture. Cut off and discard the tough stems.

5. In a wok or deep-fryer, heat the oil for deep frying, and when hot but not smoking add the chicken and frogs' leg mixture. Cook briefly, about 1 minute, stirring, then drain by scooping into a sieve-lined bowl. Do not cook through.

6. Pour off all but 1 tablespoon of the oil from the pan. Add the garlic, scallions, peppers, ginger, and mushrooms. Cook about 1 minute, then add the chicken and frogs' leg mixture. When thoroughly hot, add the chicken broth, wine, pepper, and sesame oil. Cook about 30 seconds. Blend the remaining tablespoon of cornstarch and the water and stir in. When slightly thickened, stir in the chicken fat.

YIELD: 4 to 6 servings

The following recipe calls for two spices—tsao kao and shan yau—which are difficult but not impossible to obtain in spice shops in any Chinatown. The dish is excellent, however, even if it is made without them. They are included for the sake of authenticity. This is a spicy dish, but not in the peppery sense. It is first cooked in a spice bath and later deep-fried.

This dish should be started a day or so before you plan to serve it, since the chicken should be hung to dry for twelve hours or more and then again for at least another two hours.

SING FONG CHICKEN

    4   sticks cinnamon
    6   star anise *
    2   tablespoons ordinary anise seeds
   40   whole cloves
    1   tablespoon Szechwan peppercorns *
    4   slices licorice root *
    2   tsao kao (optional)
   10   pieces shan yau (optional)
    2   quarts plus ¼ cup water
        Salt to taste (approximately 7 tablespoons)
    1   chicken (2½ to 3 pounds)
    2   tablespoons honey
    1   tablespoon red wine vinegar
        Peanut, vegetable, or corn oil for deep frying
        Watercress and/or cherry tomatoes for garnish

* Available in Chinese markets and by mail order. For more information see Chapter XI.

1. Combine the cinnamon, star anise, regular anise, cloves, peppercorns, licorice root, tsao kao, and shan yau. Pour the 2 quarts of water into a wok or kettle and add the spices and salt. Bring to a boil and cook 15 minutes.

2. Tie the neck or feet of the chicken with string to facilitate manipulating it in hot water and place the chicken, breast side down, in the liquid. The chicken legs should be in the boiling water. Spoon the hot liquid all over the chicken with a large spoon for about 3 minutes, then turn off the heat. Cover and let the chicken stand in the liquid 10 minutes or longer.

3. Uncover. Lift the chicken out while holding the string. Bring the liquid to a boil again, and when full and rolling return the chicken to the pan, this time placing it on its back. (There is no need to spoon the water over this time.) Turn off the heat again, cover, and let stand 10 minutes. Remove the chicken, leaving the string on. Hang the chicken in a cool and preferably windy place. (An electric fan in a cool room would work well—or it may be put into a garage or a cellar.) Let it hang, if possible, 12 hours or longer.

4. Put the honey, the remaining ¼ cup of water, and the vinegar into a small saucepan. Heat and stir briefly until combined. Do not brush the syrup on the chicken, but rub the chicken all over with the syrup, using your hands. Rehang the chicken for 2 hours or longer in a cool place.

5. Heat the oil in a wok or deep-fryer and add the chicken on its back. Baste with oil for about 15 seconds, then turn, basting continually. Cook, basting, for a total of about 12 to 15 minutes. Drain and cut into chopstick-size morsels. Serve hot, garnished with watercress and/or cherry tomatoes.

YIELD: 4 to 8 servings

Chicken giblets—the liver, the gizzard, and the heart—may not have universal appeal, but they are delectable stir-fried with celery cabbage, bamboo shoots, and black mushrooms.

STIR-FRY CHICKEN GIBLETS
WITH CELERY CABBAGE

3   sets of chicken giblets (3 livers, 3 gizzards, and 3 hearts)
1   tablespoon light soy sauce *
1   teaspoon dark soy sauce *
1   tablespoon cornstarch
2   tablespoons dry sherry or shao hsing wine *
4   large dried black mushrooms *
½   cup thinly sliced bamboo shoots *
¾   cup shredded celery cabbage *
1   teaspoon sugar
¼   teaspoon monosodium glutamate (optional)
    Salt to taste
⅓   cup peanut, vegetable, or corn oil
½   cup water

* Available in Chinese markets and by mail order. For more information see Chapter XI.

1. Cut the livers in half and drop into water to cover. Bring to a boil, then turn off the heat and let stand 1 minute. Drain and set aside in a mixing bowl.

2. Carefully slice off and discard the tough musclelike coating that covers the meaty part of the gizzards. Cut the meaty part into thin slices. Add to the livers.

3. Split the hearts down one side and open them. Add to the livers and gizzards.

4. Add the soy sauces, the cornstarch, and 1 tablespoon of the wine to the prepared giblets.

5. Meanwhile, put the mushrooms into a mixing bowl and add boiling water to cover. Let stand 15 to 30 minutes. Squeeze the

mushrooms to extract most of their moisture, then cut off and discard the tough stems. Cut the mushroom caps into quarters. There should be about ⅓ cup.

6. Combine the mushrooms, bamboo shoots, and cabbage. Set aside.

7. Combine the sugar, monosodium glutamate, and salt and set aside.

8. In a wok or skillet heat the oil, and when very hot add the giblets. Cook, stirring, about 30 or 40 seconds, no longer. Scoop out with a slotted spoon and set aside.

9. Pour off all but about ¼ cup of oil from the pan and add the vegetable mixture. Cook, stirring, about 30 seconds.

10. Add the sugar mixture and cook, stirring, about 15 seconds. Add the water and cook 1 minute.

11. Add the giblets and cook, stirring, about 30 seconds. Stir in the remaining tablespoon of wine and cook 1 or 2 minutes longer.

YIELD: 3 to 8 servings

We have a friend who was taught in Chinese cooking class to pluck off the tip and string end of bean sprouts—a far more elegant manner of serving bean sprouts than simply leaving them as they come from the Chinese greengrocer. He is one of those rare people who still have a devoted servant in the kitchen, but, after spending an entire afternoon at that task, she informed him that if he ever brought another mess of bean sprouts in for cleaning she, for one, was leaving. Now he does it himself. Cleaning them is time-consuming, but it is worth it. The following is an elegant banquet dish, easily made (the bean sprouts don't really have to be cleaned, although we recommend it) and impressive both in appearance and flavor.

CHICKEN SHREDS WITH BEAN SPROUTS

3   chicken breast halves, skinned and boned
2   teaspoons cornstarch
½   egg white (beat the egg white lightly, then divide in half)
2   tablespoons dry sherry or shao hsing wine *
     Salt to taste
     Peanut, vegetable, or corn oil
3   cups bean sprouts * (preferably, with the root thread and
       the curlicue at the top pinched off)
¼   cup thinly shredded fresh red or green long hot peppers *
2   teaspoons sugar
¼   teaspoon monosodium glutamate (optional)

* Available in Chinese markets and by mail order. For more information see Chapter XI.

1. Place the chicken on a flat surface and slice it thin on the bias. Shred the slices as fine as possible. (This is easier if the meat is partially frozen before slicing and the slices stacked before shredding.)

2. Using the fingers, blend the shredded chicken with the cornstarch, egg white, 1 tablespoon of the wine, and salt to taste. Refrigerate for 30 minutes.

3. In a wok or deep-fryer heat oil for deep frying, and when it is warm but not piping hot add the chicken mixture. Cook, stirring, just until the shreds separate and the chicken loses its raw look. Drain in a sieve-lined bowl to catch the drippings and set aside. Pour off all but 3 tablespoons of the oil.

4. Heat the 3 tablespoons oil, then add the bean sprouts and salt to taste. Cook, stirring constantly, about 45 seconds in all. Drain.

5. Rinse out and wipe the pan. Add 2 tablespoons of oil, and when it is hot add the hot pepper shreds. Cook briefly and add the bean sprouts, the chicken, salt to taste, the sugar, monosodium glutamate, and remaining tablespoon of wine. Stir around just to heat thoroughly. Serve hot.

YIELD: 2 to 6 servings

Among the marvelous appetizers of the Chinese table are those wonderfully seasoned morsels wrapped in paper (or other material) and deep fried. The packages may contain chicken pieces or shrimp or ham, among other ingredients—or a combination of these foods, as in the following recipe.

CHICKEN, SHRIMP, AND HAM
IN PAPER PACKAGES

¾ pound chicken breasts, boned and skinned
32 very thin slices bamboo shoots,* each slice about 1½ inches wide (the shapes may vary—squares, rectangles, etc.)
16 raw shrimps, peeled, deveined, and split in half
1 teaspoon baking soda
   Salt to taste
¼ pound ham, preferably Smithfield ham, cut into 32 very thin squares or rectangles (1½ inches wide, more or less)
4 teaspoons sugar
3 tablespoons sesame oil *
2 tablespoons rendered chicken fat (see Chapter XI) or peanut, vegetable, or corn oil
2 tablespoons oyster sauce *
1½ tablespoons dry sherry or shao hsing wine *
4 cloves garlic
3 scallions, green part included, trimmed and cut into 1-inch lengths
10 thin slices fresh ginger,* peeled
6 tablespoons water
   Waxed paper (the ordinary kind)
64 small sprigs fresh coriander leaves * (optional)
   Peanut, vegetable, or corn oil for deep frying

* Available in Chinese markets and by mail order. For more information see Chapter XI.

1. Slice the chicken breasts on the bias into 32 very thin slices. (This is easier to do if the meat is partially frozen.) The slices will vary in size and shape, of course, but they should be approximately 2 inches square. Lay each slice on a flat surface and pound lightly with the flat side of a knife or cleaver. Set aside in a mixing bowl.

2. Set aside the prepared bamboo shoots in another mixing bowl.

3. Place the shrimps in a third mixing bowl and add the soda and salt. Set aside. (The soda, which makes the shrimps crisp, will be washed off later.)

4. Place the ham in a fourth mixing bowl and add half the sugar.

5. Prepare a marinade by combining the remaining sugar, sesame oil, chicken fat or oil, oyster sauce, and wine.

6. In the container of an electric blender, combine the garlic, scallions, ginger, and water. Cover and blend thoroughly. Place a sieve over a small bowl and strain the mixture, saving the juice but discarding the pulp. Add 3 tablespoons of the juice to the marinade. Reserve the remaining juice for another use or discard it.

7. Add the chicken slices and bamboo slices to the marinade.

8. Rinse the shrimps thoroughly under cold water. Drain well and pat dry. Add to the marinade.

9. Take a length of waxed paper and fold it over and over itself, with each fold measuring 9 inches wide. Using scissors or a knife, slit the paper at both folded ends. Now cut the paper to produce 9-inch squares. Continue folding and cutting until there are 32 squares in all.

10. Place one square at a time on a flat surface and start adding the filling. First, place a sprig of coriander, if used, in the center of the square. Then make layers as follows: 1 slice of bamboo shoot, 1 piece of ham, 1 piece of chicken, ½ shrimp, and finally another sprig of coriander. Fold the paper to make a package as indicated in the drawings. Be sure to fold the paper firmly and tuck the flap in tightly in the final step so that the packages won't come apart while cooking. The packages may be refrigerated for a few hours before cooking.

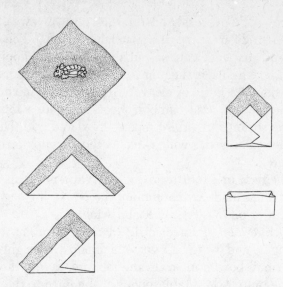

11. In a wok or deep-fryer, bring 1 quart or more of oil to piping hot and add half the packages, more or less, using your own judgment. Cook, turning each package once or twice, about 1½ minutes. The foods in the package should be cooked but not until they become dry. Drain on paper toweling and serve hot. To serve, let each guest help himself to a package and split it open with a fork or chopsticks before eating the inside.

YIELD: 5 to 12 servings

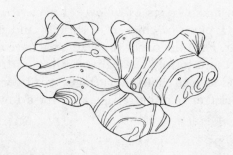

Chicken legs may be, along with the back and the wings, one of the more mundane parts of the chicken. They take on a whole new air, however, when steamed and fried and served with a sesame-flavored hot sauce.

SPICED CHICKEN LEGS WITH SESAME SAUCE

The chicken:

8   chicken legs (about 2 pounds)
2   star anise *
1   teaspoon Szechwan peppercorns *
3   1-inch broken pieces of cinnamon stick
1   1-inch piece of fresh ginger,* crushed
1   scallion, green part included, trimmed and cut into 2-inch lengths
¼   cup light soy sauce *
1   tablespoon dry sherry or shao hsing wine *
   Salt to taste
1   teaspoon sugar
¼   teaspoon monosodium glutamate (optional)
   Cornstarch for dredging
   Peanut, vegetable, or corn oil for deep frying

The sauce:

4   cloves garlic, finely chopped (about 1 tablespoon)
¼   cup light soy sauce *
3   tablespoons red wine vinegar
2   tablespoons sugar
1   teaspoon sesame oil *
½   teaspoon hot oil * (optional)
   Salt to taste

* Available in Chinese markets and by mail order. For more information see Chapter XI.

The dip:

>   Reserved marinade from the chicken
> 1   tablespoon cornstarch
> 2   tablespoons water

1. Put the chicken legs into a mixing bowl. Add the star anise, peppercorns, cinnamon pieces, ginger, scallion, soy sauce, wine, salt, sugar, and monosodium glutamate. Stir to coat the chicken parts. Let stand 2 hours or longer.

2. Place the chicken legs in a dish that will fit in the top of a steamer. Strain and reserve the marinade.

3. Place the dish with the chicken in the top of a steamer and set it over boiling water. Cover the steamer and steam 1 hour, then remove the dish and let the chicken cool. When cool, roll each piece of chicken lightly in cornstarch.

4. Heat the oil for deep frying in a wok or deep-fryer and cook the chicken until golden brown and crisp on the outside. Leave the legs whole or, preferably, use a cleaver to cut them into pieces that may be handled easily with chopsticks. Arrange the pieces on a platter.

5. To prepare the sauce, combine the garlic, soy sauce, vinegar, sugar, sesame oil, hot oil (including some of the powdered pepper residue), and salt. Pour this over the chicken pieces.

6. To prepare the dip, pour the reserved marinade into a saucepan and bring to a boil. Blend the cornstarch with the water and stir to thicken the sauce. Serve separately as a dip.

YIELD: 4 to 8 servings

Glutinous rice is, in truth, rice, but its characteristics are vastly different from those of ordinary table rice. It has, as the name states, a glutinous, sticky quality, and it has multiple uses in the Chinese kitchen. It is used here as the basis for a most appetizing and unusual stuffing for chicken.

CHICKEN STUFFED WITH GLUTINOUS RICE

 1 cup glutinous rice *
12 large dried black mushrooms *
 1 whole chicken (3 pounds), plus the gizzard and liver
 3 tablespoons plus ¼ cup peanut, vegetable, or corn oil
 ¾ cup pork, cut into ½-inch cubes
 1 teaspoon light soy sauce *
 1 teaspoon plus 3½ tablespoons dark soy sauce *
 ½ cup bamboo shoots,* cut into ½-inch cubes
 2 tablespoons sugar
    Salt to taste
 ½ teaspoon monosodium glutamate (optional)
 ½ cup thinly sliced bamboo shoots *
 6 tablespoons dry sherry or shao hsing wine *
 6 cups water
 2 scallions, green part included, trimmed and cut into 2-inch
       lengths

* Available in Chinese markets and by mail order. For more information see Chapter XI.

1. Place the rice in a mixing bowl and add cold water to cover to a depth of about 3 inches above the rice. Let soak overnight or at least 6 hours, then drain.

2. Line the top of a steamer with cheesecloth and scatter the glutinous rice over the cloth. Cover and steam over boiling water 1 hour, then let cool and set aside.

3. Place the mushrooms in a mixing bowl and add boiling water to cover. Let soak 15 to 30 minutes.

4. Remove the gizzard and liver from the chicken. Trim off the tough outer coating from the gizzard and discard it. Cut both the gizzard and liver into ⅜-inch cubes. Set aside.

5. Rinse the chicken inside and out and pat dry. Set it aside.

6. Remove 6 of the mushrooms and squeeze to extract most of the moisture. Cut off and discard the stems. Cut the caps into cubes and set aside. Reserve the remaining mushrooms and the mushroom liquid.

7. Heat the 3 tablespoons oil in a wok or skillet and add the pork. Cook, stirring, about 1 minute and add the light soy sauce and the teaspoon of dark soy sauce. Cook, stirring, about 15 seconds, then add the chicken giblets, cubed mushrooms, and cubed bamboo shoots.

8. Add 1 teaspoon of the sugar, salt to taste, and half the monosodium glutamate. Stir in 2 tablespoons of the wine and cook, stirring, over high heat about 2 minutes.

9. Stir in 2 cups of the cooked glutinous rice and let cool slightly.

10. Stuff the chicken with the mixture, and skewer it.

11. In a wok or heatproof casserole heat the ¼ cup oil and add the chicken. Cook, turning frequently to brown on all sides, about 3 minutes.

12. Add the remaining wine, the water, the remaining dark soy sauce, the remaining sugar, and the remaining monosodium glutamate. Cover and cook 1 hour, turning the chicken at 10-minute intervals. The sauce should be quite reduced.

13. Spoon out the remaining 6 mushrooms and reserve the soaking liquid. Squeeze the mushrooms to extract most of their moisture and cut off and discard the tough stems. Add them to the pan, along with ½ cup of mushroom liquid and the sliced bamboo shoots. Cook 20 minutes longer, turning the chicken occasionally. Transfer the chicken to a serving dish, remove the skewer, and pour the sauce over. Garnish with scallions.

YIELD: 4 to 8 servings

PON PON CHICKEN

1	chicken (2½ to 3 pounds), cut into serving pieces
3	tablespoons sesame paste *
2	tablespoons brewed tea
1	tablespoon hot oil *
¼	teaspoon monosodium glutamate (optional)
1	teaspoon salt, or to taste
2	teaspoons sugar
3	tablespoons chopped scallions, green part included
2½	tablespoons light soy sauce *
2	teaspoons sesame oil *
1 to 1½	tablespoons coarsely chopped garlic
2	tablespoons red wine vinegar
⅓	cup peanut, vegetable, or corn oil
¼	cup Szechwan peppercorns *
	Chopped fresh coriander leaves * (optional)

* Available in Chinese markets and by mail order. For more information see Chapter XI.

1. Place the chicken in a saucepan and add water to cover. Bring to a boil and simmer 15 minutes, or until done. Turn off the heat and let the chicken stand until cool.

2. Put the sesame paste into a mixing bowl and gradually stir in the tea. When well blended, add the hot oil, monosodium glutamate, salt, sugar, scallions, soy sauce, sesame oil, garlic, vinegar, and peanut, vegetable, or corn oil. Stir to blend well. The ingredients for the sauce may be adjusted according to taste.

3. Place the peppercorns in a small skillet and cook over moderate heat, stirring and shaking the skillet until they are roasted, then put them into the container of an electric blender and blend until fine. Add 1 tablespoon to the sauce. The remainder may be kept in a covered container indefinitely.

4. Pull the meat from the bones of the chicken and cut it into strips. Arrange them on a serving dish and pour the sauce over. Sprinkle with chopped coriander leaves and serve.

YIELD: 3 to 8 servings

Chinese chefs frequently indulge in a good deal of romance when they name their dishes. Take the one below, which in the Western world would probably be called something prosaic like "mock chicken legs," for it is actually made with finely ground or blended chicken meat mixed with ground shrimp, ham, and water chestnuts, with the whole thing shaped around chicken bones to resemble chicken legs. It is a fantasy, of course—but an exceptional fantasy.

PHOENIX AND DRAGON CHICKEN LEGS

4   chicken legs
4   chicken thighs
¾   pound raw shrimps, peeled and deveined
⅓   cup finely minced Smithfield ham
12 fresh or canned water chestnuts,* finely minced
1   small onion, finely minced (about ⅓ cup)
1½ tablespoons dry sherry or shao hsing wine *
2   tablespoons light soy sauce *
½   teaspoon monosodium glutamate (optional)
    Salt to taste
    Freshly ground pepper to taste
1   teaspoon sugar
1   tablespoon sesame oil *
    Cornstarch
1   egg
½   pound caul fat (lace fat) *
    Peanut, vegetable, or corn oil for deep frying
    Seasoned Salt (see recipe below)

* Available in Chinese markets and by mail order. For more information see Chapter XI.

1. Skin and bone the chicken legs and thighs or have them skinned and boned, but save the bones. Carefully remove all sliverlike fibers and tendons from the meat with a sharp knife. Chop the remaining chicken meat coarsely and put it into the container of an electric

blender. Blend well, then spoon and scrape the blended matter into a bowl.

2. Place the chicken bones in a kettle and add cold water to cover. Bring to a boil and simmer about 30 minutes. Drain and rinse under cold water. Carefully work with the fingers to clean the bones and make them, in effect, "bone" bare.

3. Place the shrimps on a flat surface and chop them fine, then add to the chicken. Add the ham, water chestnuts, and onion and blend. Add the wine, soy sauce, monosodium glutamate, salt, pepper, sugar, sesame oil, and 1 tablespoon of cornstarch and blend thoroughly.

4. Place the egg in a mixing bowl and beat well. Add 3 tablespoons of cornstarch and salt to taste. Beat well again.

5. Cut or trim the caul fat into 8 squares or rectangles that measure roughly 6 by 7 inches.

6. Lay out one square or rectangle at a time on a flat surface and rub it lightly with the egg and cornstarch mixture. Refrigerate for 30 minutes.

7. Spoon about ⅓ cup of the chicken mixture in the center of each square. Insert one chicken bone inside the mass and, using the fingers, mold and shape the meat around the bone to resemble a rather fat chicken leg. Leave part of the bone protruding, of course. Bring up the edges of the caul fat to envelop the meat but not the bone. Brush the outside of each "chicken leg" with the cornstarch mixture and dust lightly overall with cornstarch. (The legs may be refrigerated for a day or two at this point.)

8. Heat oil for deep frying in a wok or deep fryer and cook the legs, turning frequently in the hot oil, from 14 to 20 minutes, depending on the heat of the oil and the size of the legs. The legs should not be fried in oil that is too hot. Drain and serve hot, with the seasoned salt.

YIELD: 4 to 8 servings

SEASONED SALT

Heat ¼ cup Szechwan peppercorns (or use black peppercorns or a mixture of both) in a dry skillet. Cook, shaking the skillet, until the peppercorns start to smoke. Put into the container of an electric blender, add 2 or 3 tablespoons of salt, and blend thoroughly.

Squabs are one of the joys of the Chinese table, and they are cooked in many ways. This one, simply made, is in the Cantonese manner.

FRIED SQUABS CANTONESE STYLE

2   squabs, cleaned but preferably (to be really Chinese) with
     the heads left on
4   teaspoons salt
1   tablespoon dark soy sauce *
2   star anise *
     Peanut, vegetable, or corn oil for deep frying
     Watercress for garnish
     Seasoned Salt (see recipe; optional)

* Available in Chinese markets and by mail order. For more information see Chapter XI.

1. Rub the squabs very well inside and out with the salt and soy sauce. Place in a bowl, cover, and let stand about 3 hours.
2. Bring enough water to cover the squabs to a boil and add the star anise. Cook 10 minutes, then add the squabs. Cover and simmer over low heat, turning them occasionally in the water, for 45 minutes, then drain.
3. When cool enough to handle, attach a string around the neck of each squab. Hang them in a cold, preferably windy place (an electric fan in a cold room would work well—or they may be hung in a garage or a cellar) for an hour or longer, until dry.

4. In a wok or deep-fryer bring the oil to full heat without letting it smoke, and add the squabs, holding them by the strings. Cook, spooning hot oil over, and turning the squabs in the oil. Cut the squabs into serving pieces, including the heads, which are considered a delicacy. Serve garnished with watercress, and if desired, serve seasoned salt on the side for dipping.

YIELD: 2 to 8 servings

The squabs in the following dish are brushed with a caramel syrup before deep frying. The caramel gives them more of a mahogany look.

JUICY FRIED SQUAB

¾ cup water
¼ cup sugar
2 whole squabs, cleaned but (preferably) with heads left on
    Peanut, vegetable, or corn oil for deep frying
    Lemon wedges for garnish
    Seasoned Salt (see recipe)

1. Combine ½ cup of the water with the sugar in a saucepan. Have the remaining water at hand so it can be added immediately when needed.

2. Bring the sugar-water mixture to a boil and cook over moderately high heat. When it starts to become syrupy, stir constantly. The syrup will gradually turn from golden to light to dark brown. The syrup must be stirred constantly and watched carefully to make sure it does not burn. When the syrup becomes brownish-black, stir in the remaining water.

3. Pour this caramel syrup into a small, fairly deep dish large enough to hold the squabs when added. Let the caramel cool thoroughly, then add the squabs. Turn the squabs in the syrup occasionally so that they will be coated evenly all over.

4. Using 2 strings, one for each squab, tie the squabs by the neck. Hang them in a cool, dry, and preferably windy place. (An electric fan in a cold room would work well—or hang them in a garage or a cellar.) Let stand 3 or 4 hours, until the skin is dry.

5. In a wok or deep-fryer heat the oil for deep frying to the smoking point. Turn off the fire, then add the squabs, breast side down. Cook, turning the squabs occasionally and always spooning the oil over the exposed part of the squabs. When the squabs are lightly brown, turn on the fire to medium, and cook until the squabs are dark brown, 25 to 30 minutes. Drain. Cut up the squabs, then chop them into bite-size morsels. Garnish with lemon wedges and serve with seasoned salt on the side.

YIELD: 2 to 6 servings

Squab is a costly dish, but worth it for those whose purse can bear it. In a casserole or stir-fried it is elegant to the taste.

STIR-FRY SQUAB

2	squabs (1 pound each)
8	dried black mushrooms *
25	snow peas *
3	tablespoons dry sherry or shao hsing wine *
3	teaspoons cornstarch
	Salt to taste
1½	teaspoons sugar
4	thin slices fresh ginger,* peeled
¼	cup bamboo shoots,* cut into small pieces
3	scallions, green part included, trimmed and cut into 2-inch lengths
2	tablespoons light soy sauce *
¼	teaspoon monosodium glutamate (optional)

    1   cup peanut, vegetable, or corn oil
2 or 3   tablespoons chicken broth
    1   tablespoon water

* Available in Chinese markets and by mail order. For more information see Chapter XI.

1. Cut off the legs and wings of the squabs. Carefully cut away the breast meat. Cut away the meat from the fleshier parts of the legs and wings, discarding much but not all of the skin.

2. Cut the breast meat into very thin slices or cubes, ½ inch or smaller. Use only a small portion of the skin of the breast. Combine all the meats in a small bowl and set aside.

3. Meanwhile, place the mushrooms in a bowl and add boiling water to cover. Let stand 15 to 30 minutes or more, then drain and squeeze to extract most of the moisture. Cut away and discard the stems. Set the mushrooms aside.

4. Unless the snow peas are very young, "string" them top and bottom.

5. To the squab meat add 1 tablespoon of the wine, 2 teaspoons of the cornstarch, salt, and ½ teaspoon of the sugar. Blend and set aside.

6. Place the prepared ginger, bamboo shoots, and scallions in separate small bowls or piles and set aside.

7. Blend the soy sauce, the remaining 2 tablespoons of the wine, salt, the monosodium glutamate, and the remaining teaspoon of sugar.

8. In a wok or skillet heat the oil and add the squab meat. Cook, stirring, about 1½ minutes. Spoon out the meat, leaving the oil.

9. To the oil in the pan add the bamboo shoots and cook, stirring, about 10 seconds. Add the snow peas, cook about 5 seconds, and drain the contents of the pan, oil and all, into a sieve-lined bowl.

10. Add the sauce mixture to the pan and cook, stirring, about 10 seconds. Add the chicken broth.

11. Blend the remaining teaspoon of cornstarch with the water and stir it into the sauce. Add the squab, bamboo shoots, mushrooms, snow peas, scallions, and ginger, tossing and stirring. Cook, stirring, about 10 seconds, then spoon into a serving dish.

YIELD: 4 to 8 servings

Of all the Chinese banquet dishes commonly served in the Western world, Peking Duck is probably the best known. Oddly enough, what are sold in America as Long Island ducklings are, in truth, descendants of true Peking ducks.

PEKING DUCK I

1	duck (5 to 6 pounds, freshly killed and with head on)
½	cup red wine vinegar
1	cup water
4 to 5	tablespoons honey
6	or more scallions, green part included
40	Chinese Pancakes (or doilies; see recipe)
	Peking Duck Sauce I or II (see recipes; optional. Hoi sin sauce * thinned with a little sesame oil * may be substituted.)

* Available in Chinese markets and by mail order. For more information see Chapter XI.

1. Wash the duck thoroughly under cold running water, then pat dry with paper toweling. Pull out excess fat from the cavity of the duck and discard. Cut off the wing tips.

2. Skewer close the lower cavity of the duck tightly, as follows: Starting at one end of the cavity, push the point of a 5-inch skewer through the skin on one side of the opening.

Bring the point of the skewer around the opposite edge of skin (on the other side of the cavity) and pierce it from the outside about ¾ inch below the original puncture. Bring the point of the skewer around again and pierce the skin on the side you started on, from the outside in, about ¾ inch below the last puncture. Continue in this fashion, pushing the head of the skewer down when necessary.

When the cavity is closed, secure the skewer by pushing it through a double fold of skin. The two sides of the cavity have, in effect, been braided together with a skewer. Wind a length of twine around the top and bottom of the skewer, knot it with a single knot, and pull on it, thereby further tightening the closing. Knot the twine firmly.

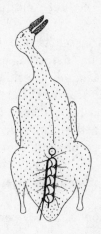

3. Pinch and pull the skin of the duck to loosen it from the meat. In the duck's neck cavity separate the skin from the flesh and insert a narrow hollow tube (see Note) into the hole you have made. Blow into the tube as if inflating a balloon until the duck is almost one and a half times bigger, pinching and plucking at the skin to allow the air in. Tie the neck cavity closed by winding twine around the neck several times and pulling tight.

Place the duck on a rack in the sink, breast side up. Pour boiling water over the duck, wait for a few seconds, and repeat. Turn the duck onto its breast and pour boiling water once over its back. Run cold water over the duck, then wipe it dry with paper toweling.

4. Combine the vinegar, water, and honey and mix thoroughly. Brush this mixture over the entire body of the duck. Hang the duck up by a cord around the neck in a cool, windy place (preferably outdoors, although an electric fan in a cold room would work well— or hang it in a garage or a cellar) and let dry for at least 10 hours.

5. When ready to cook, preheat the oven to 400 degrees. Select a 2-inch-deep roasting pan and fit a rack over it. The duck must cook about 2 inches from the bottom of the pan. Put the duck, back side down, onto the rack and put into the oven, turning the heat down to 350 degrees. Roast about one hour or longer; check at 15 minutes and turn the duck over and on its side until it is a dark even brown.

6. Meanwhile, prepare the scallions. Trim them and cut them into 2-inch lengths. Shred the tips of each length of scallions and drop them into cold water to cover. Let stand until the ends curl. When ready to serve, drain.

7. To serve the duck, carve off its skin, leaving as little meat and fat attached to it as possible, in rectangles about 3 inches long by 1 to 1½ inches wide, and place all the skin on a platter. Serve with pancakes, duck sauce, and scallions. Let each guest help himself. The procedure is to place a hot pancake on a plate, unfold it, and smear a little duck sauce in the center, using a scallion as a brush. Cover the sauce with a piece of skin, then add a scallion if you like them. Roll up the pancake and eat with the fingers. The duck meat is cut up and served in another bowl after the skin has been eaten.

YIELD: 10 servings of about 2 pieces per person

Note: Bamboo tubes that can be cut down to about the length of a flute may be purchased at the Oriental Country Store, 12 Mott Street, New York, N.Y. 10013. These tubes are useful for blowing up a duck, but a length of narrow piping or any other narrow tube of about a foot in length will be suitable.

Here is a simpler version of Peking Duck for home use.

PEKING DUCK II

1   duck (5 to 6 pounds)
   Water
2   tablespoons honey
   Peking Duck Sauce I or II (see recipes; optional. Hoi sin sauce * thinned with a little sesame oil * may be substituted.)
40   Chinese Pancakes (or doilies; see recipe)
6   or more scallions, green part included

1. Rinse the duck inside and out and pat dry.
2. Tie the duck by the neck with a long string to facilitate manipulating it in water.
3. Bring a large quantity of water to a boil in a wok or roasting pan. When the water is boiling, turn off the heat and let the water stand about 1 minute. Place the duck in the water, breast side down, and turn in the water, back and front and all over, about 1 minute. Remove.
4. Turn the heat on once more and return the water to a boil. Turn off the heat and repeat the previous step, removing the duck at the end.
5. Turn on the heat a third time, and when the water boils turn off the heat and repeat the procedure for a third time, removing the duck at the end.
6. Bring the water back to a boil and repeat the process for a fourth and final time. Remove the duck and hang it by the neck

in a cool, windy place (preferably in the open air, although an electric fan in a cold room would work well—or hang it in a garage or a cellar) for about 6 hours.

7. Combine the honey with 10 tablespoons of water and heat briefly, stirring to blend. Brush the duck all over, taking care that all areas of the skin are coated with the light syrup. Hang the duck up again for 4 hours. Brush once more all over with syrup.

8. Preheat the oven to 450 degrees.

9. Select a 2-inch-deep roasting pan and fit a rack over it. The duck must cook about 2 inches from the bottom of the pan.

10. Put the duck, back side down, on the rack and let it roast 6 to 10 minutes, until golden brown or darker. Turn it with a kitchen towel. Do not use a fork, or the duck will be punctured. Roast 8 to 10 minutes longer, but watch carefully that the duck does not burn.

11. Reduce the heat to 350 degrees and turn the duck on its back once more. Roast 20 minutes, then reduce the heat to 300 degrees.

12. Roast 10 minutes, then reduce the heat to 250 degrees.

13. The duck at this point has roasted for about 50 minutes in all. Now increase the heat once more to 450 degrees and roast 10 minutes longer, a total of about 1 hour.

14. While the duck is roasting, prepare the duck sauce, pancakes, and scallions.

15. Trim the scallions and cut them into 2-inch lengths. Shred the tips of each length of scallion and drop the scallions into very cold water to cover. Let stand. The ends should curl. When ready to serve, drain.

16. To serve the duck, carve it all over, skin and flesh, into very thin slices (if you can manage it, carve off the crisp skin first, then carve the meat). Let each guest help himself to the assorted dishes. The procedure is to place a hot pancake on a plate, unfold it, and smear a little duck sauce in the center. Cover the sauce with a piece of skin and meat, or a piece of each, then add a scallion. Wrap up the pancake to enclose the other ingredients and eat with the fingers.

YIELD: 6 to 8 servings

PEKING DUCK SAUCE I

¼ cup bean sauce * or ground bean sauce *
1 tablespoon water
1 tablespoon sugar
2 tablespoons peanut, vegetable, or corn oil
5 hot dried red peppers * (optional)
1 teaspoon sesame oil *

* Available in Chinese markets and by mail order. For more information see Chapter XI.

1. Combine the bean sauce, water, and sugar and stir to blend. If the whole bean sauce is used, mash the beans slightly.

2. Heat the oil in a small saucepan and add the peppers. Cook, stirring, about 45 seconds, then turn off the heat. Remove and discard the peppers.

3. Add the bean sauce mixture and cook, stirring, about 45 seconds. Spoon the sauce into a small serving dish and add the sesame oil.

YIELD: Slightly more than ¼ cup of sauce

PEKING DUCK SAUCE II

4 tablespoons ground bean sauce *
1 tablespoon sugar
¼ teaspoon monosodium glutamate (optional)
3 tablespoons peanut, vegetable, or corn oil

* Available in Chinese markets and by mail order. For more information see Chapter XI.

1. Blend the bean sauce with the sugar and monosodium glutamate.

2. Heat the oil in a small saucepan and add the bean sauce mixture. Cook just to the boiling point and remove from the heat.

YIELD: About ½ cup of sauce

One of the commonest sights in any Chinatown in the Western world is the roast ducks hanging from slender cords on duck hooks in the grocery stores and restaurants of the community. They are for the most part Cantonese roast ducks, and are almost invariably cooked in professional ovens. Here is a home version.

CANTONESE ROAST DUCK ❖

1   duck (5 to 6 pounds)
1   tablespoon ground bean sauce *
2   tablespoons dry sherry or shao hsing wine *
1½   tablespoons sugar
½   teaspoon five spices powder,* commercially prepared or homemade
2   tablespoons light soy sauce *
1   clove crushed garlic
½   whole star anise *
7   cups water
½   cup red wine vinegar
4   tablespoons honey or corn syrup

* Available in Chinese markets and by mail order. For more information see Chapter XI.

1. Cut off the wing tips and second joints of the duck.

2. Combine the ground bean sauce, wine, sugar, five spices powder, soy sauce, garlic, and star anise and rub the inside of the duck with the mixture. Sew carefully and securely both the neck and the tail openings. They must be closely sewed so that the sauce does not run out of the duck as it hangs or cooks.

3. Bring 6 cups of water to a boil. Place the duck on a rack in the sink and spoon 3 cups of the boiling water over the breast. Turn the duck and pour the remaining boiling water over that side. Make sure that all parts of the duck have been exposed to the boiling water.

4. Pat the duck on all sides with paper toweling to dry well all over, then place it in a jelly-roll pan or a roasting pan.

5. Combine 1 cup of water with the vinegar and honey or corn syrup and heat and stir to blend smoothly. Brush the duck all over with the mixture.

6. Slip a loop around the duck's neck and hang it to dry in a cool, dry, and preferably windy place overnight. (An electric fan in a cold room would work well—or hang it in a garage or a cellar.)

7. Preheat the oven to 450 degrees.

8. Select a 2-inch-deep roasting pan and fit a rack over it. The duck must cook about 2 inches from the bottom of the pan.

9. Put the duck, back side down, onto the rack and let it roast 6 to 10 minutes, until golden brown or darker. Turn it with a kitchen towel. Do not use a fork, or the duck will be punctured. Roast 8 to 10 minutes longer, but watch carefully that the duck does not burn.

10. Reduce the heat to 350 degrees and turn the duck onto its back once more. Roast 20 minutes, then reduce the heat to 300 degrees.

11. Roast 10 minutes, then reduce the heat to 250 degrees.

12. The duck at this point has roasted for about 50 minutes in all. Now increase the heat once more to 450 degrees and roast 10 minutes longer, a total of about 1 hour.

13. Remove the duck and serve it hot or cold.

YIELD: 6 to 8 servings

There follow two recipes for leftover roast duck, both stir-fry dishes. One is with chives, the other with bean sprouts. Either or both of these dishes may be made with leftover duck that has been roasted at home, Peking or Cantonese style, or purchased in a Chinese market.

STIR-FRY ROAST DUCK WITH CHIVES

½   roast duck with skin
2   tablespoons peanut, vegetable, or corn oil
2   tablespoons light soy sauce *
2   teaspoons sugar
1   cup shredded bamboo shoots *
3   cups chives, preferably Chinese chives,* picked over and
        cut into 2-inch lengths
    Salt to taste

* Available in Chinese markets and by mail order. For more information see Chapter XI.

1. Remove the meat, with the skin, from the duck carcass. Place the meat on a flat surface and cut it into ¼-inch shreds with a sharp knife or Chinese cleaver. There should be about 2 cups somewhat firmly packed.

2. Heat the oil in a wok or skillet, and when it is hot add the duck and cook, stirring, about 1 minute. Add the soy sauce and cook 30 seconds. Add half the sugar, cook 15 seconds, and then remove the duck. Leave the pan drippings in the pan.

3. Pour off all but 3 tablespoons of the drippings and add the bamboo shoots. Cook, stirring, about 30 seconds, then add the chives and cook about 1 minute, stirring. Add the remaining sugar and salt to taste and cook about 10 seconds, stirring. Add the duck. Toss until thoroughly hot and serve.

YIELD: 4 to 8 servings

STIR-FRY ROAST DUCK WITH BEAN SPROUTS

½	roast duck with skin
4 to 4½	cups bean sprouts *
½	teaspoon sugar
¼	teaspoon monosodium glutamate (optional)
	Salt to taste
1	tablespoon dry sherry or shao hsing wine *
6	tablespoons peanut, vegetable, or corn oil
2	tablespoons light soy sauce *

* Available in Chinese markets and by mail order. For more information see Chapter XI.

1. Remove the meat, with the skin, from the duck carcass. Place the meat on a flat surface and cut it into ¼-inch shreds with a sharp knife or Chinese cleaver. There should be about 2 cups somewhat firmly packed.

2. Rinse the bean sprouts, drain well, and set aside.

3. Blend the sugar, monosodium glutamate, salt, and wine and set aside.

4. Heat ¼ cup of the oil in a wok or skillet, and when it is quite hot add the bean sprouts. Cook over high heat, tossing quickly, about 30 seconds, then drain quickly into a sieve-lined bowl. Clean the pan.

5. Heat the remaining 2 tablespoons of oil and stir in the duck and soy sauce. Cook about 30 seconds, then add the wine mixture and cook, stirring, about 30 seconds longer. Add the bean sprouts and stir briskly until hot. The total cooking time should be 3 minutes or slightly less.

YIELD: 4 to 8 servings

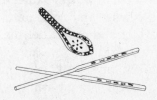

Here is another easily cooked duck dish—simply duck with onions.

CASSEROLE DUCK WITH ONIONS ❖

Peanut, vegetable, or corn oil for deep frying
1½ to 2 pounds small to medium onions (14 to 16), peeled and left whole
1 duck (5 to 6 pounds), cleaned and rinsed and patted dry inside and out
⅓ cup dry sherry or shao hsing wine *
5 to 6 cups water
5 to 6 tablespoons dark soy sauce *
Salt to taste
3 tablespoons sugar
¼ teaspoon monosodium glutamate (optional)

* Available in Chinese markets and by mail order. For more information see Chapter XI.

1. Heat the oil in a wok or deep-fryer. When it is very hot, add the onions and cook, stirring, about 3 minutes. Drain, but leave the oil in the pan.

2. Tie a string around the neck of the duck, to facilitate manipulating the duck in the oil. While holding the string, place the duck, breast side down, in the oil and cook, spooning hot oil all over the skin with a large spoon. Cook about 5 minutes, then turn the duck in the oil and continue cooking, basting the breast constantly. After 10 minutes, pull out the duck and hold it over the pan to drain whatever has accumulated in the cavity. The duck should be light brown after deep frying.

3. Place the duck in a clean wok or skillet and add the wine. Turn the duck around in the wine and cook until most of the wine has evaporated. Add the water and cover. Let the duck cook, breast side down, about 15 minutes. Add the soy sauce, salt, sugar, and monosodium glutamate, cover, and cook over medium heat until the sauce is reduced to about 3 cups, turning every 15 minutes. Turn

the flame down to very low. Add the onions and simmer, covered, about 1 hour, or until the duck and onions are tender.

4. Transfer the duck to a platter and spoon the onions around it. Bring the sauce to a boil and cook down until it is reduced to 1½ cups. Spoon the sauce over the duck and serve.

YIELD: 4 to 8 servings

Duck is a staple of the Chinese diet, and one of the most interesting duck dishes is called Red Duck. It is called that because the duck takes on a red coloring as it cooks. The seasonings include star anise with its seductive taste.

RED DUCK ❖

1	duck (5 to 6 pounds)
2 to 3	tablespoons salt, approximately
4 to 5	tablespoons red rice *
	Water
3	pieces stick cinnamon, 1 or 2 inches in length
2	whole star anise *
1½	tablespoons salt
6	tablespoons sugar
¼	teaspoon monosodium glutamate (optional)

* Available in Chinese markets and by mail order. For more information see Chapter XI.

1. Rinse the duck inside and out under cold running water. Pull off and discard loose fat and drain well.

2. Rub the inside of the duck with 1 tablespoon of salt and the outside with 2 tablespoons of salt. Or, if the duck is to be stored overnight, rub the outside with only 1 tablespoon of salt. Let the duck rest at least 1½ hours or store it overnight in the refrigerator.

3. Combine the red rice and 6 cups water in a wok or saucepan and boil twenty minutes. Fit a sieve lined with cheesecloth over a

bowl and strain the liquid through the cheesecloth. Reserve the liquid. Tie the red rice in the cheesecloth.

4. Rinse the duck well.

5. Pour the reserved red rice liquid into the pan and add four cups of cold water. Add the cheesecloth bag, cinnamon, and star anise and bring to a boil.

6. Loop a long piece of twine around the wings of the duck and tie them akimbo so that the area beneath will color. The purpose of the string is to facilitate turning and otherwise manipulating the duck as it cooks. Place the duck in the boiling liquid breast side down. When the water returns to a boil, hold the string and turn the duck onto its back in the boiling liquid. Cook for thirty minutes, turning and moving the duck frequently in the pan so that it colors easily and the skin does not stick to the pan.

7. Add the 1½ tablespoons salt, sugar, and monosodium glutamate to the pan. Cook fifteen minutes, moving the duck around occasionally to prevent sticking, then reduce the heat to medium low. Cook twenty-five minutes longer, or until the duck is tender.

8. Lift up the duck and tilt it to drain the liquid from the cavity. Set it aside to cool, and remove the string.

9. Turn up the heat and reduce the liquid in the pan to about 3½ cups. Pour the liquid into a measuring cup and cool. Discard the cheesecloth bag, anise, and cinnamon.

10. Chop and slice the duck into bite-size serving pieces and arrange on a platter (see p. 42).

11. Pour off most of the clear fat from the contents of the measuring cup, carefully guarding the dark sauce on the bottom. Stir together the remaining fat and the sauce, and brush it generously between the pieces of duck.

YIELD: 2 to 8 servings

This duck, seasoned with Szechwan peppercorns, is marvelously perfumed with star anise and cinnamon. It is steamed first, then made crisp outside by deep frying.

CRISP SZECHWAN DUCK

2   sticks cinnamon, broken
2   star anise *
1   teaspoon Szechwan peppercorns *
   Salt
1   duck (5 to 6 pounds)
1   small piece fresh ginger,* peeled
1   scallion, green part included, trimmed
   All-purpose flour for dredging
1   tablespoon dark soy sauce *
2   egg whites
3   tablespoons cornstarch
1   tablespoon dry sherry or shao hsing wine *
½   teaspoon sugar
¼   teaspoon monosodium glutamate (optional)
   Peanut, vegetable, or corn oil for deep frying
   Watercress Garnish for Duck (optional; see recipe below)
   Seasoned Salt (see recipe)

* Available in Chinese markets and by mail order. For more information see Chapter XI.

1. Combine the cinnamon, anise, peppercorns, and 2 tablespoons salt. Roast until brown, then rub all over the outside and inside of the duck. Leave the cinnamon and anise inside the duck's cavity.

2. To the cavity, add the ginger and folded scallion. Set aside and let stand 3 or 4 hours or overnight.

3. Rub flour liberally all over the skin of the duck and place it in a Pyrex dish or other plate that will fit into the top of a steamer. Place the steamer over boiling water, cover, and steam the duck 1½ to 2 hours, or until the skin is easily penetrated with a fork or chop-

sticks (the leg meat and skin also start to pull away from the bone when it is properly cooked).

4. Let the duck stand until it is thoroughly cool, then rub it all over with the soy sauce. Wrap in foil and refrigerate until ready to cook.

5. Combine the egg whites with the cornstarch, wine, sugar, salt to taste, and monosodium glutamate and blend to make a paste. Rub this all over the outside of the duck to coat. Let stand for at least 30 minutes.

6. Heat the oil in a wok or deep-fryer, and when it is very hot add the duck, back side down. Cook, spooning hot oil all over the exposed part of the duck. Ideally, enough oil to cover the duck completely should be used, but it is expensive. Cook the duck, turning occasionally, until it is quite crisp and golden brown.

7. Serve whole while hot, garnished, if desired, with watercress garnish. Carve at the table and serve with seasoned salt on the side for dipping.

YIELD: 3 to 8 servings

Note: This duck is sometimes served with Deep-Fried Chinese Bread (see recipe).

WATERCRESS GARNISH FOR DUCK

3   cups loosely packed watercress, picked over to remove tough bottom stems
1   tablespoon sesame oil *
1   tablespoon light soy sauce *
    Salt to taste
1   teaspoon sugar
¼   teaspoon monosodium glutamate (optional)

* Available in Chinese markets and by mail order. For more information see Chapter XI.

1. Rinse the watercress well and shake it dry. Blend the remaining ingredients and add the watercress.

2. Toss well and use as a garnish before the watercress wilts.

YIELD: About 3 cups

This dish must be made in a well-ventilated room, preferably with circulating air because of the smoke it creates. It must be started at least a full day before it is to be served.

SMOKED DUCK

1   duck (5 to 6 pounds)
1   tablespoon whole black peppercorns
2   tablespoons salt
1   cup dark tea leaves
1   cup raw rice
¾   cup sugar
     Peanut, vegetable, or corn oil for deep frying (optional)
     Greens for garnish

1. Pull out any excess fat from the duck and discard or use for another purpose.

2. Place the peppercorns and salt in a skillet and cook, shaking the skillet occasionally, until the peppercorns are smoking. Remove immediately and cool.

3. Rub the duck all over, inside and out, with the peppercorn mixture. Wrap tightly in waxed paper or plastic wrap and place on its back in a container. Place a heavy weight on the duck and let it stand 24 hours.

4. Rinse the duck well and place it, back side down, in the top of a steamer. Cover and steam over boiling water for 1 to 1½ hours, depending on the size of the duck.

5. Line a large wok or other steaming device with heavy-duty aluminum foil. Combine the tea leaves, rice, and sugar and sprinkle over the foil. If a wok is used, arrange 4 chopsticks in crisscross fashion or use a fairly high rack to elevate the duck so that it will be at least 1 inch above the tea mixture. Place the duck on its back and cover the pan closely with foil or a large lid covered with foil. Seal as tightly as possible.

6. Place the pan over a hot flame, which will bake the tea mixture and cause smoke inside to flavor the duck.

7. Smoke the duck over high heat for 10 minutes, then reduce the heat to medium high. The smoke should continue to circulate, however. Turn off the heat 20 to 30 minutes later, when the duck is nicely browned. Leave covered until the smoke subsides. Transfer it to a platter and cool thoroughly, at least 2 hours.

8. The duck may be served at room temperature, or it may be cooked in hot oil, as for deep frying. If the latter method is used, place the duck, back side down, in hot oil and spoon the oil over the breast as it cooks, 5 to 10 minutes. Remove and drain on paper towels.

9. Garnish the cavity of the duck with greens or carve the duck and serve it garnished with greens.

YIELD: 4 to 10 servings

There is a dish in Chinese cooking that resembles such boned fowl dishes of the Western world as galantine or ballottine of duck. But the resemblance rests largely in the preparation, for in the Chinese kitchen the duck is skinned and boned with the skin left intact to receive a stuffing that contains duck meat plus such delectable oddments as mushrooms, dates, ham, bamboo shoots, lotus seeds, and barley. The duck when stuffed is steamed and served with a white sauce.

EIGHT PRECIOUS TREASURES

1	duckling (4½ to 6 pounds)
24	chestnuts, fresh if available; otherwise dried *
⅔	cup pearled medium barley (pearl barley)
16	Chinese dates *
16 to 18	small dried black mushrooms *
¾	cup dried lotus seeds *
2	tablespoons peanut, vegetable, or corn oil
½	cup bamboo shoots,* cut into ¼-inch cubes
½	cup Smithfield ham, cut into ½-inch cubes
1	10½-ounce can gingko nuts *
3	teaspoons sugar
	Salt to taste
¾	teaspoon monosodium glutamate (optional)
2	tablespoons dry sherry or shao hsing wine *
3	tablespoons cornstarch
5	tablespoons water
1	cup chicken broth
3	tablespoons finely chopped fresh coriander leaves *

* Available in Chinese markets and by mail order. For more information see Chapter XI.

1. Skin and bone the duck according to the instructions on page 44. Reserve the carcass and bones for soup, if desired.
2. Place the pieces of duck meat on a cutting surface. Cut and trim away any tough fibers, tendons, or membrane and discard. Cut

the duck meat first into thin strips, then cut the strips into cubes, ½ inch or slightly smaller. Refrigerate.

3. Slash the tops of the chestnuts, if they are fresh, and place in a saucepan. Add cold water to cover and simmer for 30 minutes. Drain, cool, and peel. If the chestnuts are dried, put them into a saucepan in cold water to cover to a depth of 1 inch above the chestnuts. Bring to a boil and simmer 1 hour, or until the chestnuts are tender. Drain. When cool enough to handle, peel.

4. Prepare (more or less simultaneously) the barley, dates, mushrooms, and lotus seeds as indicated below.

5. Place the barley in a saucepan and add water to cover. Bring to a boil and simmer until tender, about 40 minutes. Drain. There should be about 2½ cups.

6. Soak the dates in hot water for 20 minutes. Pit them and cut into small cubes. There should be about ½ cup.

7. Pour boiling water over the mushrooms and let stand 15 to 30 minutes. Drain the mushrooms, but reserve 1 cup of the soaking liquid. Squeeze the mushrooms to extract most of the moisture, then trim off and discard the tough stems. Cut the mushroom caps into small cubes. There should be about 1 cup. Set aside.

8. Place the lotus seeds in a saucepan and boil in water to cover 30 minutes. Drain.

9. Heat the oil in a large wok or skillet and add the duck meat. Cook, stirring, about 2 minutes, then add the dates, mushrooms, lotus seeds, bamboo shoots, and ham. Drain the gingko nuts and add. Cook about 1 minute and add the chestnuts and reserved mushroom liquid. Add the sugar, salt, ½ teaspoon monosodium glutamate, and the wine.

10. Cook about 10 minutes, then add the barley. Stir and cook 10 minutes. There should be a little liquid but not a great deal, just enough to bind the ingredients when the cornstarch is added.

11. Blend 2 tablespoons of the cornstarch with 3 tablespoons of the water and stir it in to bind. Remove from the heat.

12. Stuff the duck skin with the mixture and carefully and thoroughly sew up both ends of the duck.

13. Place the duck on a platter that can be fitted inside the top of a large steamer, cover, and place over boiling water. Steam 1 hour, then carefully pour off most of the liquid that will have ac-

cumulated around the duck on the platter. Cover the steamer once more and continue to steam 1½ hours longer, a total of 2½ hours' cooking time.

14. Remove the duck carefully and place it on another serving dish. Remove the string with which the duck was sewed. Strain the drippings (including the fat) from the platter and pour them into a wok or saucepan. Add the chicken broth, salt to taste, and the remaining ¼ teaspoon monosodium glutamate. Bring to a boil. Blend the remaining 1 tablespoon of cornstarch with the 2 remaining tablespoons of water and stir into the sauce. Add the chopped coriander and pour the sauce over the duck. Serve sliced.

YIELD: 6 to 12 or more servings

Crisp fried walnuts make an impressively good contrast to a fine-fleshed duck.

WALNUT CRISPY DUCK

1   1-inch cube of fresh ginger,* crushed with a knife
1   scallion, green part included, finely chopped
¼   cup boiling water, approximately
1   tablespoon plus ½ teaspoon dry sherry or shao hsing wine *
    Salt and pepper to taste
1   duck (4½ to 5 pounds), preferably with head on, washed
      and dried
2   quarts peanut, vegetable, or corn oil
2   cups whole walnut halves
20 water chestnuts,* coarsely chopped into fine dice
5   eggs
2   teaspoons sugar
7   tablespoons cornstarch, approximately
    Caul fat (lace fat) *
2   egg whites

* Available in Chinese markets and by mail order. For more information see Chapter XI.

1. Place the ginger and scallion in a small bowl and pour about ¼ cup boiling water over them. Let stand 15 minutes.

2. In another small bowl blend the tablespoon of wine with salt, pepper, and 2 tablespoons of the ginger-scallion juice. (The rest of the ginger-scallion juice may be saved for another use.) Place the duck in a bowl and rub it all over, inside and out, with the wine mixture. Cover the duck with foil and refrigerate it for at least 2 hours or overnight.

3. Remove the foil and place the duck on a dish large enough to hold it. Place the dish in the top of a steamer and steam, covered, over boiling water 40 to 60 minutes, depending on the size of the duck. The duck should be tender but not overcooked, because it will be deep-fried later. Remove from the steamer and cool just until you can handle it. Do not let it get cold.

4. Now bone the duck. Split the skin of the duck down the backbone with a sharp knife. Using a small boning or paring knife, work the knife between the skin and carcass, pulling the flesh away with the fingers and leaving the skin intact. The wings and legs should come off with the skin; use a pair of kitchen shears where necessary to cut them off the carcass. Continue working, avoiding as much as possible piercing or tearing the skin except the initial cutting down of the backside. Leave the leg and thigh bones intact, but cut off the wing tips. Scrape off and reserve random bits, all the pieces of flesh that remain on the bones. Chop these bits and pieces into fine dice. Set aside both the skin and the meat. The carcass may be saved for soup or stock.

5. Heat 2 cups of the oil, and when it is hot add the walnut halves. Deep-fry until golden and crisp, 1 minute or less. Watch them carefully because they cook quickly. Drain on paper toweling. Chop the walnut halves into fine dice and put them into a bowl.

6. To the walnut halves add the duck meat, water chestnuts, eggs, salt to taste, the sugar, and the ½ teaspoon of wine. Blend well.

7. Place the duck skin, opened up, on a flat surface. Put 3 tablespoons of the cornstarch into a sieve and dust the inside of the duck. Add the walnut stuffing and reshape the duck with the hands. Overlap the edges of the duck and seal any tears in the skin with cornstarch.

8. Spread out a layer of caul fat on a flat surface. It should measure 1½ x 2½ feet, more or less. Trim away and discard the edges if they seem thick.

9. Blend 4 tablespoons of the cornstarch with the 2 egg whites. Rub the caul fat with a little of the mixture. Place the duck in the center of the caul fat, the opened back down. Bring up the edges of the caul fat and fold it over the duck to enclose the duck completely, except for the neck and head (if still on the duck). Rub the wrapped duck all over with the cornstarch and egg white mixture. Let stand for at least 30 minutes.

10. Heat about 1½ quarts of oil in a wok or deep-fryer, and when it is very hot carefully slip the duck in the oil. Cook about 5 minutes on one side until golden brown and crisp, then turn and cook about 4 to 5 minutes on the other. Lay it on several layers of paper toweling and drain. Transfer to a platter and serve sliced.

YIELD: 4 to 8 servings

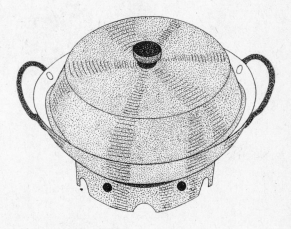

IV

Pork

There are many dishes in the Chinese repertory that can double either as an appetizer Western style or a main course for a Chinese meal. One of them is the following recipe.

DEEP-FRIED PORK BALLS

1   pound ground pork
1   tablespoon all-purpose flour
2   tablespoons cornstarch
1   teaspoon salt
¼   teaspoon monosodium glutamate (optional)
½   teaspoon sugar
1   tablespoon dry sherry or shao hsing wine *
    Oil for deep frying
    Seasoned Salt (see recipe; optional)

* Available in Chinese markets and by mail order. For more information see Chapter XI.

1. Place all the ingredients except the oil in a mixing bowl and blend, using your fingers or chopsticks. Blend thoroughly for 3 or 4 minutes.

127

2. Shape into balls about 1½ inches in diameter. In a wok or deep-fryer, heat the oil, and when it is hot and almost smoking add the balls, one at a time. Cook over moderately low heat, turning the balls occasionally so that they brown evenly, about 20 minutes. Serve, if desired, with seasoned salt on the side for dipping.

YIELD: 14 to 16 balls

The Chinese table is probably graced with more pork dishes than any other on earth. Generally the pork appears in cubes or shredded or in casseroles. A lesser-known cut is the pork chop, which also takes on special qualities when cooked in the Chinese manner. There follow two unusual pork chop dishes.

SESAME SEED PORK CHOPS

6   loin pork chops (about 1½ pounds), with bone in
2   scallions, green part included, trimmed and cut into 1-inch lengths
¼   cup coarsely chopped fresh ginger *
1   cup water
1½   tablespoons dry sherry or shao hsing wine *
1½   teaspoons sugar
    Salt to taste
½   teaspoon monosodium glutamate (optional)
¼   teaspoon ground pepper
1   tablespoon light soy sauce *
1   egg white
2   tablespoons cornstarch
2   cups white sesame seeds,* approximately
¾   cup peanut, vegetable, or corn oil, approximately

* Available in Chinese markets and by mail order. For more information see Chapter XI.

1. Place the chops on a flat surface and pound the meat lightly on both sides with a small, solid, flat object. Do not break the meat. Now, using a sharp knife, lightly score the meat to a depth of ⅛ inch on both sides.

2. Place the scallions, ginger, and water in the container of an electric blender and blend. Hold a sieve over a mixing bowl and strain. Discard the pulp in the strainer. To the liquid add the wine, 1 teaspoon of the sugar, salt, half the monosodium glutamate, the pepper, and soy sauce. Pour this mixture over the chops and let marinate, turning them occasionally, about 30 minutes.

3. Combine the egg white with the cornstarch and beat well to blend. Add the remaining ½ teaspoon sugar, salt to taste, and the remaining monosodium glutamate.

4. Drain the pork chops and brush either side with the egg white mixture.

5. Pour the sesame seeds into a flat dish and dip the pork chops, one at a time, in the seeds to coat both sides generously.

6. Pour oil in one or two skillets to cover the bottom by about ¼ inch. Heat the oil, but do not let it get piping hot or the seeds will spatter and burn.

7. Add the chops to the skillet and cook 5 to 7 minutes on one side, then turn and cook 5 to 7 minutes on the other. Cooking time will depend on the thickness of the chops. Cook on both sides until golden brown. Drain and serve immediately.

YIELD: 6 servings

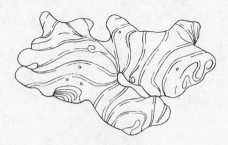

MARINATED PORK CHOPS CHINESE STYLE

6   loin pork chops (about 1½ pounds), with bone in
3   tablespoons light soy sauce *
½   teaspoon ground pepper
¼   teaspoon monosodium glutamate (optional)
     Salt to taste
1½   teaspoons sugar
3   teaspoons sesame oil *
¼   cup cornstarch, approximately
¾   cup peanut, vegetable, or corn oil, approximately

* Available in Chinese markets and by mail order. For more information see Chapter XI.

1. Place the chops on a flat surface and pound the meat lightly on both sides with the back of a cleaver. Do not break the meat. Now, using a sharp knife, lightly score the meat to a depth of ⅛ inch on both sides.

2. Combine the soy sauce, ground pepper, monosodium glutamate, salt, sugar, and sesame oil. Stir to dissolve the sugar. Spoon the mixture into a flat dish and add the chops in one layer. Let stand 30 minutes or so, turning the chops in the marinade occasionally.

3. Drain the chops, one at a time, and sprinkle one side with cornstarch, rubbing it in lightly. Turn and sprinkle the other side with cornstarch, rubbing again. Use about 2 teaspoons cornstarch per chop.

4. Pour the oil in one or two skillets to cover the bottom by about ¼ inch. Heat the oil, and when it is hot add the chops. Cook 5 to 7 minutes on each side. The cooking time will depend on the thickness of the chops. When golden brown on both sides, drain and serve immediately.

YIELD: 6 servings

Twice-cooked pork is another of those dishes all but unknown in the Western world a couple of decades ago. The pork is cooked twice, and it is well worth the effort.

TWICE-COOKED PORK

2	pounds fresh, lean, unsalted, boneless bacon with rind on (pork belly) *
4 to 6	fresh red or green long hot or sweet peppers *
4 to 6	cloves garlic, flattened but not chopped
3	tablespoons chili paste with garlic (Szechwan paste) *
1½	tablespoons bean sauce *
2	teaspoons sugar
1	tablespoon dry sherry or shao hsing wine *
¼	teaspoon monosodium glutamate (optional)
½	cup peanut, vegetable, or corn oil
3	scallions, green part included, trimmed and cut into 1-inch lengths

* Available in Chinese markets and by mail order. For more information see Chapter XI.

1. Place the pork in a kettle and add water to cover to a depth of 1 to 2 inches above the pork. Cover and simmer 1 hour, or until the meat is tender when pierced with a fork or chopsticks. Drain and let cool.

2. Core and seed the peppers, then cut into 1-inch cubes or into thin strips. Combine with the garlic.

3. Combine the chili paste with the bean sauce, sugar, wine, and monosodium glutamate. Set aside.

4. Slice the meat down through the rind wafer thin, ⅛ inch thick or less. (This is easier if the meat is partially frozen.)

5. Heat the oil in a wok or skillet, and when it is hot add the pork slices. Have a cover ready to use if necessary, because the meat tends to sputter and splatter. Cook, stirring, 7 to 8 minutes. Drain in a sieve-lined bowl and save the oil.

6. Add 2 tablespoons of the reserved oil to the pan and add the peppers and garlic. Cook, stirring, about 1 minute. Drain.

7. Add about ¼ cup of the oil to the pan and add the sauce. Cook, stirring, about 45 seconds. Add the pork, peppers, and garlic and cook, stirring, just to heat thoroughly. Add the scallions, stir, and serve without cooking more than a few seconds.

YIELD: 6 to 8 servings

Sweet and sour pork is, of course, one of the best-known dishes in all the world. Like anything else, a good sweet and sour pork is one thing and an ordinary sweet and sour pork is quite another. This is an excellent one. It is best if all the recommended ingredients are used, but license may be taken. For example, substitute fresh or canned mushrooms for the dried ones, and so on.

SWEET AND SOUR PORK

1   pound lean pork, cut into ¾-inch cubes
1   tablespoon dark soy sauce *
1   tablespoon dry sherry or shao hsing wine *
1   cup plus 2 tablespoons cornstarch
4   dried black mushrooms *
½   cup green and red sweet peppers, cut into 1-inch cubes (or use all green if red is not available)
2   tablespoons sliced carrot
½   cup onion, cut into 1-inch cubes
¼   cup thinly sliced bamboo shoots *
⅓   cup drained pineapple chunks or sliced pineapple cut into bite-size pieces
⅓   cup pickled scallions,* each cut in half (optional)
4   cloves garlic, peeled, crushed, and left whole
4   thin slices fresh ginger,* peeled
1¼   cups water

½ cup sugar
⅓ cup red wine vinegar
1 tablespoon light soy sauce *
  Salt to taste
  Peanut, vegetable, or corn oil
12 drops red food coloring

* Available in Chinese markets and by mail order. For more information see Chapter XI.

1. Using the back of a kitchen knife or cleaver, pound each piece of pork lightly, then place in a mixing bowl and add the dark soy sauce and the wine. Mix with the fingers.

2. Place 1 cup of the cornstarch on a large sheet of waxed paper and dredge the pork, one piece at a time, in the cornstarch. Dredge each piece liberally and massage gently to coat well. Discard the leftover cornstarch.

3. Place the mushrooms in a mixing bowl and add hot water to cover. Let stand 15 minutes or so until softened.

4. In a mixing bowl combine the pepper cubes, carrot, onion, bamboo shoots, pineapple, scallions, garlic, and ginger.

5. Drain the mushrooms and squeeze to extract the moisture. Cut off the stems and slice the mushrooms into thin pieces. Add them to the vegetables and set aside.

6. Heat oil for deep frying to the boiling point in a wok or deep-fryer and drop in the pork pieces, a few at a time. Cook 5 to 8 minutes, or until the pork is cooked through and golden brown and crisp. Remove and drain on paper toweling. (See Note.)

7. Pour off all but ¼ cup of the oil and add the vegetable mixture. Cook, stirring, 4 to 5 minutes.

8. Meanwhile, in a saucepan combine 1 cup of the water, the sugar, vinegar, light soy sauce, and salt. Bring to a boil and stir until the sugar is dissolved.

9. Blend the remaining 2 tablespoons of cornstarch with the remaining ¼ cup of water and stir into the simmering sweet and sour sauce. Stir in the food coloring, then stir in 2 tablespoons of fresh oil to "glaze" the sauce. Pour the sauce over the vegetables and bring to a boil.

10. Transfer the pork to a serving dish. Customarily in America the sauce and vegetables are poured over the pork before serving. We prefer to serve the pork on one platter, the sauce with vegetables separately, so that each guest may help himself.

YIELD: 4 to 8 servings

Note: The pork may be cooked twice to make the pieces crisper. Cook 5 minutes the first time, and remove the pieces. Let the oil reheat until it is almost smoking and put back the pork, cooking for 1 or 2 minutes, or until it is brown and crisp.

One of the most interesting and popular dishes in Chinese cooking is named, oddly, Lion's Head. It is basically a long-cooked combination of meat balls served on a bed of Chinese green cabbage—a dish that could, with a little imagination, be said to resemble the head of a lion. Like most dishes in Chinese cookery, this is a shared dish, and four meat balls serve eight or more.

LION'S HEAD ❖

2 to 3	pounds green, long-leaved Chinese cabbage * (or celery cabbage,* mustard greens, or regular cabbage)
1½	pounds raw, unsalted fresh bacon (pork belly) *
1	cup lightly crushed cornflakes (about two cups before crushing)
6	tablespoons water, or more, if necessary
2	tablespoons dark soy sauce *
3	tablespoons dry sherry or shao hsing wine *
1	tablespoon cornstarch
	Salt to taste
2	scallions, green parts included, trimmed and neatly chopped
1	egg, beaten

Peanut, vegetable, or corn oil for deep frying
½ teaspoon monosodium glutamate (optional)
1 tablespoon sugar

* Available in Chinese markets and by mail order. For more information see Chapter XI.

1. Rinse the green cabbage well and squeeze it between the fingers to extract as much of the moisture as possible. Reserve and set aside 3 or 4 nice leaves to cover the dish before it is cooked. Cut the remaining cabbage into thirds, or if other greens are used, cut them into rather large bite-size pieces. Set the chopped cabbage aside.

2. Trim away or have trimmed away any bones (some fresh bacon has rib bones in it) and rind from the bacon. Put the meat, fat and lean, through a meat grinder. The bacon should not be too finely ground. Or use the traditional Chinese method: cut the meat into small dice and then chop with a cleaver until the morsels of meat are the size of raw rice grains.

3. Place the ground bacon in a mixing bowl. Add the crushed cornflakes and work lightly with the hands. Add the water, half the soy sauce, 1 tablespoon of the wine, the cornstarch, and salt while kneading well with the hands. Work in the scallions.

4. Shape the mixture into 4 balls, about the size of tennis balls, and lightly flatten to cakes about 4 inches in diameter.

5. Beat the egg, then, using your hands, lightly coat each ball all over with egg.

6. Heat oil for deep frying in a wok or skillet until it is hot but not at the smoking point, about 250 degrees. Drop in one ball at a time and cook each ball for about 20 seconds, basting the top with hot oil until brown, then remove and drain. When the balls have been cooked, strain the oil and reserve all but 3 tablespoons for a later use.

7. Heat the 3 tablespoons of strained oil in the pan and add the chopped cabbage. Stir-fry about 1 minute, then add the remaining wine, the remaining tablespoon soy sauce, the monosodium glutamate, sugar, and salt. The water content of leaf vegetables varies, and if the cabbage seems too dry add about 3 tablespoons of water. Cook the cabbage in the pan, about 3 minutes' total cooking time. Cover the bottom of a 3- or 4-quart heatproof casserole with the

cabbage and spoon the cooking juices over the cabbage. Arrange the meat balls neatly over the cabbage and cover the meat with the reserved cabbage leaves. If the cabbage still seems too dry, add about 3 more tablespoons of water. Cover the casserole and cook over medium heat about 1 hour. Serve the cabbage and meat balls directly from the casserole or spoon out into a deep dish, placing the balls on a bed of cabbage.

YIELD: 8 to 12 servings

Bean curd has as many uses in China as cottage cheese does in the Western world. It is one of those neutral dishes like potatoes and snails which adapt well to assertive flavors.

SPICY PORK AND BEAN CURD

6　pads fresh white bean curd *
½　pound ground pork
1　tablespoon chili paste with garlic (Szechwan paste) *
1　tablespoon dark soy sauce *
1　teaspoon sugar
¼　teaspoon monosodium glutamate (optional)
¼　cup peanut, vegetable, or corn oil
2　tablespoons finely diced fresh ginger *
2　tablespoons finely minced garlic
½　cup chicken broth
1　tablespoon Szechwan peppercorns *
⅓　cup minced scallions, green part only
1　tablespoon cornstarch
2　tablespoons water
1　tablespoon sesame oil *
　　Fresh coriander * for garnish

* Available in Chinese markets and by mail order. For more information see Chapter XI.

1. Soak the bean curd pads in boiling water for 3 minutes, then drain and cut into ½-inch pieces.

2. Place the peppercorns in a small skillet and cook over moderate heat, stirring and shaking the skillet until they are roasted, then put them into the container of an electric blender and blend until fine. Measure out 1 teaspoon and set aside. (The remainder may be kept indefinitely in a covered container.)

3. Blend together the pork, chili paste with garlic, soy sauce, sugar, and monosodium glutamate.

4. Heat the oil in a wok or skillet and add the pork mixture. Cook, stirring to separate the grains of the meat, about 30 seconds. Add the ginger and garlic and cook briefly. Add the chicken broth and cook about 1 minute.

5. Add the bean curd pieces and stir—gently, for they break easily. Cook just to heat through, about 2 minutes. Add the peppercorn powder and scallions. Blend the cornstarch and water and add it, stirring gently. (No matter how gently you stir, the bean curd will inevitably break up to some degree.) When the dish is thickened, transfer it to a dish and sprinkle with the sesame oil. Garnish with fresh coriander.

YIELD: 4 to 8 servings

The Western world has quite decidedly had its influence in Chinese kitchens, as is evidenced in any dishes that contain tomatoes or peanuts or, more interestingly, perhaps, corn. The Chinese employ miniature ears of baby corn in their cookery, and they make a cunning addition to a dish. Mini-ears of corn are tinned in China and sold in cans in Chinese groceries and by mail order in the Western world.

STIR-FRY PORK CUBES WITH STRAW MUSHROOMS AND BABY CORN

4　small pork chops (about 1 pound)
1　tablespoon dark soy sauce *
1　tablespoon light soy sauce *
2　tablespoons dry sherry or shao hsing wine *
2　teaspoons sesame oil *
¼　teaspoon ground pepper
1　tablespoon cornstarch
1　15-ounce can straw mushrooms * (the 15-ounce can specifies that it offers 8 ounces drained weight)
1　15-ounce can miniature ears of baby corn *
¼　pound fresh snow peas * (optional)
1　teaspoon sugar
1　teaspoon monosodium glutamate (optional)
　　Salt to taste
　　Peanut, vegetable, or corn oil

* Available in Chinese markets and by mail order. For more information see Chapter XI.

1. Trim the meat from the bones, but reserve both meat and bones.
2. Using the back, blunt side of a heavy knife, pound the meat in a crisscross fashion on both sides. Cut each piece of meat into cubes that measure about 1 inch by ½ inch or slightly larger. Put the cubes and bones into a mixing bowl and add the soy sauces, 1 tablespoon

of the wine, the sesame oil, pepper, and cornstarch. Blend well to coat the pieces and set aside.

3. Drain the mushrooms and corn and combine. Set aside.

4. If the pea pods are used, string them top and bottom. Set aside.

5. Combine the sugar, monosodium glutamate, salt, and the remaining tablespoon of wine. Set aside.

6. Heat ¾ cup of oil in a wok or skillet, and when it is hot add the pork meat and bones. Cook, stirring, over high heat 3 to 4 minutes. Drain and wipe out the pan.

7. Put 3 tablespoons of fresh oil into the pan and add the mushrooms and corn. Cook about 30 seconds, stirring. Add the sugar mixture and cook about 30 seconds.

8. Return the pork to the pan and cook 2 minutes, stirring. Add the pea pods and cook about 1 minute longer, stirring. Put the bones on the bottom of a serving dish, and the meat and vegetables on top. Serve immediately.

YIELD: 6 to 8 servings

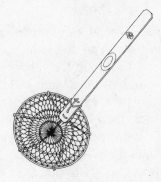

LETTUCE PACKAGE

1	large firm head iceberg lettuce
½	cup shredded bamboo shoots *
12 to 16	water chestnuts,* preferably fresh, sliced (if fresh ones are used, peel and run them under cold water before slicing)
6 to 8	dried black mushrooms *
¾	pound coarsely ground pork
1	egg, lightly beaten
1½	tablespoons dark soy sauce *
1	tablespoon plus 1 teaspoon cornstarch
2	tablespoons dry sherry or shao hsing wine *
½	cup chicken broth
1½	teaspoons sugar
¼	teaspoon monosodium glutamate (optional)
2	teaspoons salt
5½	tablespoons peanut, vegetable, or corn oil
1	cup finely diced celery

* Available in Chinese markets and by mail order. For more information see Chapter XI.

1. Discard the outside layer of the lettuce and split the head in half with a knife. Peel away 16 to 20 of the largest leaf halves and place on a serving dish. Set aside in the refrigerator.

2. Cut and chop the bamboo shoots and water chestnuts into very fine dice. Pour enough hot water over the mushrooms to cover. Let stand for 15 to 30 minutes, then drain, squeezing to extract most of the liquid. Trim off the stems and shred the mushrooms fine, then cut and chop into very fine dice.

3. Combine the mushrooms with the bamboo shoot and water chestnut mixture and set aside.

4. Combine the pork with the egg, soy sauce, and 1 tablespoon of the cornstarch. Mix well and set aside.

5. Combine the wine, half the chicken broth, the sugar, monosodium glutamate, and salt and set aside.

6. Blend the remaining teaspoon of cornstarch with the remainder of the chicken broth and set aside.

7. Heat 4 tablespoons of the oil in a wok or skillet, and when almost smoking add the pork mixture, stirring quickly and constantly to separate the bits of pork. When the pork is cooked, add the mushroom mixture and cook, stirring, about 2 minutes. Add the wine, broth, and sugar mixture and cook about 15 seconds, stirring. Stir the cornstarch mixture to make certain it is properly blended and stir into the pork. Cook, stirring rapidly, about 15 seconds. Add the celery and stir just until the celery is heated through. Add the remaining 1½ tablespoons of oil, stirring to distribute it. This will glaze the dish.

8. Turn the dish out onto a serving platter and accompany the meat with the platter of lettuce leaves. To serve, let each guest help himself to a cold lettuce leaf, the cup of which is then filled with a spoonful of the pork. It is wrapped between the fingers, then eaten while the pork is still hot.

YIELD: 4 to 8 or more servings

One of the dishes that has soared to popularity in New York's Chinatown within a comparatively few years is Mo-Shu-Ro, spelled variously and frequently listed on Chinese menus as a North China egg dish. It consists of a savory combination of exotics like "tree ears," a form of mushroom, and tiger lily stems plus pork and egg, all scrambled together and served with rice or in round white pancakes that have been steamed.

MO-SHU-RO

Chinese Pancakes (see recipe)
20 pieces dried tiger lily stems *
 3 tablespoons tree ear mushrooms *
    Peanut, vegetable, or corn oil
 ¼ pound pork, cut into very thin strips (there should be about ⅔ cup)
 2 teaspoons dark soy sauce *
 1 cup bamboo shoots,* cut into fine strips
 1 teaspoon sugar
    Salt to taste
 6 eggs, lightly beaten
 ¼ cup chicken broth
 ½ cup diced scallions, green part included

* Available in Chinese markets and by mail order. For more information see Chapter XI.

1. Make the Chinese pancakes and start steaming them.
2. Rinse the tiger lily stems in several changes of cold water and place in a saucepan. Add the tree ears and cover with boiling water. Simmer about 3 minutes, then drain. Cut off the hard tips of each tiger lily stem and cut away the hard part of each tree ear. Set aside.
3. In a wok or skillet, heat 2 tablespoons of oil, and when hot add the pork. Cook, stirring, about 1 minute. Add the soy sauce, bamboo shoots, tiger lily stems, and tree ears. Add half the sugar and salt. Cook, stirring, about 1 minute, then turn off the heat. Transfer the

mixture to a warm place and let stand briefly while the remainder of the dish is prepared.

4. Wipe out the pan and add ½ cup oil. Add the eggs and cook to the scrambled stage, stirring gently with a flat spoon or pancake turner. Add the remaining sugar and salt to taste. Cook, stirring, to the hard-scrambled stage, then return the pork mixture to the pan. Continue to cook and stir, breaking up the egg into small pieces. Add the chicken broth and cook about 45 seconds longer, stirring to blend. Add the scallions, stir quickly, and serve.

5. To serve, place one pancake flat on an individual dish and spoon a generous amount of the filling inside. Roll up to enclose the filling and fold one end over to prevent dripping. Eat from the other end. The dish may also be served without pancakes, with rice.

YIELD: 6 to 8 servings

There are numerous times when thin Chinese pancakes, sometimes called "doilies," may be left over—when they are made for Mo-Shu-Ro or Peking Duck, for example. Do not discard them, but turn them into an interesting dish of shredded pancakes with pork and vegetables. It is an omeletlike dish.

SHREDDED PANCAKES WITH PORK AND VEGETABLES

10	Chinese Pancakes (or doilies; see recipe)
½	head romaine lettuce
3	eggs
½	cup peanut, vegetable, or corn oil
¼	cup finely shredded pork
1	teaspoon dark soy sauce *
	Salt to taste
¼	teaspoon monosodium glutamate (optional)
½	teaspoon sugar

* Available in Chinese markets and by mail order. For more information see Chapter XI.

1. Stack the pancakes, a few at a time, and cut them into thin shreds. Set aside.

2. Cut off the bottom of the lettuce and discard the tough outer leaves. Separate the leaves of the lettuce, wash well, and pat dry. Stack and shred them, then set aside.

3. Beat the eggs and set aside.

4. Heat half the oil in a wok or skillet and add the pork. Cook, stirring to separate the shreds. Add the soy sauce and cook about 30 seconds. Remove the pork and set aside.

5. Add the remaining oil to the pan and add the beaten eggs. Cook, stirring in a circular motion, about 30 seconds. Add the shredded pancakes and cook about 4 seconds, stirring. Return the pork to the pan and cook, stirring, to blend all the ingredients. Cook about 2 minutes, then add the romaine and cook, stirring, about 1 minute. Add salt to taste, the monosodium glutamate, and the sugar. Cook about 2 minutes, then serve. This dish when properly made is not moist like an omelet, but on the dry side.

YIELD: 4 to 8 servings

Note: This is really a catchall dish, and almost anything could go in it: ¼ cup or so of shredded black mushrooms, bamboo shoots, bean sprouts, and so on.

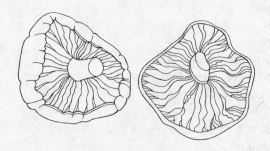

If you have ever seen those strips of roast pork hanging on skewers or hooks in Chinatown markets and wondered how they were seasoned, then wonder no more. This is a very simple, easily made dish that could not be better if it were made in Canton itself. Please note, however, the substitution of bourbon whiskey for a Chinese counterpart not available in the United States.

CANTONESE ROAST PORK

2½   pounds lean loin of pork or other boneless cut in one piece
1   tablespoon bourbon whiskey, cognac, or rum
½   cup light soy sauce *
9   tablespoons sugar
1   teaspoon five spices powder,* commercially prepared or homemade
   Salt to taste
2   tablespoons red bean curd sauce *
2   tablespoons bean sauce *
1   tablespoon sesame paste *
2   tablespoons or more dark soy sauce *
1   cup white or dark corn syrup or honey

* Available in Chinese markets and by mail order. For more information see Chapter XI.

1. Cut the meat into strips approximately 8 to 10 inches long and 1½ to 2 inches thick. The length will depend, of course, on the size of the meat. There should be about 6 strips. Place the strips in one layer in a dish just large enough to hold them.
2. Combine the liquor, ¼ cup of light soy sauce, half the sugar, the five spices powder, and salt. Blend well. Pour the sauce over the meat, turning the pieces until the meat is coated. Let stand about 30 minutes.
3. Meanwhile, blend together the red bean curd sauce, bean sauce, 1 tablespoon of the light soy sauce, 1½ tablespoons of the sugar, and the sesame paste.
4. Preheat the oven to 450 degrees.

5. Take the meat from the original marinade but do not dry. Smear each piece of meat with the red bean curd sauce mixture.

6. Place a rack on top of a roasting pan. The rack should be about 2 inches above the bottom of the pan. Arrange the pieces of meat parallel to each other but without the sides touching. Bake 30 minutes, then turn each piece of meat and bake 15 minutes longer.

7. Brush each piece of meat with approximately ½ teaspoon dark soy sauce. Bake 5 minutes.

8. Turn each piece of meat and brush that side with dark soy sauce. Continue baking 10 minutes.

9. Meanwhile, in a saucepan blend the remaining 3 tablespoons of light soy sauce, 3 tablespoons of the sugar, 1 tablespoon of dark soy sauce, and the corn syrup. Heat briefly and stir to blend. Let cool slightly, then pour the mixture into a mixing bowl.

10. When the pieces of pork are done, add them to the last sauce. Coat well and remove. Let stand 10 minutes, then dip again to coat well. Dip 3 or 4 times in all.

11. Serve thinly sliced, at room temperature.

YIELD: 8 to 12 servings

Note: Unused portions of both the red bean curd sauce and the bean sauce may be kept in properly sealed containers in the refrigerator for several weeks.

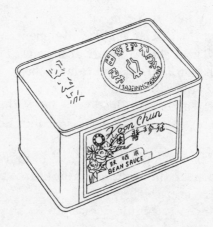

For some reason the ribs of the spareribs available in Chinese markets are almost invariably—and to their credit—smaller than those in other markets. The following recipe has such distinctive Chinese flavors as five spices powder—a commercially prepared blend of star anise, ginger, fennel, clove, and cinnamon; red bean curd sauce; hoi sin sauce; and sesame seed paste.

CHINESE BARBECUED SPARERIBS ❖

1   lean rack of spareribs (3 pounds), the smaller the bones the better
6   tablespoons sugar
2   tablespoons red bean curd sauce *
1   teaspoon five spices powder,* commercially prepared or homemade (see Chapter XI)
3   tablespoons light soy sauce *
2   tablespoons ground bean sauce *
3   tablespoons hoi sin sauce *
2   tablespoons sesame paste (sesame seed paste) *
    Peanut, vegetable, or corn oil

* Available in Chinese markets and by mail order. For more information see Chapter XI.

1. Cut the spareribs into individual ribs or leave the rack whole.
2. Place the ribs in a suitable dish, such as a shallow baking dish, and rub all over with 1 tablespoon of the sugar. Let stand 30 minutes.
3. Preheat the oven to 450 degrees.
4. Blend the red bean curd sauce, the remaining sugar, the five spices powder, soy sauce, ground bean sauce, hoi sin sauce, and sesame seed paste in a bowl. Use half the sauce to rub over the rack of spareribs or the individual ribs.
5. Fit a baking dish large enough to hold the ribs with a rack. Add a cup or so of water to the bottom of the dish. Arrange the rack of spareribs or the individual ribs on the roasting rack.
6. Place the baking dish in the oven and bake 30 minutes, then brush the ribs with oil and turn them.

7. Reduce the oven heat to 350 degrees and bake 15 minutes longer. Brush the ribs with oil, then brush lightly with more of the sauce. Bake 15 minutes, then turn. Brush that side lightly with oil, then with more sauce.

8. Bake 30 minutes or longer, turning the ribs occasionally and basting lightly with oil and sauce. When ready to serve, the ribs should be appetizingly brown and on the well-done side.

YIELD: 6 to 10 servings

This is the simplest, most easily made recipe in this book. It may be the simplest in any book. And yet it is a substantial and creditable dish.

BOILED PORK WITH GARLIC SAUCE ❖

1   piece of pork loin (3 pounds), with bone in
6   tablespoons finely minced garlic
2   tablespoons sesame oil *
¾   cup light soy sauce *

* Available in Chinese markets and by mail order. For more information see Chapter XI.

1. Place the pork in a kettle with 3 quarts water. Do not add salt. Bring to a boil, partially cover, and simmer 1½ hours. Cool to room temperature and slice into ⅛-inch slices.

2. Serve with the sauce—made by combining the garlic, sesame oil, and soy sauce—on the side as a dip.

YIELD: 6 to 12 servings

There are numerous Chinese dishes that are well suited for Western-style buffets because they are not to be served immediately and should be served at room temperature. Some of them can be made to advantage a day or so in advance, including this pork casserole.

SPICY FRESH PORK CASSEROLE ❖

1   fresh uncured ham or pork butt (4 pounds), with bone in and skin on
2½ quarts cold water
6   tablespoons dry sherry or shao hsing wine *
5   tablespoons dark soy sauce *
5   tablespoons sugar
    Salt to taste
2   1-inch sticks cinnamon
1   scallion, green part included, trimmed
½   teaspoon monosodium glutamate (optional)
5 to 6 star anise *
4   ¼-inch-thick round slices of fresh ginger,* peeled
1   teaspoon peanut, vegetable, or corn oil (optional)

* Available in Chinese markets and by mail order. For more information see Chapter XI.

1. Place the pork in a kettle and add water to cover. Bring to a boil, simmer 2 minutes, and drain. Run under cold running water.

2. Return to the kettle and add the 2½ quarts of cold water. Bring to a boil and add the wine, soy sauce, sugar, salt, cinnamon sticks, scallion, monosodium glutamate, star anise, and ginger. Cover and cook for 2 hours, turning the meat often in its cooking liquid.

3. Uncover and continue cooking over medium high heat, taking care that the meat does not stick. Cook 1½ to 2 hours longer, until the meat is tender.

4. Remove the meat. Strain the liquid into a wok or other open vessel, discarding the herbs and spices, and cook over high heat, stirring often, until the sauce is syrupy, 15 to 20 minutes. Glaze with

1 teaspoon oil, if desired, and pour over the pork. Let stand to room temperature. Serve, sliced like a ham, in the gravy.

YIELD: 8 to 12 servings

This is a robust, easily made, traditional country dish that is delicious if you like very rich dishes. Remember, however, that it is made with pork belly, which is quite fat, and it is therefore not a dish for those who normally shun butter, cream, and lard.

RED-COOKED PORK ❖

1   3-pound square unsalted fresh bacon (pork belly),* with
     bones in, containing generous stripes of lean
½   cup dry sherry or shao hsing wine *
1   quart cold water
3   tablespoons dark soy sauce *
3   tablespoons sugar
     Salt to taste

* Available in Chinese markets and by mail order. For more information see Chapter XI.

1. Leave the skin on the bacon. Split the square of bacon in half, cutting from the rind downwards, then cut each half into 2-inch squares (a total of about 12 or 14 pieces). Place the meat in a flameproof casserole or a wok and add water to cover. Bring to a boil and simmer about 5 minutes, then drain.
2. Run the pork briefly under cold water and drain. Return it to the casserole or wok and add the wine. Cook, stirring, 4 or 5 minutes. Add the 1 quart cold water and bring to a boil. Cover and cook over medium heat about 30 minutes, stirring and turning the meat occasionally as it cooks. Add the soy sauce, cover again, and cook about 30 minutes. Add the sugar and salt, cover, and cook about 30 minutes, stirring occasionally to prevent burning. Turn the heat to very low and cook, covered, 30 minutes to 1 hour longer,

or until the skin is soft, the meat and fat are tender, and the sauce
is syrupy and reduced to about ¾ cup.

YIELD: About 6 to 12 servings

The Chinese, like the French and the Germans and many another
nationality, appreciate the marvelous but uncommon parts of the
pig, including the feet. This is a robust pigs' feet casserole.

PIGS' FEET CASSEROLE ❖

2   pigs' feet (about 2½ pounds)
5   cups cold water
5   tablespoons dark soy sauce *
4   ounces (about ½ cup) rock sugar (rock candy) * or ¼ cup
        sugar
¼   teaspoon monosodium glutamate (optional)

* Available in Chinese markets and by mail order. For more information see
Chapter XI.

1. Have the pigs' feet split in half lengthwise, then have each
piece cut into serving pieces (this had better be done by the butcher,
but it can be done at home with a heavy, sharp cleaver).
2. Rinse the pieces well and drain.
3. Bring enough water to a boil to cover the pieces, then add them.
Bring to a boil, drain, and rinse well under cold water.
4. In a heatproof casserole combine the pieces with the 5 cups
cold water and cook over high heat 10 minutes. Turn the heat down
to medium and cook about 50 minutes. Add the soy sauce, sugar,
and monosodium glutamate. Turn the heat to low and simmer until
the pork is well cooked, about 1½ to 2 hours. While cooking, turn the
meat a few times. Serve from the casserole or transfer to another
serving dish.

YIELD: 4 to 8 servings

The following Cantonese dish has an interesting background. It was—and perhaps still is—a dish customarily eaten every day for a month by the ladies of Canton after giving birth—and by the guests calling on them. Perhaps it is the nutritious nature of the pigs' feet, or perhaps it is the spicy sweet and sour nature of the dish that kindles the appetite. The sauce left in the pot is used as the base for the next day's dish, with fresh pigs' feet and seasonings added, so that it becomes richer and mellower as the month wears on.

PIGS' FEET WITH GINGER ❖

2 to 4   pigs' feet (about 3 pounds), preferably with hock left on
4   quarts cold water
Salt to taste
2   cups red wine vinegar
1   pound dark brown sugar
1¼   pounds fresh ginger,* peeled and cut into 1-inch chunks
1   tablespoon dark soy sauce *

* Available in Chinese markets and by mail order. For more information see Chapter XI.

1. When you buy the pigs' feet, have them split in half. Then ask the butcher to cut each half into 2-inch lengths.
2. Place the pigs' feet in a kettle and add cold water to cover. Bring to a boil and simmer 1 minute, then drain immediately and run under cold water. Drain again.
3. Return the pigs' feet to the kettle and add the 4 quarts cold water. Cover and cook about 50 minutes.
4. Add the salt, vinegar, brown sugar, ginger, and soy sauce.
5. Do not cover, but cook for 1¾ to 2 hours.
6. Using a slotted spoon, ladle out the pigs' feet and spoon about 2 cups of sauce over them.

YIELD: 4 to 8 servings

In most Chinese restaurants and presumably in homes where Chinese food is prepared in America, Smithfield ham is generally used as a substitute for aged Chinese hams, which are not as of now available in the United States. Chinese hams are exceptional in their flavor and, unlike the vast majority of Smithfield hams, they are not cured with smoke. Hams play a coveted role in Chinese cooking, and one of the most desirable ways of eating ham per se is as in the following recipe. But despite the name, the ham here is sweetened with pineapple and crushed rock sugar rather than honey.

HONEY HAM

1   round 2-pound Smithfield ham section, with bone in and rind on
3   tablespoons rock sugar (rock candy, finely crushed) *
1   8-ounce can pineapple rings
½   teaspoon dark soy sauce *
1   tablespoon cornstarch
3   tablespoons water
1   tablespoon peanut, vegetable, or corn oil

* Available in Chinese markets and by mail order. For more information see Chapter XI.

1. Put the ham into a kettle with enough water to cover to a depth of about 1 inch above the top of the ham. Simmer 1½ hours, then drain.

2. Carefully cut away and discard the rind from the ham. Cut the ham into ½-inch thick slices, including the fat. Discard the bone, or save for another purpose.

3. Neatly arrange the ham slices, standing them on end, one against the other, in a round or square mold in which they will fit snugly. Sprinkle them with the rock sugar and the juice from the can of pineapple. Place the mold in the top of a steamer and cover with the steamer lid. Place over boiling water and steam 20 to 30 minutes, until the sugar has melted.

4. Pour off and reserve the accumulated liquid from the mold.

5. Unmold the ham slices onto a platter and garnish with halved pineapple rings.

6. Bring the reserved liquid to a boil and add the soy sauce.

7. Blend the cornstarch with the water and stir it into the liquid. When thickened, stir in the oil and immediately pour over the ham.

YIELD: 4 to 8 servings

The following is a fascinating recipe in which a ground pork filling is stuffed inside thin, small omeletlike pancakes. The pancakes are made, curiously enough, by swirling a little beaten egg inside a soup ladle over low heat until the egg sets. The ladle, in effect, is the Chinese answer to the French crêpe pan. The technique requires a little practice, but once mastered it is easy.

PORK AND EGG DUMPLINGS ❖

½	pound ground pork
1	teaspoon chopped fresh ginger * (optional)
¼	cup chopped scallions, green part included
	Salt to taste
	Dark soy sauce *
2	teaspoons dry sherry or shao hsing wine *
1	tablespoon cornstarch
¼	teaspoon monosodium glutamate (optional)
1¼	teaspoons sugar
1	tablespoon water
3	dried black mushrooms *
4	eggs
	Peanut, vegetable, or corn oil
10 to 12	leaves celery cabbage,* trimmed
1½	cups chicken broth

* Available in Chinese markets and by mail order. For more information see Chapter XI.

1. First make the dumpling mixture. In a mixing bowl combine the ground pork, ginger, scallions, salt, 2 teaspoons of dark soy sauce, wine, cornstarch, monosodium glutamate, ¼ teaspoon of the sugar, and the water. Blend well with the fingers, then set aside.

2. Place the mushrooms in a small bowl and pour boiling water over them to cover. Let stand 15 to 30 minutes, or until soft, then drain and squeeze to remove most of the moisture. Trim off and discard the tough stems. Set the mushrooms aside.

3. Meanwhile, beat the eggs with a fork until well blended, about 2 minutes. Set aside.

4. Brush the inside of a soup ladle with oil. The ladle should have a diameter of about 4 inches, a depth of about 2 inches, and a smooth inside surface.

5. Place the bottom of the ladle over moderate to low heat, and when it is hot spoon about one tablespoon of the beaten egg into it. Immediately start turning the ladle in a circular motion, around and around, so that the egg will set around the bottom and sides in one thin layer. When the egg is set, unmold the pancake thus formed onto a flat surface. With the fingers, smooth it out like any pancake. If the egg should stick to the surface of the ladle, add a little salt and wipe clean with paper toweling. Add a little more oil and start again. As noted above, this technique may seem difficult in the beginning, but once mastered it is simple.

6. As the pancakes are made, pile them on top of each other on a dish and cover the pile with damp cheesecloth. To each pancake add a little of the dumpling mixture, fold over the edges of the pancake to enclose the filling, and press the edges together to seal. If they do not seal properly, brush a little beaten egg yolk around the edges of the pancake, then seal by pressing lightly with the fingers. Continue until all the pancakes have been filled.

7. Cut the cabbage leaves into 2-inch squares. There should be about 9 or 10 cups.

8. Heat 6 tablespoons of oil in a large wok or skillet, and when it is hot add the cabbage. Cook and stir over high heat about 2 minutes, then add the mushrooms and 1½ tablespoons dark soy sauce. Add the chicken broth and cook, stirring, 1 minute. Cover and steam 5 minutes.

9. Arrange the pork and egg dumplings over the vegetables and sprinkle with the remaining teaspoon of sugar and salt to taste. Cover closely and cook about 30 minutes, or until the cabbage is well cooked.

YIELD: 4 to 8 servings

The following recipe is an excellent luncheon dish, or it could be used with almost any combination of Chinese dishes for a large meal. It consists of steamed seasoned pork with salted duck eggs on top.

STEAMED PORK WITH SALTED EGGS ❖

¾   pound ground pork
1   egg, lightly beaten
¼   cup water
1½   tablespoons light soy sauce *
       Salt to taste
1   tablespoon cornstarch
1   tablespoon dry sherry or shao hsing wine *
3   salted duck eggs *
2   tablespoons chopped scallions, green part included

* Available in Chinese markets and by mail order. For more information see Chapter XI.

1. Select a shallow plate with a rim—preferably one with a 7- or 8-inch diameter—that will fit inside a steamer. Have the steamer ready, with water boiling in the bottom.

2. Combine the ground pork, beaten egg, water, soy sauce, salt, cornstarch, and wine and mix well with your hands. Spread the mixture inside the plate and smooth it on top. Make three depressions in the pork to contain the yolks of the duck eggs.

3. Break the eggs, one at a time, and deposit one yolk in each depression, allowing the whites to cover the surface. Sprinkle with

the scallions. Set the dish, uncovered, in the top of the steamer and cover the steamer. Steam 30 minutes.

YIELD: 3 to 8 or more servings

This is a recipe that is only for the genuine connoisseurs, those with the palate of Beelzebub, for it is fiery hot to the taste. This is a dish to make strong men cough, and Texans, unless they are of the proper ilk and enthusiasm, weep capsicum. Heed well this warning. And further, if you have fastidious friends who are addicted to only the mildest, blandest digestibles, warn them to stay away. Even the fumes as the dish cooks give the uninitiated the shakes. It is a fantastic blend of ground pork and hot peppers, finely minced and quickly cooked. They say it will last forever in the refrigerator—but not in the kitchens of those who dote on peppery food, for it is irresistible.

GROUND PORK WITH HOT PEPPERS

½ pound fresh red or green long hot peppers,* preferably
   mixed
¼ cup peanut, vegetable, or corn oil
1 pound ground pork
2 tablespoons dark soy sauce *
   Salt to taste
2½ teaspoons sugar

* Available in Chinese markets and by mail order. For more information see Chapter XI.

1. Cut off and discard the stem ends of the peppers and split the peppers in half. Cut away the white membrane and discard the seeds. Mince the peppers as fine as possible but without making a pulp or puree. The tiny pieces should be identifiable. There should be about 1½ cups chopped. Set aside.

2. In a wok or skillet heat the oil to very hot and add the ground pork. Turn off the heat and cook the pork, stirring, until the grains separate and the pork loses its color. Do not brown.

3. Add the soy sauce and cook over high heat, stirring constantly, 3 or 4 minutes. Add the salt and sugar and stir quickly. Add the minced peppers and cook, always over high heat, about 3 minutes. Serve. Store leftover pork with hot peppers in glass jars, well sealed. Refrigerated, it will keep for at least a week. It is good cold, too.

YIELD: About 3 pints

For those who favor spiced dishes, this pork with hot peppers is as excellent as it is simple; it is a shade less fiery than the preceding recipe using ground pork.

PORK WITH HOT PEPPERS

10 to 15	fresh red or green long hot peppers *
½	pound lean pork
2	teaspoons dark soy sauce *
2	teaspoons cornstarch
1	teaspoon sugar
¼	teaspoon monosodium glutamate (optional)
	Salt to taste
3	tablespoons peanut, vegetable, or corn oil
¾	cup finely shredded bamboo shoots *
1	tablespoon dry sherry or shao hsing wine *

* Available in Chinese markets and by mail order. For more information see Chapter XI.

1. Core the peppers and remove the seeds. Cut the peppers into fine shreds or into 2-inch pieces.

2. Place the pork on a flat surface and, using a sharp knife, cut it into the thinnest possible slices. Cut the slices into the finest possible shreds. There should be about 1 cup. Place the shreds in a mixing bowl and add the soy sauce and cornstarch. Blend thoroughly.

3. Combine the sugar, monosodium glutamate, and salt. Set aside.

4. Heat the oil in a wok or skillet, and when it is hot add the pork mixture. Cook, stirring, to separate the shreds, about 3 minutes.

5. Add the bamboo shoots and sugar mixture. Cook, stirring, about 30 seconds. Add the peppers and cook, stirring, about 1 minute longer. Add the wine and cook, stirring, about 15 seconds. Serve hot.

YIELD: 4 to 6 servings

Corned Pork is a very special, easily made banquet dish from the region of Yang Chao. It keeps well for several days in the refrigerator and can be served as an appetizer or main dish.

CORNED PORK ❖

The pork:

1   fresh uncured ham (8 pounds)
10   tablespoons kosher salt
3½   teaspoons saltpeter (available in drugstores)
     Water
5   tablespoons salt
¼   cup dry sherry or shao hsing wine *
¼   cup sugar
2   scallions, green part included, cut into 2-inch lengths
¼   cup peeled, thinly sliced fresh ginger *
6   star anise *
4   3-inch sticks cinnamon
     Fresh coriander leaves * or parsley for garnish

The dipping sauce for each individual serving:

2   tablespoons loosely packed fresh ginger,* peeled and cut into the finest strips (julienne)
4   tablespoons red wine vinegar

* Available in Chinese markets and by mail order. For more information see Chapter XI.

1. Have the fresh ham boned but leave the skin intact.

2. Open the ham, boned side up, and prick the meat all over and quite deeply with a sharp, thin knife, or skewer, to allow the salt and saltpeter to penetrate. Do not go through the skin. Rub it well inside and out with kosher salt. Blend the saltpeter with 1 tablespoon of water and rub this all over the ham. Roll the ham and tie it with string. Place it in an enamel, earthenware, or stainless steel vessel and cover with heavy weights. Let stand in a cool place for 3 or 4 days.

3. Remove the weights, then drain the ham and rinse it well. Soak it in cold water for 1 hour.

4. Place the ham in a kettle and add water to cover, about 4 quarts. Add the salt, wine, sugar, scallions, ginger, star anise, and cinnamon. Bring to a boil and simmer, covered, for 3 to 4 hours, or until tender. Set aside and cool.

5. Place the ham in a basin and rinse it with a little of the cooking liquid, not water.

6. Place the ham in a bowl, strain the remaining cooking liquid, discarding the spices, and add enough to cover the ham. Weight the ham down once more and let stand one day in a cool place. Remove the ham and serve. Leftover ham can keep in the refrigerator for a week to 10 days.

YIELD: 24 to 48 servings

One novelty—at least to the Western palate—is the number of Chinese dishes that employ rice powder. The powder is made of ordinary, long-grain rice that is cooked until brown with star anise, after which these are blended in an electric blender. Today, that is. It was formerly ground between stones, of course. The powder has the interesting and altogether appealing flavor of the star anise and, after steaming, a covetable soft graininess. The dish below is one example.

FRESH BACON STEAMED WITH RICE POWDER ❖

1 cup raw long-grain rice
2 whole star anise *
2 pounds fresh bacon (pork belly), with bones included and the skin left on
4½ tablespoons dry sherry or shao hsing wine *
4½ tablespoons plus 1 teaspoon dark soy sauce *
1½ tablespoons plus 1 teaspoon sugar
  Salt to taste
¾ teaspoon monosodium glutamate (optional)
4 slices fresh ginger,* peeled
3 scallions, green part included, cut into 2-inch lengths
½ cup water

* Available in Chinese markets and by mail order. For more information see Chapter XI.

1. Rinse the rice well under cold running water. Drain thoroughly and put into a wok or skillet without oil. Add the star anise and cook, stirring, over high heat. (A pancake turner is good in Western homes for stirring this.) Continue cooking and stirring and shaking the pan for about 7 minutes, always over high heat, until the rice takes on the color of dark cereal. (It probably should be cooked longer and over higher heat than the average non-Chinese would think.) When the rice is ready, continue stirring off the heat, because otherwise it will continue to cook from retained heat.

2. Spoon the rice and star anise into the container of an electric blender and blend on high speed until the mixture is like fine sand. Do not overblend. It should not be as fine as talcum powder.

3. Cut the fresh bacon into 14 to 16 pieces, each piece about ¾ inch wide, cutting down through the rind and through the bones.

4. Combine the wine, the 4½ tablespoons soy sauce, the 1½ tablespoons sugar, salt, monosodium glutamate, ginger, and scallions. Add the bacon and mix well to coat the pieces of meat. Let stand about 1 hour.

5. Select a round bowl that will fit inside the top of a steamer when the steamer is covered. Place about half the rice powder in a dish. Remove the pork pieces, one at a time, from the marinade without draining, and dip them in the rice powder, coating each piece well. As the pieces are coated arrange them in the bowl close together. Use more rice powder as necessary.

6. When all the pieces have been arranged in the bowl, pour the remaining marinade over all. Blend the water, salt to taste, the remaining teaspoon soy sauce and the remaining teaspoon sugar and pour over the pork.

7. Place the bowl in the top of the steamer and cover. Place the whole over boiling water and steam for at least 4 hours (the longer the better). This dish can be reheated. And leftover rice powder will keep indefinitely if stored in a jar with a tight-fitting cover in the refrigerator.

YIELD:　8 to 12 servings

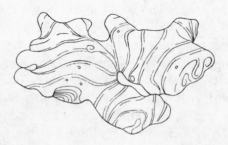

There are numerous amusing—if not to say misleading—names in Chinese cooking, and one of these is Tinkling Bells. It is not a dessert or other frivolity as one might suppose. It is a dish in which ground pork is wrapped in soy bean sheets and deep-fried until the coating is crisp. The name comes about because the exterior is supposed to crackle when you bite into it.

TINKLING BELLS

1   pound ground pork
2   tablespoons chopped scallions, green part included
1   tablespoon finely minced fresh ginger *
    Cornstarch
1   tablespoon dark soy sauce *
1   tablespoon dry sherry or shao hsing wine *
½   teaspoon sugar
    Salt to taste
¼   teaspoon monosodium glutamate (optional)
1   egg
3   tablespoons chicken broth or water
4   dried bean curd sheets *
    Peanut, vegetable, or corn oil for deep frying
    Seasoned Salt (see recipe)

* Available in Chinese markets and by mail order. For more information see Chapter XI.

1. Combine the pork, scallions, ginger, 1 tablespoon of cornstarch, the soy sauce, wine, sugar, salt, monosodium glutamate, egg, and broth or water. Mix thoroughly.

2. Bean curd sheets are semicircular, and some are apt to be broken. They can be easily repaired by fitting the pieces together on a flat surface, with the broken edges overlapping. The edges will stick together after the sheet is moistened.

3. Moisten a sheet of bean curd with water, using just enough to dampen slightly. Fold over the two sides of the half-moon-shaped

sheet to form a rough square with a rounded top. Spoon about ½ cup
of the pork mixture onto the sheet and shape it with the fingers into
a sausage shape at the bottom of the sheet but not to the ends of the
bean curd. Roll up the sheet jelly-roll fashion. Repeat until all the
meat and bean curd sheets have been used.

4. Cut each roll into 1½- to 2-inch lengths. Dip each cut end into
cornstarch.

5. In a wok or deep-fryer, heat the oil, and when hot deep-fry the
"tinkling bells" until crisp and cooked through. Serve hot, with
seasoned salt.

YIELD: 6 to 10 servings

PORK WITH SZECHWAN PRESERVED VEGETABLE

1 to 3	pieces Szechwan preserved vegetable *
¾	pound lean pork
1	tablespoon dark soy sauce *
2	teaspoons sugar
¼	teaspoon monosodium glutamate (optional)
1	tablespoon dry sherry or shao hsing wine *
¼	cup peanut, vegetable, or corn oil

  * Available in Chinese markets and by mail order. For more information see
Chapter XI.

1. Rinse the vegetable well under cold running water and pat dry.
Slice it thin, then cut it into fine shreds. There should be about 1¼
to 1½ cups.

2. Place the pork on a flat surface and slice it against the grain
into the thinnest possible slices. Carefully cut each slice into fine
shreds. Put the shreds into a mixing bowl and add the soy sauce.

3. Blend the sugar with the monosodium glutamate and wine and
set aside.

4. Heat the oil, and when it is hot add the pork. Cook, stirring,
just until the pork loses its raw color, about 1 minute. Make a well

in the center of the pork shreds and add the preserved vegetable. Cook, stirring, about 10 seconds, then add the sugar mixture. Cook, stirring, over high heat about 5 to 6 minutes. Cook until almost all the liquid has evaporated. Serve hot.

YIELD: 4 to 8 servings

V
Beef

One of the sublime cold dishes with which the Chinese often begin a meal is Aromatic Spiced Beef. The beef, cooked until tender with that subtle seasoning called star anise, is served cold with the natural, dark liquid that forms as it cooks and that jells as it sets. Not only excellent as a first course, it is especially fine for picnics. It is enormously simple to prepare.

AROMATIC SPICED BEEF ❖

 3 pounds boneless shin of beef (since it's 3 pounds after
      boning, it will doubtless require 2 shins)
10 cups water
 6 star anise *
 5 tablespoons dark soy sauce *
 5 tablespoons sugar
 2 tablespoons salt
 3 tablespoons dry sherry or shao hsing wine *
      Fresh coriander leaves * or Italian parsley for garnish

* Available in Chinese markets and by mail order. For more information see Chapter XI.

1. Trim the beef of any fat and tough membrane covering.
2. Bring the water to a boil in a kettle and add the anise. Add the meat and boil rather briskly about 1½ hours.

3. Add the soy sauce, sugar, and salt. Cover and cook 2½ hours, then add the wine and cook, uncovered, over medium high heat, turning the meat in the sauce as it cooks. Cook about 40 minutes, or until the beef is tender and there is about 1 cup of sauce remaining. Transfer the beef to a casserole and strain the sauce into a saucepan. Cool both the beef and the sauce, then cover and refrigerate. Cut the meat into quarter-inch or slightly thicker slices and arrange the pieces on a platter. Cut the jelly into cubes and arrange the pieces over the meat. Garnish with the fresh coriander and serve cold.

YIELD: 8 to 12 servings

As we have noted before, the Chinese kitchen is based to a great degree on some of the more economical cuts of meat in the world. Another case in point is oxtails, which can be gently spiced with the likes of star anise and cinnamon.

SPICED OXTAIL CASSEROLE ❖

1½ to 2	pounds oxtails, cut into serving pieces
2	quarts water
2	star anise *
2	1-inch sticks cinnamon
3	tablespoons dark soy sauce *
¼	teaspoon monosodium glutamate (optional)
2	tablespoons sugar

* Available in Chinese markets and by mail order. For more information see Chapter XI.

1. Place the oxtails in a wok or kettle and add water to cover. Bring to a boil and simmer 5 minutes. Drain and rinse under cold running water.

2. Return the oxtails to the wok or kettle and add the 2 quarts

water, star anise, and cinnamon. Cover, bring to a boil, and cook over moderately high heat 45 minutes. Add the soy sauce, monosodium glutamate, and sugar and continue cooking 2½ to 3 hours.

3. Remove the meat to a shallow bowl or mold; putting the largest pieces on the bottom. Cook the sauce down over high heat until reduced to about ½ to ¾ cup. Turn out the oxtail onto a serving plate, pour the sauce over it, and serve.

YIELD: 4 to 8 servings

Meat balls seem to exist in almost every known cuisine. Here is a tender steamed version from China.

STEAMED BEEF BALLS ❖

½ pound ground sirloin
1 tablespoon fresh ginger,* finely chopped
   Salt to taste
¼ teaspoon monosodium glutamate (optional)
1 tablespoon cornstarch
½ tablespoon dry sherry or shao hsing wine *
¼ cup cold water

* Available in Chinese markets and by mail order. For more information see Chapter XI.

1. In a mixing bowl combine the beef with the ginger, salt, monosodium glutamate, cornstarch, and wine. Blend, stirring with one hand in a circular motion. Gradually add the water, always stirring in one direction.

2. Shape the meat mixture into 16 balls.

3. Bring water in the bottom of a steamer to a boil. Lightly oil a dish that will fit in the top of a steamer and arrange the balls on it.

4. Put the dish into the top of the steamer, cover with the steamer lid, and steam over boiling water 15 minutes.

YIELD: 2 to 8 servings

Scallions are quite obviously one of the mainstays of Chinese cooking, at times a dominant or at least semidominant ingredient. They go well with short ribs of beef in this slow-simmered casserole dish. The dish could and should be cooked in advance and reheated.

SHORT RIBS OF BEEF WITH SCALLIONS ❖

2½ to 3   pounds short ribs of beef (6 to 8 small short ribs of beef)

1   pound scallions (about 35 to 40)
Peanut, vegetable, or corn oil for deep frying

4   cups water

2   tablespoons dry sherry or shao hsing wine °

3   tablespoons dark soy sauce °

2   tablespoons sugar
Salt to taste

° Available in Chinese markets and by mail order. For more information see Chapter XI.

1. Rinse the beef in cold water and pat dry.

2. Trim off and discard the ends of the scallions, but otherwise leave them whole.

3. Heat the oil in a wok or deep-fryer, and when it is hot add the scallions. Cook over high heat, stirring and turning the scallions occasionally until they are wilted. Continue cooking, stirring and turning until the scallions become quite brown and crisp, about 10 minutes in all. Remove the scallions to drain but leave the oil in the pan.

4. Add the beef to the hot oil in the pan and cook over high heat, turning the pieces in the oil until they are lightly browned, about 2 minutes. Remove the meat and pour off all the fat.

5. Wipe out the pan or use a fresh casserole and add the beef. Add the water, wine, soy sauce, sugar, and salt. Bring to a boil and add the scallions. Cover and cook for about 2 hours, until the meat is fork tender. Cool, then chill. Remove the hardened fat and reheat. When ready to serve, spoon out the meat and scallions and reduce

the sauce to a syrupy consistency. Pour over the meat and scallions and serve hot.

YIELD: 2 to 8 servings

We have often remarked that, although shin of beef is one of the lesser-known and -used cuts of beef in the Western world, it is one of the tastiest and, if cooked long enough, one of the best textured. It gives off a good amount of natural gelatin, which is good for sauces. This recipe is a home dish made with shin of beef and white Chinese turnip.

SHIN OF BEEF AND WHITE TURNIP CASSEROLE ❖

1½ pounds boneless shin of beef (weight after boning) cut into 2-inch cubes (available at most Chinese butchers and at many Western butchers on request)
8 cups water
½ cup dry sherry or shao hsing wine *
1 2-pound white Chinese turnip *
Salt to taste
½ teaspoon monosodium glutamate

* Available in Chinese markets and by mail order. For more information see Chapter XI.

1. Add to a kettle enough water to cover the beef to a depth of about 2 inches above the meat. Bring the water to a boil and add the beef.

2. When the water returns to a boil, simmer 1 minute. Drain well and run under cold water.

3. Place the meat in a casserole and add the wine. Turn the beef in the wine until it is coated all over. Add the 8 cups water and bring to a boil. Cover and simmer 1½ hours.

4. Meanwhile, trim and pare the turnip. Cut it into 2- to 3-inch cubes.

5. When the meat has cooked the 1½ hours, add the turnips. Partially cover, cook 15 minutes, and add salt and the monosodium glutamate. Continue cooking 1½ to 2 hours, or until the meat is thoroughly tender.

YIELD: 6 to 12 servings

One of the most basic and easily prepared beef with vegetable dishes is this one.

BEEF WITH ONIONS

    1   pound flank steak
    2   tablespoons dark soy sauce,* or more to taste
    1½ tablespoons cornstarch
        Peanut, vegetable, or corn oil
    3   medium onions, peeled, cut in half, and thinly sliced (about
            3½ cups sliced)
    ½   cup plus 2 tablespoons water
    2   finely shredded fresh red long hot peppers * (optional)
        Salt to taste
    ¼   teaspoon monosodium glutamate (optional)
    1   tablespoon dry sherry or shao hsing wine *

* Available in Chinese markets and by mail order. For more information see Chapter XI.

1. Cut the flank steak against the grain into very thin slices, then shred the slices. (This is easier to do if the meat is partially frozen before cutting and the slices are stacked before shredding.) Place the meat in a small mixing bowl and add half the soy sauce, 1 tablespoon of the cornstarch, and 1 tablespoon oil. Stir to blend. Set aside.

2. Heat 1½ cups oil in a wok or skillet, and when it is warm add the beef, stirring to separate the shreds. Cook briefly, no more than

20 or 30 seconds, until separated. Remove the beef and drain it in a sieve-lined bowl to catch the drippings. Pour off all but ⅓ cup of the oil from the pan.

3. Add the onions and cook, stirring, about 2 minutes. Add the ½ cup water and cook 1 minute longer. Add the remaining tablespoon of soy sauce and the hot peppers.

4. Add the beef to the onions and add salt to taste, the monosodium glutamate, and the wine. Blend the remaining water with the ½ tablespoon cornstarch and add. Bring the beef to a boil and serve hot.

YIELD: 4 to 8 servings

BEEF AND GREEN PEPPERS

4 to 5	medium sweet green peppers
1	pound lean, tender beef, preferably flank steak, although another cut may be used
2	tablespoons cornstarch
2	tablespoons dark soy sauce *
1	cup peanut, vegetable, or corn oil
¾	teaspoon sugar
1	tablespoon dry sherry or shao hsing wine *
¼	teaspoon monosodium glutamate (optional)
2	tablespoons water
½	teaspoon salt, or to taste

* Available in Chinese markets and by mail order. For more information see Chapter XI.

1. Core and seed the peppers. Cut them into thin strips lengthwise and set aside.

2. Slice the meat across the grain into thin strips 1½ to 2 inches long. Place it in a bowl and add the cornstarch, soy sauce, and 2 tablespoons of the oil. (The oil prevents the meat from sticking together while cooking.) Let stand at least 10 minutes.

3. Heat the remaining oil in a wok or skillet and cook the meat, stirring, about 30 seconds, until separated. Drain the meat in a sieve-lined bowl to catch the drippings and reserve the oil.

4. Wipe out the pan and return 2 tablespoons of the oil to it. Heat the oil and cook the peppers, stirring, until they are crisp tender. Add the sugar, wine, monosodium glutamate, water, and salt. Add the beef and cook quickly, stirring, until just heated through. Serve hot.

YIELD: 4 to 8 servings

A quickly cooked, simple, and delicious dish.

STIR-FRY BEEF WITH BEAN SPROUTS

½   pound flank steak
1   tablespoon dark soy sauce *
½   tablespoon plus 1 teaspoon cornstarch
     Peanut, vegetable, or corn oil
4   cups bean sprouts,* total volume whether they have been
         picked over to remove the end bits or not
     Salt to taste
1   teaspoon sugar
¼   teaspoon monosodium glutamate (optional)
1   tablespoon water

* Available in Chinese markets and by mail order. For more information see Chapter XI.

1. Place the beef on a flat surface and cut it across the grain into the thinnest possible slices. (This is easier to do if the meat is partially frozen.) Put the meat into a mixing bowl and add the soy sauce, the ½ tablespoon cornstarch, and ½ tablespoon oil.

2. Rinse and drain the bean sprouts well and set aside.

3. In a wok or skillet heat 1 cup oil, and when it is warm add the

beef and cook, stirring, about 20 seconds, just to separate the slices. (The oil should not be hot or the meat will stick together in a lump.) Remove the meat with a slotted spoon and drain in a sieve-lined bowl to catch the drippings. Press down to remove excess oil.

4. Pour out all but 1 tablespoon of oil from the pan. Heat it and add the bean sprouts. Cook, stirring, about 20 seconds. Pour off all but about ½ cup of liquid from the pan.

5. Add salt, the sugar, and the monosodium glutamate to the bean sprouts. Add the beef and toss over high heat for about 1 minute. Do not overcook the beef or it will toughen. Add the 1 teaspoon cornstarch blended in the water. Stir quickly until thickened and serve.

YIELD: 3 to 8 servings

They are called variously "bean thread," "vermicelli," "cellophane noodles," and "transparent noodles" (actually they are translucent). Whatever the name, they go well with many things, including beef. This is an incredibly simple dish to prepare.

BEEF WITH CELLOPHANE NOODLES

¾   pound flank steak, well trimmed
1   tablespoon plus 1 teaspoon dark soy sauce *
5   tablespoons peanut, vegetable, or corn oil
1   tablespoon cornstarch
2   ounces cellophane noodles (bean thread, transparent noo-
      dles) *
1   teaspoon sugar
1   teaspoon salt
¼   teaspoon monosodium glutamate (optional)
⅓   cup chicken broth

* Available in Chinese markets and by mail order. For more information see Chapter XI.

1. Place the beef on a flat surface and, using a sharp knife, cut it across the grain into the thinnest possible slices. Cut each slice into very fine shreds. (This is easier to do if the meat is partially frozen before slicing and stacked before shredding.) Put into a mixing bowl. There should be about 1½ cups shredded meat.

2. To the meat add the 1 tablespoon soy sauce, 1 tablespoon of the oil, and the cornstarch. Set aside.

3. Meanwhile, place the noodles in a bowl and pour boiling water over them to cover. Let stand about 1 hour. Drain. Cut the noodles in half.

4. In a wok or skillet heat the remaining oil and add the beef. Stir over high heat until the meat loses its color. Push the meat to one side of the pan and add the noodles. Stir about 30 seconds, then blend with the meat. Sprinkle with the sugar, salt, and monosodium glutamate. Cook about 10 seconds, then add the broth. Cook about 15 seconds, then add the remaining 1 teaspoon soy sauce. Cook 2 minutes, stirring occasionally, and serve hot.

YIELD: 3 to 8 servings

No one cooks beef with vegetables with more authority than the Chinese. The beef is usually flank steak that is cut against the grain. The important thing is that both the beef and the vegetables be cooked quickly.

BEEF WITH ASPARAGUS

1	pound flank steak
1½	tablespoons dark soy sauce *
	Peanut, vegetable, or corn oil
1	tablespoon cornstarch
12	asparagus spears
1	teaspoon sugar
1	teaspoon salt

¼   teaspoon monosodium glutamate
2   tablespoons dry sherry or shao hsing wine *
2   tablespoons chicken broth

* Available in Chinese markets and by mail order. For more information see
Chapter XI.

1. Place the beef on a flat surface and, using a sharp knife, cut it
against the grain into very thin slices. (This is easier to do if the
meat is partially frozen.) Combine the beef with the soy sauce, 1
tablespoon of the oil, and the cornstarch. Work the mixture with the
fingers and set aside.

2. Cut off the tough ends of the asparagus, then scrape with a
swivel-bladed paring knife, leaving the tips intact. Rinse well. Drop
the asparagus into boiling water to cover and simmer about ½ to 1
minute, depending on the age and size of the asparagus. Drain and
immediately run under cold running water to chill. Cut the asparagus on the bias into 1-inch lengths, and put the pieces into a bowl
of cold water till all are cut up. Drain.

3. Heat 2 cups of oil in a wok or skillet, and when it is warm add
the beef, stirring to separate the slices. (If the oil is hot the meat will
stick together in a lump.) Cook briefly, no more than 20 or 30 seconds. Drain in a sieve-lined bowl to catch the drippings and discard
all but 2 to 3 tablespoons of the oil.

4. Combine the sugar, salt, and monosodium glutamate and set
aside.

5. Heat the 2 to 3 tablespoons of reserved oil in the pan, and when
it is almost smoking add the asparagus pieces. Sprinkle with the
sugar mixture and cook, stirring, about 10 seconds. Add the beef
and stir to blend. Add the wine and broth and cook 1 minute or less,
stirring, until the sauce is almost absorbed in the beef.

YIELD: 4 to 8 servings

Beef with Oyster Sauce may not be the ultimate easily and rapidly cooked dish to prepare in Chinese cookery, but it would certainly be a contender for the title.

BEEF WITH OYSTER SAUCE

¾ pound flank steak (trimmed weight)
1   cup peanut, vegetable, or corn oil
1   tablespoon dark soy sauce *
1   teaspoon sugar
3   teaspoons cornstarch
1   tablespoon shredded fresh ginger *
1   scallion, green part included, trimmed and shredded
2   tablespoons oyster sauce *
1   tablespoon dry sherry or shao hsing wine *
2   tablespoons water

* Available in Chinese markets and by mail order. For more information see Chapter XI.

1. Place the flank steak on a flat surface and, using a sharp knife, cut it across the grain into the thinnest possible slices. (This is easier to do if the meat is partially frozen.) Place the meat in a mixing bowl and add 1 tablespoon of the oil. Add the soy sauce, sugar, and 2 teaspoons of the cornstarch.
2. In a wok or skillet heat the remaining oil until warm but not hot. (If the oil is hot the meat will stick together in a lump.) Add the beef mixture and cook, stirring, about 30 seconds. The meat should be only half cooked. Remove and drain the meat well in a sieve-lined bowl to catch the drippings, but leave about 1 tablespoon of oil in the pan. Add the ginger and scallion and cook about 10 seconds over high heat, then add the oyster sauce. Blend the remaining teaspoon of cornstarch with one tablespoon water. Add the beef, wine, and the remaining tablespoon water and stir in the cornstarch mixture. Stir to thicken and serve hot.

YIELD: 4 servings

Peanuts are a quite common and delicious adjunct to the Chinese cuisine. This recipe calls for beef with peas—and peanuts.

BEEF WITH PEAS AND PEANUTS

2   cups peanut, vegetable, or corn oil
½   cup raw shelled and hulled fresh unsalted peanuts *
1   pound ground round steak
1   tablespoon dark soy sauce *
2   tablespoons dry sherry or shao hsing wine *
4   teaspoons cornstarch
1   10-ounce package frozen peas, slightly thawed to separate (or, if available, 1 cup very fresh, briefly cooked green peas)
    Salt to taste
6   tablespoons water
1   teaspoon sugar
¼   teaspoon monosodium glutamate (optional)

* Available in Chinese markets and by mail order. For more information see Chapter XI.

1. Heat about 1½ cups oil in a small saucepan almost but not quite to the smoking point. Turn off the heat, add the peanuts, and let stand about 30 seconds, until they are golden brown. Be careful not to let them burn, since they brown very fast. Drain them and save the oil for another use.

2. Combine in a mixing bowl the ground meat, soy sauce, half the wine, 1 tablespoon oil, and half the cornstarch. Blend well with the fingers.

3. Heat 4 tablespoons of oil in a wok or skillet, and when warm, not hot, add the beef mixture, stirring just to separate the pieces. (If the oil is hot the meat will stick together in a lump.) Remove the beef from the pan and set aside.

4. Add 3 tablespoons of oil to the pan, and when it is hot add the peas, salt to taste, and the meat, cooking and stirring. Add 4 tablespoons of the water, the remaining wine, the sugar, and the mono-

sodium glutamate. Blend the remaining 2 teaspoons of cornstarch with the remaining 2 tablespoons of water and stir it into the beef. When the mixture is piping hot and thickened, transfer it to a serving dish and sprinkle with the peanuts. Serve hot.

YIELD: 4 to 8 servings

Here is another of those Szechwan dishes that have achieved such rare popularity in the Western world within the past decade. But a dish of the following authenticity is hard to find in restaurants because the beef reduces considerably in cooking and is therefore expensive to prepare.

SZECHWAN STIR-FRY BEEF WITH HOT PEPPERS

1	flank steak (2 pounds)
1	tablespoon light soy sauce *
1	tablespoon dark soy sauce *
1	tablespoon dry sherry or shao hsing wine *
2	teaspoons sugar, or more to taste
¼	teaspoon monosodium glutamate (optional)
	Salt to taste
1	carrot
2 to 6	ribs celery
2 to 6	fresh red long hot peppers *
8 to 16	hot dried red peppers,* left whole
1	cup peanut, vegetable, or corn oil

* Available in Chinese markets and by mail order. For more information see Chapter XI.

1. Split the flank steak in half. Slice each half against the grain into the thinnest possible slices, then cut these slices into the finest possible shreds. (This is easier if the meat is partially frozen before cutting and the slices stacked before shredding.) There should be about 4 cups of shredded meat.

2. In a bowl blend the soy sauces, wine, sugar, monosodium gluta-mate, and salt to taste. Set aside.

3. Scrape the carrot and celery ribs with a swivel-bladed vegetable peeler. Cut each into 2-inch lengths and thinly slice both carrot and celery lengthwise. Cut the thin slices of carrot and celery into very fine shreds (julienne). There should be about 1 cup of each vege-table. Combine in a bowl and set aside.

4. Trim the fresh red hot peppers and split them in half. Cut these, too, into fine shreds (julienne). Add to the carrot-celery bowl.

5. Have the hot dried red peppers ready.

6. Heat the oil in a wok or skillet and add the beef. Cook, stirring, over high heat 8 to 10 minutes, until the meat is quite dry. Drain thoroughly in a sieve-lined bowl.

7. Pour off all but 1 tablespoon of oil from the pan and heat over high heat. Add the hot dried red peppers and cook, stirring, until the peppers start to smoke and look rather burned, about 1 minute. Remove and discard the peppers.

8. Add the beef and soy sauce mixture. Cook, stirring, about 5 minutes, then add the carrot mixture and continue to cook and stir about 3 minutes. Add salt to taste and, if desired, about 1 teaspoon more sugar.

YIELD: 4 to 8 servings

The following dish is a kind of curry made with a bottled seasoning, found in Chinese markets, called Barbecue Sauce, which, according to the label, consists of the following ingredients: chili, garlic, oil, and salt. If the commercial sauce is not available, curry powder may be substituted.

SAND BEEF

1   pound flank steak, well trimmed
    Peanut, vegetable, or corn oil
1   tablespoon cornstarch
1   tablespoon dry sherry or shao hsing wine *
1   tablespoon dark soy sauce *
¼   cup finely chopped onion
2   tablespoons chopped scallion, green part included
3   tablespoons chopped fresh red or green long hot peppers *
1   teaspoon sugar
    Salt to taste
¼   teaspoon monosodium glutamate (optional)
¼   cup commercially prepared Barbecue Sauce or 2 tablespoons
        curry powder, or more to taste
2   tablespoons chicken broth

* Available in Chinese markets and by mail order. For more information see Chapter XI.

1. Place the meat on a flat surface and slice across the grain into the thinnest possible slices. (This is easier to do if the meat is partially frozen.) Place it in a mixing bowl and add 1 tablespoon of oil, the cornstarch, wine, and soy sauce. Work well so that the meat is thoroughly blended with the other ingredients.

2. Combine the onion, scallion, and red or green hot peppers and set aside.

3. In a wok or skillet heat 2 cups of oil, and when it is hot but not smoking add the beef. Cook, stirring, just until the meat changes color. Drain in a sieve-lined bowl to catch the drippings, and discard all but 2 tablespoons of the oil.

4. Return the reserved oil to the pan and add the onion mixture. Add the sugar, salt, and monosodium glutamate and cook about 30 seconds, then add the Barbecue Sauce or curry powder. Return the meat to the pan and add the chicken broth. Cook, stirring, until blended and thoroughly hot. Do not overcook.

YIELD: 4 to 6 servings

The name "steak" on a Chinese menu always sounds slightly anachronistic, but the following steak has a decidedly Chinese flavor.

STIR-FRY STEAK WITH MUSHROOMS

1   shell steak or club steak (1½ pounds)
2   tablespoons light soy sauce *
2   tablespoons dry sherry or shao hsing wine *
2   teaspoons sugar
    Salt to taste
¼   teaspoon ground pepper
1   teaspoon sesame oil *
2   teaspoons cornstarch
6   small dried black mushrooms *
½   cup thinly sliced bamboo shoots *
¼   pound green snow peas,* trimmed and "stringed"
2   scallions, green part included, trimmed and cut into 2-inch
      lengths
½   cup peanut, vegetable, or corn oil
¼   teaspoon monosodium glutamate (optional)

* Available in Chinese markets and by mail order. For more information see Chapter XI.

1. Trim the steak of fat and bone if there is any. Cut it into 1½-inch cubes and pound each cube lightly on all sides with the blunt edge of a heavy kitchen knife. Place the meat in a bowl and add the soy sauce, half the wine, half the sugar, salt, pepper, sesame oil, and cornstarch. Stir and blend well, then set aside.

2. Place the mushrooms in a mixing bowl and add boiling water to cover. Let stand 15 to 30 minutes, then drain, squeezing to extract most of the moisture. Cut off and discard the tough stems.

3. Combine the mushrooms, bamboo shoots, snow peas, and scallions. Set aside.

4. Heat the oil in a wok or skillet and add the steak. Cook over high heat about 2 minutes (or a little longer if you insist on very well-done meat). Drain the steak in a sieve-lined bowl to catch the drippings, and discard all but about 3 tablespoons of oil.

5. Heat the reserved oil in the pan. Add the vegetable mixture and cook 1 minute, stirring. Add the remaining teaspoon of sugar, salt to taste, and the monosodium glutamate and cook 1 minute, stirring. Add the remaining wine and the steak and cook, stirring, about 2 minutes.

YIELD: 4 to 8 servings

What on earth would the Chinese kitchen do without fresh ginger? It is as basic as soy sauce and goes beautifully with beef.

GINGER BEEF

¾ pound flank steak, well trimmed
2 teaspoons cornstarch
1 tablespoon dark soy sauce *
   Peanut, vegetable, or corn oil
¾ cup finely shredded fresh ginger *
1 teaspoon salt
½ teaspoon sugar
1 tablespoon dry sherry or shao hsing wine *
¼ teaspoon monosodium glutamate (optional)
3 cups loosely packed fresh coriander leaves,* rinsed and patted dry

* Available in Chinese markets and by mail order. For more information see Chapter XI.

1. Place the beef on a flat surface and slice it across the grain as thin as possible. Put it into a mixing bowl and add the cornstarch, soy sauce, and ½ tablespoon oil.

2. Put the ginger into a mixing bowl and add 1 teaspoon salt. Let stand 10 minutes, then drain and squeeze to extract most of the moisture that will have accumulated.

3. In a wok or skillet heat 1 cup of oil and turn off the heat. Add the beef and turn the heat on again. Cook, stirring, just until the pieces are separated and the meat loses most of its red color. Do not overcook or it will toughen. Drain in a sieve-lined bowl to catch the drippings and discard all but 2 tablespoons of the oil.

4. Blend the sugar, wine, and monosodium glutamate and set aside.

5. Heat the 2 tablespoons of oil in the pan and add the ginger. Cook, stirring, about 15 seconds, then add the beef and cook about 15 seconds longer. Stir in the coriander leaves and cook about 5 seconds. Add the wine mixture and stir just to blend well. Serve hot.

YIELD: 4 to 8 servings

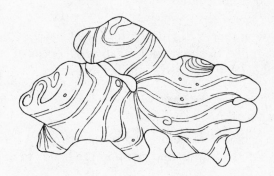

Bean curd—that staple of the Chinese kitchen—has a somewhat meaty characteristic. It is also interesting when blended with a meat such as beef and seasoned with ginger and hot pepper.

GINGER BEEF AND BEAN CURD
WITH HOT PEPPER

    5   pads fresh white bean curd *
    3   dried black mushrooms *
    ½   cup chopped scallions, green part included
    ½   tablespoon chopped garlic
    1   tablespoon finely chopped fresh ginger *
    2   tablespoons chopped fresh red or green long hot peppers *
    2   or more hot dried red peppers,* chopped
    2   tablespoons peanut, vegetable, or corn oil
    ¼   pound ground lean beef
    2   tablespoons light soy sauce *
    1   cup plus 2 tablespoons chicken broth
    ½   teaspoon monosodium glutamate (optional)
    1   tablespoon cornstarch
        Salt to taste
    1   tablespoon rendered chicken fat (see Chapter XI; optional)
    ½   cup chopped fresh coriander leaves * (optional)
        Hot oil * (optional; see Note below)

    * Available in Chinese markets and by mail order. For more information see Chapter XI.

1. Rinse the pads of bean curd and place them in a bowl. Soak in cold water briefly, then drain and crush in the hands to make a pulp. Set aside.

2. Place the mushrooms in a mixing bowl and add boiling water to cover. Let stand 15 to 30 minutes, then drain, squeezing to extract most of the moisture, and cut off the tough stems. Chop the mushrooms.

3. Combine the mushrooms, scallions, garlic, ginger, and the chopped fresh and dried peppers.

4. Heat the oil in a wok or skillet, and when it is hot add the beef. Stir quickly to separate the pieces, then add the soy sauce. Stir quickly and add the mushroom and scallion mixture. Add the 1 cup chicken broth, and when it boils add the crushed bean curd. Cook, stirring, about 1 minute, then add the monosodium glutamate. Cook, stirring, about 3 minutes.

5. Blend the cornstarch with the remaining 2 tablespoons of chicken broth and stir until thickened. Add salt to taste. Just before serving, spoon the chicken fat over the dish to glaze it and, if you wish, sprinkle with the coriander.

YIELD: 2 to 6 servings

Note: If you want a spicier dish, add a few drops of hot oil or as much as you wish.

There may be no dish on earth more typically Cantonese than bitter melon in one form or another. The "melon" is really a vegetable, cucumber shaped and as bitter as gall. It is dark green and has a rough, wartlike skin. On first taste it may seem, to some palates, utterly abhorrent. But like most tastes that are acquired, once admired it is something to hunger for and covet.

BITTER MELON WITH BEEF

1	bitter melon * (¾ pound)
5	tablespoons fermented salted black beans *
3	tablespoons water, approximately
5 to 10	small fresh red or green long hot peppers *
3	cloves garlic, peeled and flattened but left whole
¾	pound flank steak
½	tablespoon cornstarch
	Peanut, vegetable, or corn oil
1	tablespoon dark soy sauce *
2½	teaspoons sugar
¼	teaspoon monosodium glutamate (optional)
	Salt to taste
1	tablespoon dry sherry or shao hsing wine *

* Available in Chinese markets and by mail order. For more information see Chapter XI.

1. Trim off and discard the ends of the bitter melon. Split the vegetable in half. Place each half cut side down and cut into thin slices, about ¼ inch or slightly thicker. Using a paring knife or a melon ball cutter, cut out and discard the white center portion of each slice. Reserve the pieces of green outer shell.

2. Bring to a boil enough water to cover the pieces of bitter melon. Drop the slices in the water and cook 3 minutes. Drain and immediately run under cold running water. Drain well.

3. Soak the black beans in the 3 tablespoons of water and crush them lightly with the back of a spoon. Set aside.

4. Cut off the stem ends of the peppers and slice in half. Remove the seeds and cut the pepper into very fine strips (julienne). Combine the pepper strips and garlic and set aside.

5. Put the beef on a flat surface and, with a sharp knife, cut into the thinnest possible slices. (This is easier to do if the meat is partially frozen.) Put the beef slices into a mixing bowl and add the cornstarch, 1 tablespoon oil, and the soy sauce.

6. Heat 1 cup of oil, and when it is hot but not smoking add the beef and cook, stirring to separate the slices. Cook only until half done, about 20 to 30 seconds. Drain well in a sieve-lined bowl to catch the drippings.

7. Heat about 3 tablespoons of oil and add the black beans. Stir. Add the pepper strips and garlic and cook about 15 seconds, stirring. Add the bitter melon and cook about 30 seconds, stirring. Stir in the sugar, then add the monosodium glutamate and salt. Cook and stir about 15 seconds, then add the wine.

8. Add the beef and cook, stirring, just to heat through.

YIELD: 4 to 6 servings

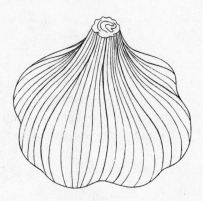

Tripe, like snails and sea slugs, is not for all palates, but then again neither is peanut butter and jelly. Tripe is an "occasional" dish that appears in all the world's great cuisines, be they French, Italian, or Chinese. The last named, at times, combines it in a stir-fry dish with coriander leaves—complementary flavors indeed.

TRIPE WITH CORIANDER

1   pound tripe, cut into large squares or rectangles measuring
    4 or 5 inches to a side
1   bunch fresh coriander *
4   hot dried red peppers *
1   tablespoon dry sherry or shao hsing wine *
    Salt to taste
½   teaspoon sugar
½   teaspoon monosodium glutamate (optional)
⅛   teaspoon ground pepper
¼   cup peanut, vegetable, or corn oil
¼   cup shredded fresh ginger *

   * Available in Chinese markets and by mail order. For more information see Chapter XI.

1. Rinse and drain the tripe and put it into a kettle or deep heatproof casserole with water to cover. Cover with a lid and simmer 30 minutes or longer, until tender. The cooking time will vary, since the toughness of tripe varies from one batch to the next. Drain, and when cool enough to handle pick over the pieces to remove any excess fat.

2. Cut the tripe into strips about ⅜ inch wide and 2 inches long. Pat dry.

3. Pick over the coriander, pulling off and discarding the tough stems. Reserve only the leaves and tender stems. Rinse well and shake in a salad basket or pat in a towel to remove excess moisture. Pack the leaves into a measuring cup. There should be about 2 cups loosely packed.

4. Using a pair of kitchen scissors, cut the peppers lengthwise. Remove and discard the seeds. Cut the peppers into thin strips and set aside.

5. Blend the wine, salt, sugar, monosodium glutamate, and ground pepper. Set aside.

6. In a wok or skillet, heat the oil, and when it starts to smoke add the tripe, peppers, and ginger. Cook, stirring, about 20 seconds. Add the wine mixture and cook, stirring rapidly, about 30 seconds. Add salt to taste and the coriander leaves. Cook until the sauce is almost totally reduced, and serve immediately.

YIELD: 4 to 8 servings

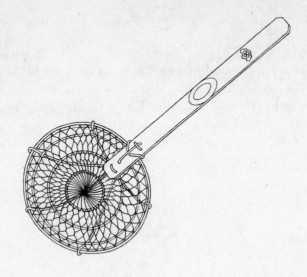

VI

Seafood

The infinite uses and varied virtues of sesame seeds are splendid in the Chinese repertoire of cooking—and put to good use as a coating for many foods, including fresh fish fillets.

DEEP-FRIED FISH FILLETS
WITH SESAME SEED COATING

Fillets of non-oily fish such as sole, flounder, striped bass, or sea bass (¾ to 1 pound)
1   1-inch piece fresh ginger,* crushed lightly
1   scallion, green part included, trimmed and crushed lightly
¼   cup water, approximately
2   tablespoons dry sherry or shao hsing wine *
    Salt to taste
½   teaspoon five spices powder,* commercially prepared or home made
1   egg white
3   tablespoons cornstarch
¼   teaspoon sugar
1   cup or more white sesame seeds *
    Peanut, vegetable, or corn oil for deep frying

* Available in Chinese markets and by mail order. For more information see Chapter XI.

197

1. Place the fish fillets on a flat surface and cut them on the bias, holding the knife at an angle close to the board. Cut into very thin slices measuring about 3 by 4 inches, more or less. There should be about 16 to 18 pieces. Set aside.

2. Put the ginger and scallion into a small bowl and add the water. Let stand 30 minutes.

3. Combine the wine, salt, and five spices powder in a mixing bowl. Add the liquid from the ginger and scallion and discard the ginger and scallion.

4. Add the fish to the wine mixture, stirring so that the pieces are well coated.

5. Blend the egg white with the cornstarch, more salt to taste, and sugar.

6. Pour the sesame seeds into a flat dish.

7. Drain the fish slices. Dip them first into the cornstarch mixture, then coat liberally on both sides with sesame seeds. Refrigerate at least 30 minutes.

8. Pour enough oil for deep frying into a wok or deep-fryer. In the beginning the oil should be only moderately hot; otherwise, the seeds will cook too fast and spurt.

9. Cook until almost but not quite brown and transfer the fish slices to a colander. (Placed in a dish and covered well, the fillets can be refrigerated overnight at this point.) When ready to serve reheat the oil to quite hot, add the fish, and cook quickly until golden brown.

YIELD: 4 to 8 servings

This dish bears the peculiar name of "roof brick," because some ancient chef decided that the pieces of carp resembled the bricks on the roof of his house. It is a most appetizing dish served under a blanket of fried noodles and topped with a sweet and sour garlic and ginger sauce.

ROOF BRICK CARP

1   carp (3 pounds)
     Salt
2   tablespoons dry sherry or shao hsing wine *
6   tablespoons all-purpose flour
1½   cups plus 3 tablespoons water
1   tablespoon dark soy sauce *
½   teaspoon monosodium glutamate (optional)
6   tablespoons red wine vinegar
7   tablespoons sugar
1½   tablespoons cornstarch
1   packet from a 1-pound package of banshu somen (Japanese dried noodles) *
     Peanut, vegetable, or corn oil
2   tablespoons finely chopped garlic
2   tablespoons finely chopped fresh ginger *
3   scallions, green part included, trimmed and chopped
3   tablespoons finely chopped fresh red long hot peppers * (optional)

* Available in Chinese markets and by mail order. For more information see Chapter XI.

1. Cut off and discard the head and tail of the fish. Split the fish down the middle lengthwise, along the backbone. Cut each half of the fish into 2 pieces crosswise, if it is a small fish, and into 4 pieces if the fish is large. The pieces should be about 4 to 5 inches long.

2. Rub the more or less rectangular pieces of fish with salt and place in layers in a mixing bowl. Add the wine and let stand for an hour or longer, then coat each piece with flour.

3. To start the sauce, combine in a saucepan the 1½ cups water, soy sauce, salt to taste, monosodium glutamate, vinegar, and sugar. Bring to a boil and stir until the sugar is dissolved. This may be done in advance and set aside.

4. Blend the cornstarch and remaining 3 tablespoons of water in a small cup and set aside.

5. Place the banshu somen in a container and add boiling water to cover. Let soak until soft, about 15 minutes. Drain and cover with cold water to keep the strands separate.

6. Heat oil for deep frying in a wok or deep-fryer and add the pieces of fish. Cook, turning the pieces in the oil, until golden brown and cooked through, about 7 to 8 minutes. Arrange the pieces on a hot platter and keep warm. Let the oil remain in the pan for cooking the banshu somen. Heat it to smoking.

7. With your hands pull the noodles out of the water, shake off excess water, and drop them straight—without draining—into the oil so that they make a skeinlike pattern. For some reason the wet noodles do not spatter much, but stand back anyway. As the noodles cook they will firm themselves into a round, skeinlike cake. Turn this cake in the oil a few times until it is uniformly brown. (If the oil is new, this may take longer than you would expect. Foods brown more quickly in oil that, while still fresh, has been used a few times before.)

8. When the noodles are done, drain them and arrange them over the fish.

9. To finish making the sauce, heat 2 tablespoons of oil in a wok or saucepan, add the garlic and ginger, and stir quickly over high heat. Add the sweet and sour sauce and stir until the sauce boils. Stir the cornstarch and water mixture and add to the sauce. When thickened, add the scallions and peppers and immediately pour the sauce over the noodles and fish. Serve hot.

YIELD: 6 to 8 servings

Oyster sauce is one of those curious (if delectable) ingredients that adapts itself to many basic foods. Not the least of these is abalone, an engaging ingredient in itself.

ABALONE WITH OYSTER SAUCE

2   15-ounce tins of abalone *
    Chicken broth
2   tablespoons peanut, vegetable, or corn oil
1   tablespoon dry sherry or shao hsing wine *
¼   teaspoon ground white pepper
1   tablespoon cornstarch
2   tablespoons water
2½ tablespoons oyster sauce *
¼   teaspoon sugar
1   tablespoon rendered chicken fat (see Chapter XI)
½   teaspoon sesame oil *

* Available in Chinese markets and by mail order. For more information see Chapter XI.

1. Drain the abalone and place in a saucepan. Add enough chicken broth to cover, 2 or 3 cups. Bring to a boil and simmer 1 hour. Drain and discard the broth.

2. Slice the abalone into oval slices, each about ¼ inch thick. Arrange neatly on a serving platter.

3. Heat the oil in a wok or saucepan, and when it is hot add the wine. Cook briefly, then add 1 cup of chicken broth and the white pepper.

4. Blend the cornstarch with the water and stir into the sauce. Add the oyster sauce and sugar and stir to blend. Add the chicken fat and sesame oil. Pour the sauce over the abalone and serve immediately.

YIELD: 4 to 6 servings

The following dish, well known in Chinese cooking, is called Squirrel Fish because, through a wild stretch of its creator's imagination, the fish looked like squirrel when it was cooked. It is a northern dish, and in the north it is made with yellowfish. Whiting serves the purpose nobly.

SQUIRREL FISH

4	whiting (about ½ pound each), filleted but with the skin left on
¼	cup dry sherry or shao hsing wine *
1	tablespoon plus 1 teaspoon light soy sauce *
	Salt to taste
6 to 8	dried black mushrooms *
¼	cup ham, cut into ¼-inch cubes
¼	cup bamboo shoots,* cut into ¼-inch cubes
¼	cup raw shrimps, cut into ¼-inch cubes
¼	cup coarsely chopped hot or sweet green peppers
	All-purpose flour for dredging
	Peanut, vegetable, or corn oil
½	cup sugar
⅓	cup red wine vinegar
2	tablespoons chopped fresh ginger *
¼	teaspoon monosodium glutamate (optional)
1¼	cups water
4	teaspoons cornstarch
2	tablespoons chopped scallions, green part included
	Fresh coriander * for garnish

* Available in Chinese markets and by mail order. For more information see Chapter XI.

1. Place the fish, skin side down, on a cutting surface. Score the flesh of the fish fairly deeply, cutting on the diagonal, at ½-inch intervals, without cutting through the skin. Next score each fish lengthwise, making a diamond pattern.

2. Combine 3 tablespoons of the wine with 1 tablespoon of the

soy sauce and salt to taste. Add the pieces of fish and rub lightly with the marinade. Let stand 20 to 30 minutes.

3. Meanwhile, pour boiling water over the mushrooms and soak them for 15 to 30 minutes. Drain the mushrooms, squeezing to extract most of the moisture, and cut off and discard the stems. Cut the mushrooms into ¼-inch cubes, place them in a mixing bowl, and add the ham and bamboo shoots. Set aside.

4. Combine the shrimps and hot or sweet peppers and set aside.

5. Remove the fish from the marinade and coat each fillet generously with flour.

6. Heat oil for deep frying in a wok or deep-fryer and deep-fry the fillets, 2 or 3 at a time, until golden all over. Drain. Return the fillets to the hot oil and cook briefly once more. This will make them crisp. Drain and place on a serving dish.

7. Heat ¼ cup of oil in a wok or skillet and add the mushroom mixture. Cook, stirring, about 1 minute and add the shrimps and hot or sweet peppers. Blend the sugar and vinegar and add, then stir in the remaining wine and soy sauce. Add the ginger and monosodium glutamate. Add 1 cup water.

8. Blend the cornstarch with the remaining ¼ cup water. Stir it in and bring to a boil. Pour the sauce over the fish and garnish with the chopped scallions and fresh coriander.

YIELD: 6 to 10 servings

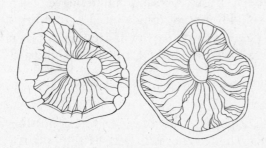

This is an odd but gratifying recipe in which fillets of fish are cooked on thin sheets of unsalted pork fat and sometimes served on a bed of deep-fried chrysanthemum leaves. These leaves are not the florist's kind but the kind sold fresh in Chinese groceries.

WINE AND GINGER FISH

4 to 6 very thinly sliced unsalted fresh pork fat, each slice measuring about 5 by 7 inches

4 to 6 small flounder fillets

4 scallions, green part included, trimmed and cut into 1-inch lengths

2 tablespoons coarsely chopped fresh ginger *

1 clove garlic, coarsely chopped

½ cup water

2 tablespoons plus 1 teaspoon dry sherry or shao hsing wine *

¼ teaspoon ground pepper

Salt to taste

1½ teaspoons sugar

1 egg white

Cornstarch

¼ teaspoon monosodium glutamate (optional)

Peanut, vegetable, or corn oil

1 bunch fresh chrysanthemum leaves,* trimmed, thoroughly rinsed, drained and patted dry (optional) or several large leaves of fresh lettuce, or a bunch of watercress, washed, trimmed, and dried

* Available in Chinese markets and by mail order. For more information see Chapter XI.

1. The slices of pork fat should be as thin as possible and as large as or slightly larger than the fish fillets. If the butcher is agreeable, have him slice the pork fat for you on his professional slicing machine. A machine is all but essential to get the slices thin enough.

2. Place the fish fillets in a bowl and set aside.

3. Put the scallions, ginger, garlic, and water into the container of an electric blender and blend. Hold a sieve over a mixing bowl and strain the liquid. Discard the pulp in the strainer.

4. Spoon 1 tablespoon of the scallion-ginger-garlic liquid into a mixing bowl. Reserve the remaining liquid for another recipe or discard it.

5. Add the 2 tablespoons wine, pepper, salt, and sugar to the scallion-ginger-garlic liquid. Pour this over the fish and stir to coat the fillets. Set aside.

6. Combine the egg white with the remaining 1 teaspoon wine, 2 tablespoons cornstarch, monosodium glutamate, and salt to taste.

7. Place one slice of pork fat at a time on a flat surface and brush the top with the egg-white mixture.

8. Remove one fish fillet at a time and dredge lightly on both sides in cornstarch. Place it neatly on the pork fat. Using a sharp knife, carve around the pork fat to approximately the shape of the fillet but leaving a small border of fat. Continue until all the slices of pork fat are topped with fish.

9. Heat about ⅛ inch of oil in one or two skillets and place the fish fillets, pork side down, in the oil. Cook over gentle heat, without turning, 10 to 12 minutes, or until the fish fillets are tender and cooked through.

10. Meanwhile, if chrysanthemum leaves are used, heat oil for deep frying in a wok or deep-fryer and drop in the leaves. Cook, stirring, until they are cooked through and crisp, 3 to 6 minutes, depending on the tenderness of the leaves. Drain well. Arrange the leaves on an oval or round platter. Otherwise, make a bed of fresh lettuce or watercress on the platter.

11. Drain the fish and cut each fillet into bite-size pieces. Arrange the pieces on the bed of chrysanthemum leaves or greens and serve immediately.

YIELD: 4 to 8 servings

MASTER RECIPE FOR STEAMED FISH

1   white-fleshed, non-oily fish (1 to 1½ pounds) such as sea bass
    or flounder, with head and tail left on, but cleaned, scaled,
    and with the spongy matter inside the head (gills) re-
    moved
    Dry sherry or shao hsing wine *

* Available in Chinese markets and by mail order. For more information see
Chapter XI.

1. Rinse the fish inside and out with a small quantity of wine.
2. Select a round or oval platter large enough to hold the fish, but
one that will fit inside the top of a steaming utensil. The utensil
could be a traditional Chinese bamboo or metal steamer, or a Western-style clam steamer.
3. Bring a large quantity of water to a boil in the bottom of the
steamer.
4. Place the fish on the platter and set the platter in the top of the
steamer. Cover and steam over the boiling water 10 to 15 minutes,
depending on the size of the fish. When cooked, remove the platter
and pour off the liquid that has accumulated around the fish.

YIELD: 3 to 6 servings

There is no food more delicate than genuinely fresh fish steamed properly, Chinese fashion. It has a purity that is perfectly complemented by whatever sauce is served with it. Two of the most interesting sauces for fish are a "meat" sauce (made with a bottled meat sauce) and a bean sauce.

STEAMED FISH WITH "MEAT" SAUCE

 1 fish (1 to 1½ pounds) such as sea bass or flounder, steamed according to the Master Recipe for Steamed Fish (see preceding recipe)
 2 tablespoons meat sauce such as A-1 or Escoffier
 2 tablespoons light soy sauce *
 2 tablespoons oyster sauce *
 2 tablespoons bean sauce *
 2 tablespoons hoi sin sauce *
 2 teaspoons sugar
    Salt to taste
 2 tablespoons coarsely chopped garlic
 1½ tablespoons minced fresh ginger *
 4 small fresh red long hot peppers,* finely chopped (optional)
 2 tablespoons chopped scallions, green part included
 ¼ cup peanut, vegetable, or corn oil
 ½ cup finely slivered scallions for garnish

* Available in Chinese markets and by mail order. For more information see Chapter XI.

1. Steam the fish, and while it is cooking prepare the sauce by combining all the ingredients except the oil and finely slivered scallions.

2. Heat the oil in a wok or saucepan, and when it is hot add the meat sauce mixture. Cook, stirring, just until the sauce boils.

3. Pour the sauce over the fish. Sprinkle with the slivered scallions and serve hot.

YIELD: 3 to 6 servings

STEAMED FISH WITH BEAN SAUCE

1   fish (1 to 1½ pounds) such as sea bass or flounder, steamed according to the Master Recipe for Steamed Fish (see recipe)
¼   cup bean sauce *
3   cloves garlic, coarsely chopped (about 2 tablespoons)
2   tablespoons chopped scallions, green part included
2   tablespoons finely minced fresh ginger *
2   teaspoons sugar
¼   cup peanut, vegetable, or corn oil

* Available in Chinese markets and by mail order. For more information see Chapter XI.

1. Steam the fish, and while it is cooking prepare the sauce by combining all the ingredients except the oil.
2. Heat the oil in a wok or saucepan, and when it is hot add the bean sauce mixture. Cook, stirring, until the sauce boils.
3. Pour the sauce over the fish.

YIELD: 3 to 6 servings

The Chinese method of steaming fish is one of the purest because the flavor of the fish, through steaming, is left intact. In the recipe that follows, the fish, after steaming, is served with a tremendously complementary, somewhat piquant sauce made with wine and soy sauce.

STEAMED FLOUNDER

The fish:

2   large dried black mushrooms *
1   flounder (1 to 1½ pounds; the number may be doubled if

the steamer is large enough to accommodate two), with head and tail left on but cleaned, scaled and with the spongy matter inside the head (gills) removed
Dry sherry
⅓　cup finely shredded pork (approximately ⅛ pound)
2　tablespoons rendered chicken fat (see Chapter XI)
¼　cup finely shredded fresh ginger *
4　cloves garlic, finely shredded
⅓　cup shredded bamboo shoots *
3　scallions, green part included, trimmed
Fresh coriander * for garnish (optional)

The sauce:

3　tablespoons dry sherry or shao hsing wine *
7　tablespoons peanut, vegetable, or corn oil
3　tablespoons light soy sauce *
1½　teaspoons sugar
1½　teaspoons salt, or to taste
¼　teaspoon monosodium glutamate (optional)

* Available in Chinese markets and by mail order. For more information see Chapter XI.

1. Pour boiling water over the mushrooms and let stand for 15 to 30 minutes.

2. Select an oval or round plate with a rim large enough to hold the fish and fit inside the steamer.

3. Rinse the fish inside and out with a little dry sherry and pat dry.

4. Place the flounder, dark skin side up, on the plate (if 2 flounders are used, place them side by side).

5. Bring an ample quantity of water to a boil in the bottom of the steamer. The water level should be close to the steamer top.

6. Scatter the shredded pork, chicken fat, ginger, garlic, and bamboo shoots over the fish.

7. Drain the mushrooms, then squeeze them to extract much of the liquid. Cut off and discard the stems and slice the mushrooms thin. Scatter them over the fish.

8. Place the dish in the top of the steamer. Cover and steam 10 to 15 minutes, or until the fish is tender when poked with chopsticks or a fork.

9. Meanwhile, combine all the ingredients for the sauce in a small skillet.

10. Cut the scallions into 2-inch lengths, then shred each piece.

11. When the fish is done, carefully pour off the liquid that has accumulated in the plate. Scatter the scallions over the fish. Bring the sauce to a boil and pour it over the fish. Garnish with sprigs of fresh coriander, if desired.

YIELD: 2 to 8 servings

Carp, the fresh-water fish that if uncaught lives to a great age and sometimes weighs forty pounds or more, is one of the favored fish of the Chinese kitchen. The following sweet and sour dish is known as West Lake Carp because the dish originated in Hangchow, with fish caught in the West Lake there. The carp available in the Western world is not identical, but it serves the purpose well.

WEST LAKE CARP

1   fresh carp (2 to 2½ pounds), with head on
2   cups water
1   cup sugar
⅔   cup red wine vinegar
1   tablespoon plus ½ teaspoon dark soy sauce *
3   tablespoons peanut, vegetable, or corn oil
1   teaspoon salt, or to taste
2   tablespoons cornstarch
¼   cup finely chopped fresh ginger *
2   teaspoons ground white pepper

* Available in Chinese markets and by mail order. For more information see Chapter XI.

1. Have the fish man leave the fish whole but remove the spongy red matter (gills) from inside the head. The fish must be cleaned and well scaled.

2. Unless you are expert in such matters, have the fish man open up the fish from the back, once it is cleaned, and place it on a flat surface. Have him split the fish along the inside of the backbone from head to tail, without severing the bone or otherwise cutting through the fish. Have him crack open the head bone. This will permit the fish to lie flat when opened up.

3. In a large wok or roasting pan bring enough water to a boil to cover the fish when added. Place the fish, opened up, and boned side down, in the water, and simmer 7 to 10 minutes, or until done. Do not overcook.

4. Meanwhile, in a saucepan combine the 2 cups water with the sugar, vinegar, soy sauce, 2 tablespoons of the oil, and salt. Bring to a boil. Blend the cornstarch with 3 tablespoons of water and stir the mixture into the sauce until thickened. Add the ginger and gradually stir in the remaining tablespoon of oil.

5. Carefully remove the fish from the pan to a large oval serving platter. Pour the sauce over the fish and sprinkle with the pepper. Serve hot.

YIELD: 4 to 8 servings

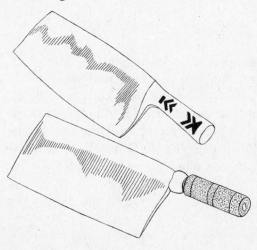

This dish is jocularly called Grand Old Man because the Chinese at times use a technique in pouring boiling water over fresh fish to make the gill fins stand straight out like a grand old man's whiskers or mustache. It is a delectable dish in which the steamed fish is served with a savory combination of herbs and spices.

GRAND OLD MAN
(Steamed Red Snapper with Herbs)

1   red snapper (2½ to 3 pounds), head and tail on
2   quarts water, approximately
⅓   cup finely shredded fresh ginger *
½   cup shredded white part of scallions
½   cup shredded green part of scallions
½   cup peanut, vegetable, or corn oil
¼   cup thinly shredded, seeded fresh red or green sweet or hot
        peppers
1   cup chicken broth
¼   teaspoon monosodium glutamate (optional)
        Salt to taste
1   tablespoon cornstarch
¼   cup cold water

* Available in Chinese markets and by mail order. For more information see Chapter XI.

1. Place the red snapper in the sink.
2. Bring about 2 quarts of water to a boil. Pour about half of the water all over one side of the fish. Turn the fish and pour the remaining water over the other side. Using a brush (or fingernails if they are sharp), go carefully all over the skin of the fish, scraping lightly but diligently as you go. This will clean off the red color of the fish. This is done more for aesthetic reasons than for flavor. If properly done, the fish will no longer look like a red snapper.
3. Place the fish in a plate and fit the plate inside the top of a steamer. Fit the top over the bottom of the steamer and steam the fish over boiling water for exactly 15 minutes.

4. Remove the fish and pour off any liquid that has accumulated around it. Scatter the ginger and half the scallions and peppers over the fish.

5. Heat the oil in a small skillet, and when it is almost piping hot but not smoking pour it over the fish.

6. Bring the broth to a boil and add the monosodium glutamate and salt. Blend the cornstarch with the water and stir it into the sauce. When thickened, pour the sauce over the fish. Scatter the remaining scallions and peppers over the fish and serve hot.

YIELD: 4 to 8 servings

In this dish the popular carp is spicily sauced with hot peppers, ginger, scallions, and garlic.

BROWN SAUCE CARP

1   carp (3 pounds), with head and tail left on but cleaned, scaled, and with spongy matter inside the head (gills) removed
3   tablespoons dark soy sauce *
6   dried black mushrooms *
    Peanut, vegetable, or corn oil
½   cup finely shredded pork
6   thin slices fresh ginger,* peeled
3   cloves garlic, peeled and flattened with the side of a knife
¼   cup thinly sliced bamboo shoots *
2   cups water
2   tablespoons dry sherry or shao hsing wine *
    Salt to taste
1   teaspoon sugar
½   teaspoon monosodium glutamate (optional)
4   small fresh red long hot peppers,* cored and seeded (optional)
3   scallions, green part included, trimmed and cut into 2-inch lengths
    Fresh coriander leaves * for garnish (optional)

* Available in Chinese markets and by mail order. For more information see Chapter XI.

1. Rinse the carp well inside and out and pat it dry. It must be very dry. Rub it inside and out with 2 tablespoons of the soy sauce and let stand about 20 minutes.

2. Meanwhile, pour boiling water over the mushrooms and let stand 15 to 30 minutes. Remove the mushrooms, but reserve about ½ cup of the soaking water. Squeeze the mushrooms to extract most of the water, then trim off and discard the stems. Slice the mushrooms.

3. In a wok or deep-fryer large enough to hold the fish heat about 2 quarts of oil over very high heat. The oil must be very, very hot before the fish is added, or it will stick to the bottom of the cooker.

4. Slide the fish into the oil, and as it cooks continually spoon oil over the top of the fish. If enough oil were used to cover the fish entirely, the spooning would not be necessary, but oil is expensive. After about 1 minute, turn the fish in the oil and continue cooking and spooning oil over for about 2 minutes. Lift the fish from the oil and transfer it to a platter. Pour off the oil (which may be re-served for other cooking). Wipe out the pan.

5. In the same pan heat ¼ cup of oil. Add the pork and cook, stir-ring, until the pork changes color. Add the ginger, garlic, and bamboo shoots. Cook, stirring, about 30 seconds, then add the fish. Add the remaining tablespoon of soy sauce, the 2 cups water, the mushroom water, and the wine. When the sauce boils, add the salt, sugar, and monosodium glutamate. As the sauce cooks, spoon it constantly over the fish, about 4 minutes. Cover and cook about 3 minutes, then add the hot peppers. Uncover and cook 4 minutes or so longer, or a total cooking time of about 15 minutes. Transfer the fish to a platter. Add the scallions to the sauce and immediately spoon the sauce over the fish. Garnish with fresh coriander leaves if desired, and serve immediately.

YIELD: 4 to 8 servings

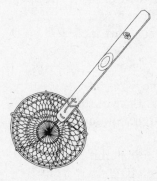

In America at least, perhaps the most popular fish in the Chinese reportoire—for the Western palate that may shun such delicacies as sea slugs and dried squid and abalone—is the sea bass. It is infinite in its adaptability, whether simply steamed or in a sweet and sour sauce.

The following recipe requires that the fish be split in two and boned. It is not a simple task, but the hardest part can be avoided by having your fish market split the head in two—or you can even have the head cut off altogether.

SWEET AND SOUR SEA BASS

1   whole sea bass (2 to 4 pounds), with head and tail left on but cleaned, scaled, and with the spongy matter inside the head (gills) removed
2   eggs, beaten
     Salt
¼   teaspoon monosodium glutamate (optional)
     Cornstarch
4   dried black mushrooms *
1   small onion, peeled and cut into 1-inch "petals" or cubes (about ¾ cup)
6   thin slices fresh ginger,* peeled
5   cloves garlic, peeled and flattened but left whole
2   fresh red sweet or long hot peppers,* seeded, halved, and cut into 1-inch cubes or smaller (about ¾ cup)
8   pickled scallions *
2   scallions, green part included
2¼   cups water
1   cup sugar
⅔   cup red wine vinegar
1   tablespoon dark soy sauce *
1   tablespoon light soy sauce *
1   teaspoon salt
3   tablespoons cornstarch
     Peanut, vegetable, or corn oil

* Available in Chinese markets and by mail order. For more information see Chapter XI.

1. First butterfly the fish. To do this, use a sharp knife or cleaver and start cutting and slicing along one side of the backfin, holding the knife as close to the bone structure as possible.

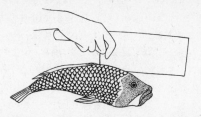

Cut down following the bone lines almost but not through to the bottom of the fish. Now cut through the top half of the fish behind the tail. Cut the head in two, using a rubber mallet to force the knife through the bone. You should now be able to open the fish like a book, with the bottom of the fish still hinged together with joining flesh and skin.

2. Bone the fish. First, using a sharp knife, your fingers, and a pair of kitchen shears, cut out the spine and the attached smaller bones in one piece, trying to leave as much flesh on the fish as possible.

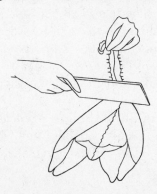

With a knife or shears remove as many of the bones left in the fish as you can see. You will not be able to get all the bones, and diners should be warned about this when the fish is served.

3. Score the flesh of the fish where it has been boned fairly deeply, but without puncturing the skin, at 1-inch intervals—less if the fish is small. The scoring should be from about ½- to 1-inch deep, depending on the thickness and size of the fish. Place the fish, opened up, skin side down, in a utensil large enough to hold it.

4. Blend together the eggs, salt to taste, and monosodium glutamate. Pour this over the fish and rub it into the opened-up, scored surface, then turn the fish and rub the egg mixture over the scaled side.

5. Spoon a tablespoon or so of cornstarch into a sieve and shake it over one side of the fish. Rub it in. Shake another tablespoon over and rub it in. Continue doing this on both the scaled and boned sides of the fish until the fish is liberally coated with cornstarch, including the area between the scored parts. Let the fish stand for 15 minutes or longer.

6. Meanwhile, place the mushrooms in a bowl and add boiling water to cover. Let stand 15 to 30 minutes. Drain, then squeeze the mushrooms to extract most of the moisture. Cut off and discard the tough stems and cut the mushroom caps in half. Put them into a bowl.

7. Add the onion, ginger, garlic, peppers, and pickled scallions.

8. Trim the scallions and cut them into 2-inch lengths. Shred the ends of each length of scallion with a sharp knife. Drop the scallion pieces into cold water and let stand until the ends curl.

9. Combine 2 cups of the water, the sugar, vinegar, soy sauces, and 1 teaspoon salt. Set aside. In a small bowl blend the 3 tablespoons cornstarch with the remaining water and set aside.

10. Heat to almost smoking about 2 quarts of oil in a large wok or other large pan suitable for deep frying. If the oil is not hot enough, the fish will stick. Add the fish skin side down. Cook over high heat, constantly spooning the oil over the exposed part of the fish. Move the fish around in the pan as it cooks to make sure the head, body, and tail cook evenly. Cooking time will vary from about 15 to 20 minutes, more or less, depending on the size of the fish.

The outside of the fish must be crisp; the inside still moist but cooked. Drain the fish and place it on a large platter.

11. Heat ¼ cup oil in a clean wok or saucepan and add the mushrooms, onion, ginger, garlic, peppers, and pickled scallions. Stir about 1 minute, then add the sugar and vinegar mixture and bring to a boil. Stir in the cornstarch mixture. Cook and stir until blended and smooth, about 1 minute or less.

12. Pour the sauce over the fish and serve garnished with the prepared fresh scallions.

YIELD: 4 to 8 servings

For that expanding segment of the public that enjoys—if not to say dotes on—fiery hot dishes made with fresh green or red long hot peppers, the following recipe is an ultimate joy.

FISH-STUFFED CHILI PEPPERS

The dish:

8	raw shrimps, peeled and deveined
¼	pound fillet of flounder
¼	cup ground pork
3	tablespoons chopped unsalted pork fat
	Salt to taste
½	teaspoon sugar
	Cornstarch
1	egg white
1	tablespoon dry sherry or shao hsing wine,* approximately
¼	teaspoon monosodium glutamate (optional)
16 to 20	fresh red or green long hot peppers,* or use sweet or hot red cherry peppers (the number will vary according to size)
	Beaten egg
3	tablespoons peanut, vegetable, or corn oil, approximately

The sauce:

2	tablespoons fermented salted black beans *
1	tablespoon dry sherry or water
3	tablespoons peanut, vegetable, or corn oil
1½	tablespoons chopped garlic
1½	tablespoons finely chopped fresh ginger *
1	cup chicken broth
1	teaspoon sugar
1	tablespoon light soy sauce *

3 tablespoons oyster sauce *
1 tablespoon cornstarch
2 tablespoons water

* Available in Chinese markets and by mail order. For more information see
Chapter XI.

1. Place the shrimps on a flat surface and chop them coarsely with
a sharp knife. There should be about 5 tablespoons chopped. Put into
a mixing bowl.

2. Place the flounder on the surface and chop it. There should be
about ¾ cup. Add to the mixing bowl.

3. Add the pork, pork fat, salt, sugar, 1 tablespoon cornstarch, egg
white, wine, and monosodium glutamate.

4. Cut a thin slice off the top of each of the peppers. Carefully
remove the veins and seeds from inside. Dust the inside of each
pepper with cornstarch, shaking out any excess. Carefully stuff each
pepper with the fish mixture, smoothing off the top, then lightly
brush each top with a little beaten egg.

5. Heat the 3 tablespoons of oil, or enough to cover the bottom,
in a wok or skillet and add the stuffed peppers, bottom side down
(filled side up). Cook on the bottom until nicely brown, about 5
to 7 minutes. Carefully turn the peppers and cook the other side
4 to 5 minutes, or until the filling is cooked through and the peppers
are tender yet crisp.

6. Meanwhile, prepare the sauce. Place the black beans in a small
bowl and add the sherry or water. Mash the beans lightly.

7. Heat the oil in a wok or skillet and add the beans, garlic, and
ginger. Cook about 45 seconds. Add the broth and bring to a boil.
Add the sugar, soy sauce, and oyster sauce and simmer briefly. Blend
the cornstarch with the water and stir in. Cook, stirring, until the
sauce thickens.

8. Transfer the peppers, stuffed side up, to a serving dish and
pour the hot sauce over all.

YIELD: 4 to 8 servings

Shrimps, chicken, pork, and beef are the principal ingredients for most Chinese dishes. The following shrimp dish is one of the simplest dishes to prepare.

QUICK PAN-FRY SHRIMPS

2 pounds shelled and deveined small shrimps (about 3 cups), preferably the small river shrimps available frozen in Chinese groceries
  Salt
½ teaspoon baking soda
2 teaspoons cornstarch
½ egg white (beat the egg white lightly, then divide in half)
1 tablespoon dry sherry or shao hsing wine *
½ teaspoon sugar
¼ teaspoon monosodium glutamate (optional)
6 thin slices fresh ginger,* peeled
2 scallions, green part included, trimmed and cut into 2-inch lengths
  Peanut, vegetable, or corn oil for deep frying

* Available in Chinese markets and by mail order. For more information see Chapter XI.

1. Rinse the shrimps well and place in a bowl, then add 2 teaspoons salt. Let stand about 30 minutes. Drain once more and pat dry.

2. Return the shrimps to the bowl and add the soda. Blend to distribute. (The soda will be rinsed away thoroughly before cooking, but it makes the shrimps crisp.) Let stand until ready to cook, 30 minutes or longer.

3. Place the shrimps in a colander and rinse thoroughly in cold running water to remove all traces of the soda. Press to extract most of the moisture.

4. Place the shrimps in a mixing bowl and add the cornstarch and egg white. Blend with the fingers and refrigerate at least 30 minutes.

5. Blend the wine, salt to taste, sugar, and monosodium glutamate. Set aside.

6. Combine the ginger and scallions and set aside.

7. In a wok or deep-fryer heat the oil, and when moderately hot add the shrimps and stir to separate. Cook about 1 minute, then drain.

8. Use the same pan to finish the dish, but do not add oil; there is enough oil left on the shrimps. Add the scallions, ginger, and shrimps and cook, tossing and stirring, for a few seconds. Add the wine mixture and cook, tossing and stirring, 30 seconds longer.

YIELD: 4 to 8 servings

The following is a savory shrimp dish made piquant with a light vinegar, garlic, and ginger sauce. It is named after that ubiquitous official who gave his name to Kung Pao Chicken.

KUNG PAO SHRIMP

14 to 16	large shrimps (about 1 pound)
1	tablespoon cornstarch
¼	cup vinegar
	Salt to taste
2	tablespoons light soy sauce *
5	teaspoons sugar
¼	teaspoon monosodium glutamate (optional)
4	cloves garlic, finely minced
2	tablespoons chopped white part of scallions
1½	tablespoons finely chopped fresh ginger *
3	cups peanut, vegetable, or corn oil

* Available in Chinese markets and by mail order. For more information see Chapter XI.

1. Shell, devein, and rinse the shrimps. Pat them dry with kitchen toweling. Place the shrimps in a small mixing bowl and add the cornstarch. Work with the fingers until all the shrimps are lightly coated. Set aside.

2. In another small mixing bowl, combine the vinegar, salt, soy sauce, sugar, and monosodium glutamate. Set aside.

3. Combine the garlic, scallions, and ginger and set aside.

4. Heat the oil in a wok or skillet, and when it is hot add the shrimps. Cook, stirring, about 1½ minutes. Drain in a sieve-lined bowl to catch the drippings. Discard all but about 1½ tablespoons of oil.

5. Return the 1½ tablespoons oil to the pan. When hot, add the ginger mixture, stirring. Add the vinegar sauce, and when it boils add the shrimps. Stir until the shrimps are well coated with sauce. When thoroughly hot, serve.

YIELD: 4 to 6 servings

BUTTERFLY SHRIMP

The shrimp:

20   medium shrimps (about 3 inches long)
    Salt to taste
1   teaspoon baking soda

The sauce:

1   tablespoon peanut, vegetable, or corn oil
2   tablespoons catsup
1   teaspoon tomato paste
1   cup plus 3 tablespoons water
1   tablespoon light soy sauce *
3   tablespoons white vinegar
    Salt to taste
¼   cup sugar
1½   tablespoons cornstarch

The batter:

1   cup all-purpose flour
1   cup water

½   teaspoon salt
2   teaspoons baking powder
    Peanut, vegetable, or corn oil for deep frying

* Available in Chinese markets and by mail order. For more information see Chapter XI.

1. Remove the shells of the shrimps, leaving on the tails. Slice the shrimps down the back, almost but not quite in half lengthwise. This is to butterfly them. Rinse well and remove the dark vein from each, then drain and pat dry. Add salt and the soda. Let stand 30 minutes or longer. The soda makes the shrimp crisp. It will be rinsed off before the shrimps are cooked.

2. To make the sauce, place the oil, catsup, and tomato paste in a saucepan and cook, stirring, about 1 minute. This precooking will make the color come out.

3. Stir the 1 cup water into the catsup mixture and add the soy sauce, vinegar, salt, and sugar. Blend the cornstarch with the 3 tablespoons water and stir this into the simmering sauce. Cook briefly, until slightly thickened.

4. For the batter, place the flour in a mixing bowl and stir in the water. Blend until smooth. If it is lumpy, strain it. Add the salt and baking powder.

5. Rinse the shrimps under cold running water to remove the soda. Drain well.

6. Heat about 2 quarts of oil in a wok or deep-fryer. The oil should be hot almost to smoking. Dip the shrimps, one at a time, in the batter and then drop them into the oil. Cook until golden brown and crisp. Drain on several layers of paper toweling. Serve the hot shrimp with the hot sauce.

YIELD: 2 to 6 servings

VELVET SHRIMP

28 medium raw shrimps, peeled
1½ tablespoons plus 2 teaspoons cornstarch
1 cup chicken broth
8 egg whites
½ teaspoon sugar
1 teaspoon salt
2 tablespoons dry sherry or shao hsing wine *
¼ teaspoon monosodium glutamate (optional)
3 tablespoons water
2 cups peanut, vegetable, or corn oil
½ cup fresh or frozen peas
¼ cup ham, chopped fine, almost to a powder

* Available in Chinese markets and by mail order. For more information see Chapter XI.

1. Split the shrimps in half and rinse well to remove the dark vein down the back. Pat dry. Place the shrimps, a few at a time, on a flat, clean surface and pound to a pulp with a heavy mallet or the bottom of a clean skillet. There should be about 1¼ cups of shrimp pulp.

2. Put the 1½ tablespoons cornstarch into a bowl and gradually blend in about ⅔ cup of the chicken broth.

3. Place the egg whites in a mixing bowl and stir in the chopped shrimps with chopsticks until smooth and combined. Stir in the chicken broth and cornstarch mixture, and add the sugar, salt, half the wine, and the monosodium glutamate. Refrigerate for 30 minutes.

4. Have a colander ready to receive the shrimp mixture when it is cooked.

5. Combine the remaining 2 teaspoons of cornstarch with the water and set aside.

6. Heat the oil in a wok or deep-fryer, and when it is hot and almost smoking turn off the heat. Wait about 10 seconds, then pour in the shrimp mixture. Turn the heat on and stir quickly and gently until the shrimp mixture turns white, using a folding motion to

bring the bottom of the mixture to the top. Scoop the mixture from the pan and into the colander to drain.

7. Pour off the oil from the pan and reserve it (the rest may be reserved for another frying). Wipe the pan dry.

8. Add 2 tablespoons of the reserved oil to the pan. Add the remaining tablespoon of wine and cook, stirring, about 20 seconds, then add the peas. Return the shrimp mixture to the pan and add the remaining ⅓ cup of broth. Stir in the cornstarch mixture and cook until slightly thickened. Spoon the velvet onto a serving dish and garnish with the ham.

YIELD: 6 to 8 servings

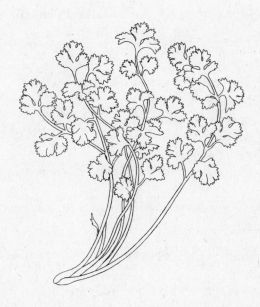

The electric blender is perhaps the most revolutionary kitchen gadget of the twentieth century. It boggles the mind to think of the multitude of good things that might have been conceived if—given the chefs of the past several hundred years—it had a more ancient history. One of the most delicate ingredients for elegant soups—or stir-fry dishes, for that matter—is a paste easily made in the blender. The paste is pushed through a pastry tube into boiling water to make shrimp "noodles." The result is remarkably like an ordinary noodle, but with an interesting texture and the delicate flavor of shrimp.

SHRIMP NOODLES

½ pound raw shrimps, shelled and deveined
1 1-inch piece fresh ginger,* peeled
1 scallion, green part included
   Water
1 tablespoon dry sherry or shao hsing wine *
   Salt to taste
2½ tablespoons cornstarch
1 egg white
2½ tablespoons milk
¼ teaspoon monosodium glutamate (optional)

* Available in Chinese markets and by mail order. For more information see Chapter XI.

1. Cut the shrimps into cubes and add them to the container of an electric blender.
2. Crush the ginger and scallion and put them into a small bowl. Add 2 tablespoons cold water and set aside 30 minutes.
3. To the shrimp add the wine, salt, cornstarch, egg white, milk, and monosodium glutamate. Add 1 tablespoon of the ginger water, discarding the rest or saving it for another recipe.
4. Blend the shrimp mixture, stirring down as necessary with a rubber spatula to make a smooth paste. Add another tablespoon of

water gradually if the mixture is stiff and sticks to the sides and beaters. It should move freely in the blender.

5. Spoon the shrimp into a pastry bag that has been fitted with a number 6 pastry tube.

6. Bring 2 quarts of water to a boil in a wok or skillet and turn off the heat. Immediately squeeze the shrimp mixture into the water in a round and round motion. If necessary, turn on the heat. The object is to heat the noodles just until they set, but without excessive cooking. Drain immediately and run under cold water. The noodles can be used immediately or stored, covered with cold water, for up to 3 days in the refrigerator.

YIELD: About 3 cups of noodles

The shrimp noodles described in this book are excellent when stir-fried with crab meat as in the following.

STIR-FRY SHRIMP NOODLES WITH CRAB MEAT

Shrimp Noodles (made with ½ pound shrimps; see recipe)
½ pound fresh lump or backfin crab meat
4 dried black mushrooms *
3 tablespoons peanut, vegetable, or corn oil
¾ cup celery cut into 2-inch lengths, then cut into very fine strips (julienne)
⅔ cup chicken broth
1 tablespoon cornstarch
3 tablespoons water
Salt to taste
½ teaspoon finely chopped garlic
1 tablespoon finely chopped fresh coriander leaves *
1 teaspoon chopped scallion, green part included
1 tablespoon pureed carrot (optional; see Note)

* Available in Chinese markets and by mail order. For more information see Chapter XI.

1. Prepare the shrimp noodles and set aside.

2. Pick over the crab to remove all traces of shell and cartilage.

3. Place the mushrooms in a mixing bowl and add boiling water to cover. Let stand 15 to 30 minutes, then squeeze the mushrooms to extract most of the moisture. Cut off and discard the tough stems. Cut the mushrooms into thin strips (julienne) and set aside.

4. Heat the oil in a wok or skillet and add the mushrooms, celery, and ½ teaspoon salt. Cook, stirring, about 15 seconds. Add the crab meat and cook, stirring, about 30 seconds.

5. Add half the chicken broth and bring to a boil. Add the shrimp noodles, then add the remaining broth. When the mixture boils, blend the cornstarch and water and stir it in. Add more salt to taste if needed.

6. Cook, stirring and tossing, about 1 minute. Spoon the mixture onto a serving dish and garnish by sprinkling with the garlic, coriander, and scallion. If desired, dot the dish with pureed carrot, which resembles crab roe.

YIELD: 4 to 8 servings

Note: To puree carrots for this dish, blanch about 12 thin slices of scraped carrot. Blend briefly or put through a food mill.

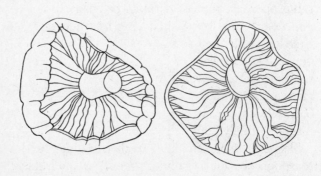

Fresh bean curd has a texture and flavor distinctly its own. It blends admirably with a host of other flavors and textures, including fresh shrimps.

STIR-FRY SHRIMPS WITH BEAN CURD

⅓   pound raw shrimps, approximately
4   teaspoons cornstarch
5   pads fresh white bean curd * (about 1 pound)
1   cup chicken broth
    Salt to taste
½   teaspoon sugar
1   tablespoon dry sherry or shao hsing wine *
1   tablespoon light soy sauce *
¼   teaspoon monosodium glutamate (optional)
1   tablespoon water
2   tablespoons peanut, vegetable, or corn oil
    Finely chopped garlic to taste or ¼ cup finely chopped scallions, green part included

* Available in Chinese markets and by mail order. For more information see Chapter XI.

1. Peel and devein the shrimps, rinse well, and pat dry. There should be about 1 cup. Add half the cornstarch and, using the fingers, stir to blend. Set aside.

2. Cut each pad of bean curd into thirds or quarters. Set aside.

3. Blend the chicken broth, salt, sugar, wine, soy sauce, and monosodium glutamate. Set aside.

4. In another bowl blend the remaining 2 teaspoons cornstarch with the water. Set aside.

5. Heat the oil in a wok or skillet, and when it is hot add the shrimps and cook, stirring over high heat about 10 seconds. Push the shrimps aside and add the bean curd. Cook, stirring, about 30 seconds, until thoroughly hot.

6. Stir the reserved chicken broth mixture and add it. Cook, stirring, about 3 minutes.

7. Stir the cornstarch mixture into the shrimp and bean-curd mixture. Spoon the dish onto a serving platter and serve sprinkled with garlic or scallions.

YIELD: 4 to 8 servings

There is an incredibly simple Cantonese way of cooking shrimps, in which the shrimps, still in the shell, are soaked in salt water to season and then deep fried. They are sprinkled with a salt and pepper mixture and served hot. Chinese eat this dish by putting the whole shrimps into their mouths and spitting out the shells. However, you can peel them first with your fingers or a knife and fork.

CANTONESE-FRIED SHRIMPS

1 pound shrimps (about 2½ inches long), in the shell
2 cups water
  Salt to taste (about 2½ teaspoons)
1 teaspoon freshly ground white or black pepper
¼ teaspoon sugar
  Peanut, vegetable, or corn oil for deep frying

1. Do not shell the shrimps, but use a pair of kitchen scissors and cut off the small feelers on the underside. Devein by cutting open a small section of the back and pulling out the vein with a skewer or toothpick.
2. In a mixing bowl, combine the water with about 2 teaspoons salt. Add the shrimps and let stand about 1 hour. Drain and pat with a clean cloth or paper toweling until very dry.
3. Combine ½ teaspoon salt, the pepper, and sugar and set aside.
4. In a wok or deep-fryer, heat the oil and add the shrimps. Fry, stirring, about 1½ minutes—no longer.
5. Drain the shrimps in a sieve-lined bowl and pour off the oil from the pan. Do not wash the pan.

6. Return the shrimps to the pan and sprinkle with the salt and pepper mixture. Toss over high heat about 15 seconds. Spoon into a serving dish and serve plain.

YIELD: 4 to 8 servings

One of the most famous Szechwan dishes is Szechwan Shrimp. It is spicy, as many Szechwan dishes are, and for those who enjoy such food, this dish is guaranteed to titillate the palate. The shrimps here are cooked and served in the shell.

SZECHWAN SHRIMP

1	pound shrimps, in the shell
½	cup finely minced fresh ginger *
2	tablespoons chopped garlic
¼	cup shredded or cubed small fresh red or green long hot peppers *
1	cup Fermented Rice (see recipe)
1	tablespoon plus 1 teaspoon dark soy sauce *
1	tablespoon light soy sauce *
½	teaspoon sugar, or to taste
	Salt to taste
½	teaspoon monosodium glutamate (optional)
1	quart peanut, vegetable, or corn oil
¼	pound ground pork
2	tablespoons chili paste with garlic (Szechwan paste) *
1	cup water
1	bunch scallions, chopped (about 1 cup), green part included
	Hot oil * to taste (optional)

* Available in Chinese markets and by mail order. For more information see Chapter XI.

1. Do not peel the shrimps. Using scissors or a sharp knife, cut through one section of the back of the shell without cutting the vein.

Pull out the dark vein of each shrimp with a toothpick or skewer and discard. Wash the shrimps well, cut off and discard the feet, and drain. Pat the shrimps dry.

2. In a small bowl, combine the ginger, garlic, and hot peppers and set aside.

3. In another bowl, combine the fermented rice, soy sauces, sugar, salt to taste, and monosodium glutamate.

4. Heat the oil in a wok or skillet and add the shrimps. Cook, stirring, until they turn pink, about 1½ to 2 minutes. Drain the shrimps in a sieve-lined bowl to catch the drippings and pour off all but about 5 tablespoons of oil from the pan. Add the pork to the oil in the pan and cook, stirring, just until the strands of pork are separated and the pork loses its pink color. Add the chili paste with garlic and cook, stirring, about 1 minute. Add the ginger and garlic mixture and cook, stirring, about 45 seconds.

5. Add the fermented rice mixture and cook about 15 seconds. Add the water and ¼ cup of the scallions. Bring to a boil, stirring, and cook about 3 minutes, or until the sauce is slightly thickened. Add the shrimps and remaining scallions. Cook about 1 minute, then stir in the hot oil, if used, and serve.

YIELD: 4 to 8 servings

A very good dish for quick cooking is the following.

SHRIMPS IN BLACK BEAN SAUCE
WITH GINGER AND SCALLIONS

1   pound raw shrimps, in the shell
    Salt
2   tablespoons fermented salted black beans *
2   tablespoons dry sherry or shao hsing wine *
3   scallions, green part included, trimmed and cut into 1½-inch
    lengths

4   cloves garlic, peeled and flattened
12   thin slices fresh ginger,* peeled
2   cups peanut, vegetable, or corn oil
½   teaspoon sugar

* Available in Chinese markets and by mail order. For more information see Chapter XI.

1. Rinse the shrimps but do not peel. Using a pair of kitchen scissors, cut open one segment along the backside of each shrimp, leaving the shell on. Pull out the dark vein with a toothpick or skewer and discard. Rinse the shrimps under cold running water, then cover them with cold water and stir in about 2 tablespoons salt. Let stand 1 hour, then drain and rinse under cold water.

2. Combine the black beans with 1 tablespoon of the wine and crush lightly with a spoon.

3. Set the scallions, garlic, and ginger aside in separate bowls.

4. In a wok or skillet heat the oil, and when hot and almost smoking add the shrimps. Cook over high heat, stirring, about 3 minutes. Drain in a sieve-lined bowl and discard all but 3 tablespoons of the oil.

5. Add the black beans to the pan. Cook over high heat about 10 seconds. Add the garlic and ginger and cook about 5 seconds, stirring. Add the shrimps, sprinkle with salt to taste, and cook about 30 seconds, stirring. Add the sugar and the remaining wine and cook, stirring, until piping hot, about 10 seconds. Add the scallions and toss quickly, about 45 seconds, and serve hot.

YIELD: 4 to 6 servings

For those unaccustomed to the dish, shrimps with kidney slices might seem a most unlikely combination. It isn't. It is a Shanghai dish, and it is exceptionally good with those contrasting textures and flavors.

SHRIMPS WITH KIDNEY SLICES

1   pound pork kidneys (4 to 6, depending on size)
½   pound raw shrimps, shelled and deveined
     Salt
½   teaspoon baking soda
1   tablespoon egg white (beat the egg white lightly and
         measure)
6   teaspoons cornstarch
4   dried black mushrooms *
½   tablespoon light soy sauce *
1½   tablespoons dark soy sauce *
½   teaspoon sugar
¼   teaspoon monosodium glutamate (optional)
1   tablespoon dry sherry or shao hsing wine *
2   tablespoons water
1   cup peanut, vegetable, or corn oil
¼   cup thinly sliced bamboo shoots *
¼   cup water chestnuts,* cut into rounds about ¼ inch thick
2   scallions, green part included, trimmed and cut into 1½-inch
         lengths

* Available in Chinese markets and by mail order. For more information see Chapter XI.

1. The most important step in this recipe is the proper preparation of the kidneys. First, pull away the thin, transparent membrane surrounding each kidney.

2. Place the raw kidneys flat on a cutting surface and split them neatly in half. Place the two halves cut side up. Holding the knife parallel to the cutting surface, carefully cut away and discard the core. Have a basin of cold water ready for the kidney slices.

3. Score each kidney half with a sharp knife. Score only the cut side and not the shiny outer surface. Score in one direction at ⅛-inch intervals, then crosswise at ⅛-inch intervals. Slice each kidney into 1- by 2-inch pieces, and drop the pieces as they are cut into cold water. Let stand in cold water to bleed the slices, changing the water several times.

4. Put the peeled, deveined shrimps into a mixing bowl and add 1 teaspoon of salt and the soda. Let stand 15 minutes, then rinse well under cold running water.

5. Blend the egg white with 2 teaspoons of the cornstarch and stir into the shrimp. Put into a bowl and refrigerate for at least 30 minutes.

6. Drain the kidney pieces well and put them into a saucepan or casserole. In another pan bring enough water to a boil to cover the slices. Pour the water over the kidneys and let stand about 40 seconds, no longer. Drain immediately in a colander. Quickly run cold water over them until they are chilled. Drain and put them into a mixing bowl. Add the light soy sauce and 3 teaspoons of the cornstarch. Blend.

7. Pour boiling water over the mushrooms and let them stand 15 to 30 minutes. Drain and squeeze dry, then cut off and discard the stems. Cut the caps into ½-inch cubes.

8. In a cup combine the dark soy sauce, sugar, salt to taste, monosodium glutamate, and wine. Set aside.

9. Blend the remaining teaspoon of cornstarch with the 2 tablespoons water and set aside.

10. In a wok or skillet heat the oil. Add the shrimps and cook, stirring quickly to separate the pieces, about 45 seconds. Drain in a sieve-lined bowl to catch the drippings, discarding all but about 2 tablespoons of oil from the pan.

11. Over high heat add the bamboo shoots, water chestnuts, mushrooms, and scallions. Add the dark soy sauce mixture, then stir the cornstarch and water, and add it, stirring. Bring to a boil, then add the kidneys and cook about 5 seconds. Add the shrimps. Stir and toss everything together for about 30 seconds, then serve.

YIELD: 6 to 8 servings

It almost goes without saying that lobster Cantonese style is one of the best known and most liked of Chinese dishes in America.

LOBSTER CANTONESE

1 live lobster (2 pounds)
3 large cloves garlic
1 cup plus 2 tablespoons peanut, vegetable, or corn oil
¼ pound ground pork (about ½ cup)
1 cup chicken broth
1 tablespoon coarsely chopped fresh ginger *
1 tablespoon dry sherry or shao hsing wine *
Salt to taste
1½ teaspoons sugar
¼ teaspoon monosodium glutamate (optional)
1 tablespoon cornstarch
2 tablespoons water
3 scallions, green part included, trimmed
2 whole eggs
All-purpose flour for dredging

* Available in Chinese markets and by mail order. For more information see Chapter XI.

1. Quickly chop or break off the tail of the lobster to sever the tail from the body and kill the lobster.
2. Cut the tail in half lengthwise, then cut each half into 2 or 3 pieces.
3. Break off the large claws and set aside.
4. Split the body or "chest" portion in half and remove and discard the small tough sac near the eyes. Cut each half into 2 or 3 pieces. Use a pair of kitchen shears to cut off and discard the "feelers" or small claws.
5. Chop the large claws in half lengthwise. Crush the small joints attached to the large claws to facilitate eating.
6. Peel the garlic and pound lightly to flatten. Set aside.
7. Have ready the oil, pork, broth, and ginger.

8. Blend together the wine, salt, sugar, and monosodium glutamate and set aside.

9. Blend together the cornstarch and water and set aside.

10. Cut the scallions into 2-inch lengths and set aside.

11. Place the eggs in a cup and set aside. Do not beat.

12. Dredge the cut portion of each lobster piece lightly in flour. When coated, set aside.

13. Heat the 1 cup of oil in a wok or large skillet, and when it is hot add the garlic. Cook briefly, then remove but reserve the garlic.

14. To the oil add the lobster and cook, spooning the oil over the pieces so that they cook evenly. Turn the pieces gently. Cook for a total of 5 to 7 minutes, depending on the heat and the size of the pieces. As each piece is suitably cooked, transfer to a serving dish.

15. In a clean wok or skillet (or the same one properly washed and dried) add the 2 tablespoons of oil. Add the reserved garlic and cook, stirring, about 10 seconds. Remove the garlic.

16. Add the pork to the pan and cook, stirring, over high heat to break up the morsels.

17. Add the chicken broth and ginger, and when the liquid boils add the wine mixture. Skim the surface as necessary to remove scum and foam. Stir the cornstarch mixture and add it. When thickened, add the scallions and cook briefly. Turn off the heat and gradually add the eggs. Cook until the egg whites are set. Spoon the sauce over the lobster, allowing the egg yolks to break and run over the sauce. Serve immediately.

YIELD: 6 to 8 servings

The combination of lobster and shrimps in a single dish is by no means uncommon in Chinese cooking, but this is one of the more delicate, subtly flavored combinations.

STIR-FRY LOBSTER AND SHRIMPS

1 live lobster (1½ pounds)
2 jumbo or 4 medium to large shrimps, peeled and deveined
¾ cup peanut, vegetable, or corn oil, or more
1 tablespoon dry sherry or shao hsing wine *
1 tablespoon plus 1½ teaspoons cornstarch
Salt to taste
¼ teaspoon sugar
½ teaspoon monosodium glutamate (optional)
1 scallion, green part included, trimmed and cut into 2-inch lengths
6 egg whites
½ teaspoon sesame oil *
1 tablespoon water

* Available in Chinese markets and by mail order. For more information see Chapter XI.

1. Use a sharp knife to cut through the section where the lobster tail and body join to quickly sever them and kill the lobster. Do not cut the tail section lengthwise.

2. Break off the lobster claws. Crack the large claws so that the meat may later be easily removed. Crush the small claw joints. Split the body or "chest" of the lobster in half lengthwise. Remove and discard the tough small sac inside the body near the eyes.

3. Remove the coral or roe and liver from the lobster body and put into a mixing bowl. Save the body halves if desired for garnish.

4. Butterfly the shrimps; that is to say, split each of them down the back, using a sharp knife, but do not cut them all the way through. Cut just enough to open them up. Add the shrimps to the bowl with the coral and liver.

5. Heat ¼ cup of the oil in a wok or skillet and add the lobster tail, claws, and claw joints. Cook briefly, stirring, just until the shell becomes bright red. This should take only seconds, for the meat will be cooked later on. Drain immediately in a sieve-lined bowl and let cool.

6. When the lobster shell is cool enough to handle, crack or cut open the tail without cutting into the tail meat. Remove the tail meat in one piece. Cut it into thin slices crosswise (not lengthwise) and add it to the bowl with the shrimps.

7. Remove the claw meat and the meat from the claw joints and add them also.

8. To the lobster and shrimps add the wine, 1 tablespoon cornstarch, salt, sugar, and half the monosodium glutamate. Blend well with the fingers. Add the scallion.

9. Blend the egg whites with salt to taste, the remaining monosodium glutamate, and the sesame oil. Stir to blend.

10. Heat another ¼ cup of oil, and when it is hot but not boiling add the lobster-shrimp and scallion mixture. Cook about 1 minute, no longer, stirring. Remove the lobster and shrimp mixture.

11. If the two pieces of body shell are to be used for garnish, add a little more oil and cook them briefly until they turn bright red. Drain.

12. Wipe out the pan and add the remaining ¼ cup of oil. Add the egg whites and cook, stirring, about 10 seconds, no longer. The whites should just start to set.

13. Add the lobster and shrimp mixture and cook, stirring as gently as possible with a folding motion, about 30 seconds. Stir in the 1½ teaspoons cornstarch blended with the 1 tablespoon water, let boil, and serve immediately. Serve hot. The lobster when cooked may not look done, but it is.

YIELD: 2 to 8 servings

The Chinese have what may be the most effective way of ridding steamer clams of sand. They put them into a basin of cold water with salt and a little oil. The clams seem to reach for the oil, and in doing so they emit their sand.

STEAMER CLAMS WITH HOT SAUCE

16   steamer clams (an arbitrary number, but it is the number that goes with the quantity of sauce to be made here)
¼   cup salt
2   tablespoons peanut, vegetable, or corn oil
2   tablespoons thinly sliced fresh green or red long hot peppers *
¼   cup light soy sauce *
2   teaspoons sesame oil *

* Available in Chinese markets and by mail order. For more information see Chapter XI.

1. Place the clams in a basin of cold water and add the salt and oil. Let stand several hours. (If you have time, drain once and repeat with more water, salt, and oil.)

2. Drain the clams and rinse individually. Place them in a saucepan with cold water to barely cover. Cover and cook until the clams open—or steam them in the usual fashion.

3. Blend the remaining ingredients and serve the clams with the sauce as a dip.

YIELD: 2 servings

This is an incredibly good, somewhat exotic dish that must be made with fresh clams in the shell. Its exotic nature is derived from a blend of ingredients including the fresh juice of the clams, garlic, ginger, soy sauce, black beans, and oyster sauce.

CLAMS IN BLACK BEAN AND OYSTER SAUCE

40	littleneck or cherrystone clams
2½	tablespoons fermented salted black beans *
1	tablespoon dry sherry or shao hsing wine *
2	small fresh red long hot peppers,* split down the sides and seeds removed
1½	tablespoons grated lemon rind
1½	teaspoons grated fresh ginger *
3	cloves garlic, finely minced (about 1 tablespoon)
1	teaspoon sugar
1	tablespoon light soy sauce *
1½	tablespoons oyster sauce *
3	tablespoons peanut, vegetable, or corn oil
1	tablespoon water chestnut powder * or cornstarch
¼	cup water

* Available in Chinese markets and by mail order. For more information see Chapter XI.

1. Open or have the fish man open the clams and remove the top shell. Do not separate the clam from the bottom shell. Be sure to reserve all the juices from the opened clams, although in dire circumstances bottled clam juice could be substituted. The clams should be opened as close to cooking time as possible, preferably only a few minutes before. As the clams are opened, drop them into a mixing bowl. Juice will accumulate in the bowl. Use this juice. In all there should be about 1½ cups of accumulated clam juice. Set the clams and juice aside.

2. Combine the beans and wine in a small mixing bowl and let stand at least 10 minutes.

3. Cut the red peppers up fine and set aside.

4. In a small bowl or cup, combine the lemon rind, ginger, and garlic. Set aside.

5. To the bowl with the beans and wine, add the sugar, soy sauce, and oyster sauce. Stir to dissolve the sugar. Add the clam juice and set aside.

6. Heat the oil in a wok or skillet, and when it is hot add the peppers and ginger-garlic mixture, stirring rapidly, about 5 seconds. Add the clams and stir until heated through, but cook quickly or the clams will toughen.

7. Add the clam juice and soy sauce mixture and bring to a full boil.

8. Stir the water chestnut powder or cornstarch with the water and add this to the clams, stirring. When the mixture thickens, serve immediately.

YIELD: 8 to 12 servings

Scallops, both fresh and dried, are much prized in the Chinese kitchen. The following is a succulent, subtle, and quickly made dish of bay scallops and vegetables lightly flavored with soy sauce.

STIR-FRY BAY SCALLOPS

6   dried black mushrooms *
1   pound fresh bay scallops
1   tablespoon plus 2 teaspoons cornstarch
½   cup bamboo shoots,* cut into small bite-size pieces
⅓   cup thinly sliced carrots
¼   cup or more fresh long hot or sweet red or green peppers,*
     cut into shreds or cubes
1   scallion, green part included, trimmed and cut into 1½-inch
     lengths
½   cup water chestnuts,* cut into thin, round slices
1   tablespoon dark soy sauce *

1½ tablespoons vinegar
1½ tablespoons sugar
    Salt to taste
¼   teaspoon monosodium glutamate (optional)
3   cups peanut, vegetable, or corn oil
2   tablespoons water

* Available in Chinese markets and by mail order. For more information see Chapter XI.

1. Pour boiling water over the mushrooms and let stand 15 to 30 minutes, then drain and squeeze to remove most of the moisture. Cut off and discard the tough stems. If small, leave the mushrooms whole; if large, slice in half. Place in a mixing bowl.

2. Rinse the scallops in cold water and drain well. Place in a mixing bowl and add the 1 tablespoon cornstarch and stir to blend well. Set aside.

3. To the mushrooms add the bamboo shoots, carrots, peppers, scallion, and water chestnuts. Set aside.

4. In another bowl blend the soy sauce with the vinegar, sugar, salt, and monosodium glutamate and set aside.

5. Put the oil into a wok or kettle, and when it is hot add the scallops, stirring gently. Cook about 1 minute and drain well in a sieve-lined bowl to catch the drippings. Reserve the oil.

6. In the same pan or in a skillet, return about 2 tablespoons of the reserved oil and add the vegetable and mushroom mixture and salt to taste. Cook about 1 minute, then remove.

7. In the same pan or skillet heat about 2 more tablespoons of the reserved oil. Add the soy sauce mixture and stir about 10 seconds. Blend the 2 teaspoons cornstarch with the water and stir it into the sauce. Add the scallops and stir. Add the mushrooms and vegetables and cook, stirring, until all is heated through and coated.

YIELD: 4 to 6 servings

Westerners mostly think of mussels in terms of what the French call *moules marinières* or perhaps in that delectable cream of mussel soup called *billi bi*. The Chinese, too, have a fine way with steamed mussels, as in the following recipes.

MUSSEL OMELET

1½　quarts fresh, well-scrubbed mussels (about 2 pounds), in the shell
3　eggs
　　Salt to taste
½　teaspoon monosodium glutamate (optional)
½　teaspoon sugar
6　tablespoons peanut, vegetable, or corn oil
1　cup cleaned, fresh chives (preferably Chinese chives *), cut into 1-inch lengths

* Available in Chinese markets and by mail order. For more information see Chapter XI.

1. Place the mussels in a kettle or large saucepan and add about ½ cup water. Cover closely and steam until the mussels open, 5 to 10 minutes. Remove from the heat and let cool.

2. When cool enough to handle, remove the mussels from their shells. There should be about 1 cup. Using a pair of scissors, cut away the tough, slender band attached to one side of the mussels. This could be pulled off with the fingers, but the mussels hold their shape better if it is cut away.

3. Break the eggs into a mixing bowl, and when well beaten add the mussels, salt, monosodium glutamate, sugar, and 1 tablespoon of the oil. Stir to blend.

4. In a wok or skillet, heat the remaining oil and add the chives. Cook briefly, stirring, and add the egg mixture. Cook and stir very gently in a folding motion, pushing from the bottom to redistribute the egg mixture. Cook about 1 minute, or just until the eggs are set. Spoon out onto a hot platter and serve.

YIELD: 4 to 6 servings

STIR-FRY MUSSELS WITH CHIVES

3 quarts fresh, well-scrubbed mussels (about 4 pounds), in the shell

2 cups cleaned, fresh chives (preferably Chinese chives *), cut into 1-inch lengths

3 tablespoons peanut, vegetable, or corn oil

¼ pound lean pork, cut into very thin shreds (about ¾ cup)

1 tablespoon light soy sauce *

1 teaspoon dark soy sauce *

Salt to taste

1 teaspoon sugar

¼ teaspoon monosodium glutamate (optional)

* Available in Chinese markets and by mail order. For more information see Chapter XI.

1. Place the mussels in a kettle or large saucepan and add 1 cup water. Cover closely and steam until the mussels open, 5 to 10 minutes. Remove from the heat and let cool.

2. When cool enough to handle, remove the mussels from their shells. There should be about 2 cups. Using a pair of scissors, cut away the tough, slender band attached to one side of the mussels. This could be pulled off with the fingers, but the mussels hold their shape better if it is cut away.

3. Combine the chives and mussels and set aside.

4. In a wok or skillet heat 1 tablespoon of the oil and add the pork, stirring. Cook until no pink shows, about 45 seconds. Add the soy sauces and cook, stirring, until the pork shreds are coated. Remove the pork and wipe out the pan.

5. Into the same pan put the remaining 2 tablespoons of oil and add the chives and mussels. Cook, stirring, about 10 seconds, no longer. Add the pork, salt, sugar, and monosodium glutamate. Cook, stirring, about 30 seconds. Serve.

YIELD: 3 to 8 servings

Hard-shell crabs have some of the sweetest flesh known to mankind, and it is probably best when freshly steamed without seasoning. The Chinese do not add salt except to purge the crabs. When steamed, the crabs are served with a piquant sauce made with vinegar, soy sauce, and ginger, a superb foil for the crab meat. Female crabs are more choice than male crabs, although either will do.

STEAMED WHOLE CRABS WITH GINGER SAUCE

Place any reasonable number of hard-shell blue crabs in a basin or a sink and run cold water over them. Add ¼ cup of salt or more and let stand at least 1 hour. This will rid the crabs of much of their sediment. Drain and rinse the crabs.

Transfer the crabs to the top of a steamer and steam, covered, over boiling water for 20 minutes. Pour the hot crabs onto a serving platter and serve hot with Ginger Sauce (see recipe below).

Yield: Depends on the number of crabs

GINGER SAUCE

    3   teaspoons chopped fresh ginger *
    4   teaspoons sugar
    3   teaspoons soy sauce *
    3   teaspoons red wine vinegar

* Available in Chinese markets and by mail order. For more information see Chapter XI.

Combine all the ingredients and stir to blend.

YIELD: 1 serving

Hard-shell crabs are a great delicacy both in this country and China. They are available, particularly on America's East Coast, from about late April until November. September is their peak period.

CANTONESE STIR-FRY CRABS

  6 large live hard-shell blue crabs, preferably female
    Salt
  2 tablespoons all-purpose flour
  2 tablespoons fermented salted black beans *
  2½ tablespoons plus ⅓ cup water
  1 egg
  ½ cup peanut, vegetable, or corn oil
  ½ cup ground pork
  2 tablespoons coarsely chopped fresh ginger *
  1½ tablespoons finely minced garlic
  2 tablespoons dry sherry or shao hsing wine *
  2 tablespoons light soy sauce *
  2 teaspoons sugar
  2 scallions, green part included, cut into 2-inch lengths

* Available in Chinese markets and by mail order. For more information see Chapter XI.

1. Place the crabs in a basin of cold water and add about 2 tablespoons of salt. Let them stand about 30 minutes or longer to clean themselves. Drain. Pull off the large claws of the crab while the crabs are alive, but take care that you are not clawed.

2. Slide a small knife under the "apron" on the underside of each crab and, with your fingers, pull the apron off. Using your fingers, pull to separate the body from the crab's back shell. Pull off and discard the spongy, feathery lungs on either side of the pried-off body. Leave the back shells whole.

3. Split the body section in half down the middle and cut off and discard the small claws at either extremity of the body.

4. Place the larger claws on a flat surface and crack them, one at a time, lightly with a mallet. This will facilitate eating later.

5. Spoon the flour onto a length of waxed paper and dip the cut portions of the body into the flour. Coat only the cut portions; do not dredge all over. Set aside.

6. Put the black beans into a small bowl and add the 2½ tablespoons water. Mash coarsely with a spoon.

7. Break the egg into a small bowl and have it ready.

8. Heat the oil in a wok or skillet and cook the crab pieces, spooning the oil over, about 2 minutes. Remove the pieces but leave the oil in the pan. Add the crab back shells and cook, spooning the oil over, about 45 seconds, or until the shells are red.

9. Remove the back shells and add the claws. Cook, stirring, about 15 seconds. Remove the claws.

10. Add the pork and cook, stirring constantly, about 20 seconds. Add the ginger and garlic and cook, stirring, about 30 seconds. Add the black beans and cook, stirring, about 10 seconds. Turn off the heat and add the crabs—bodies, backs, claws, and all—to the sauce. Add the ⅛ cup water, wine, soy sauce, and sugar. Cook, stirring, about 30 seconds. Add salt to taste, cook 30 seconds, then stir in the egg. Cook, stirring, about 15 seconds, or until the egg sets. Add the scallions, toss briefly, and serve hot.

YIELD: 6 to 8 servings

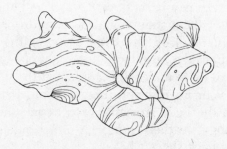

Here is another crab dish of exceeding elegance and delicacy. It is simply crabs with fresh eggs.

CRAB MEAT WITH STIR-FRY EGGS

1   pound fresh lump crab meat
4   eggs
1   cup chicken broth
2   tablespoons light soy sauce *
1½   tablespoons dry sherry or shao hsing wine *
1   teaspoon sugar
    Salt to taste
¼   teaspoon monosodium glutamate (optional)
1½   tablespoons cornstarch
¼   cup water
½   cup peanut, vegetable, or corn oil
2   tablespoons finely chopped fresh ginger *
3   tablespoons chopped scallion, green part included
1½   tablespoons red wine vinegar
3   tablespoons rendered chicken fat (see Chapter XI)

* Available in Chinese markets and by mail order. For more information see Chapter XI.

1. Pick over the crab meat to remove all bits of shell and cartilage if there are any.

2. Beat the eggs in a mixing bowl as if you were making scrambled eggs and add the chicken broth, then add the soy sauce and the crab meat.

3. Blend together the wine, sugar, salt, and monosodium glutamate. Set aside.

4. Blend together the cornstarch and water. Set aside.

5. Heat 3 tablespoons of the oil in a small saucepan and add the ginger. Cook briefly, then set aside.

6. Heat the remaining oil in a wok or skillet and add the egg and crab mixture. Stir very gently and slowly to cook. After 1½ minutes,

when it starts to set, add the ginger and the wine mixture and stir. After cooking about 2½ to 3 minutes longer, add the scallions and the cornstarch mixture. Stir in the vinegar and 1 tablespoon of the chicken fat. The total cooking time for the egg and crab mixture should be about 4 to 5 minutes, no longer. When cooked, spoon the mixture onto a serving dish and sprinkle with the remaining chicken fat.

YIELD: 6 to 8 servings

STIR-FRY CRAB MEAT

¾   pound fresh lump crab meat
4   egg whites
¾   cup chicken broth
½   cup peanut, vegetable, or corn oil
1   tablespoon finely chopped fresh ginger *
1½ tablespoons light soy sauce *
1½ tablespoons dry sherry or shao hsing wine *
¼   teaspoon monosodium glutamate (optional)
     Salt to taste
1   teaspoon sugar
1   tablespoon cornstarch
2   tablespoons water
3   tablespoons rendered chicken fat (see Chapter XI)
¼   cup finely chopped scallion, green part included
     Fresh coriander leaves,* if available

* Available in Chinese markets and by mail order. For more information see Chapter XI.

1. Pick over the crab meat to remove all traces of shell or cartilage. Set aside.
2. Beat the egg whites in a mixing bowl and add the chicken broth. Set aside.
3. In a wok or skillet heat the oil, and when it is hot add the ginger. Add the crab meat and stir briefly. Add the soy sauce, wine, monosodium glutamate, salt, and sugar. Turn the heat to low and

gradually stir in the egg white mixture. Stir by gently bringing the food from the bottom to the top in a folding motion. When almost set, blend the cornstarch with the water and stir in. When thickened, dribble the chicken fat over all and add the chopped scallion. Transfer to a serving dish and garnish with fresh coriander leaves. Serve with white vinegar and minced ginger on the side.

YIELD: 3 to 8 servings

As noted numerous times herein, fresh crab in many forms is a major pleasure of the Chinese table. Here it is stir-fried with shrimp. It is good served with Deep-Fried Chinese Bread (see recipe).

STIR-FRY CRAB MEAT WITH SHRIMPS

⅛   pound unsalted fresh pork fat
½   pound fresh lump crab meat
2   tablespoons finely minced fresh ginger *
2   tablespoons chopped scallions, green part included
1   cup peeled and deveined small shrimps (about ⅓ pound; if
      large shrimps are used, cut them in half or quarter them)
2   teaspoons plus 1 tablespoon cornstarch
3   tablespoons water
2   cups peanut, vegetable, or corn oil
4   cloves garlic, crushed
2   tablespoons dry sherry or shao hsing wine *
½   cup chicken broth
     Salt to taste
½   teaspoon monosodium glutamate (optional)
½   teaspoon sugar
1   tablespoon light soy sauce *
1   tablespoon dark soy sauce *
¼   cup green part of scallions, cut into 1-inch lengths
¼   teaspoon finely ground pepper, preferably white pepper

* Available in Chinese markets and by mail order. For more information see Chapter XI.

1. Drop the pork fat into boiling water to cover and simmer about 20 minutes. Drain and cool until it can be handled.

2. Meanwhile, pick over the crab meat to remove all traces of shell or cartilage.

3. Mince the pork fat fine and put it into a mixing bowl. Blend in the crab meat, half the ginger, and all the chopped scallions. Set aside.

4. Blend the shrimps with the 2 teaspoons cornstarch and mix well. Set aside.

5. Blend the remaining tablespoon of cornstarch with the 3 tablespoons water and set aside.

6. Heat the 2 cups of oil in a wok or skillet, and when it is warm add the shrimps and cook, stirring, about 30 seconds. Drain in a sieve-lined bowl to catch the drippings, leaving 3 tablespoons of oil in the pan. Add the garlic to the oil and brown, then remove and discard the garlic. Add the crab mixture and cook, stirring, about 30 seconds, then add the wine. Cook 30 seconds and add the chicken broth.

7. Immediately add the salt, monosodium glutamate, sugar, and soy sauces. Cook 1 minute and add the cornstarch-water mixture. Cook just until thickened, then add the shrimps, and cook about 30 seconds to cook the shrimp through. Turn out onto a serving plate and serve sprinkled with the remaining ginger, scallions, and ground pepper.

YIELD: 4 to 8 servings

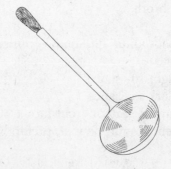

One of the nicest gifts of America's East Coast within recent years is the crab meat and crab claw packaged in tins. Although they have been pasteurized they are a perishable product and must be kept refrigerated. When opened, the meat tastes, remarkably, as fresh as the day it came off the docks. This recipe uses to handsome advantage the crab claws. The meat of the claw is wrapped in a shrimp mixture, and the crab claw itself is used as a handle to facilitate eating.

DEEP-FRIED CRAB CLAWS WITH SHRIMPS

1	pound raw shrimps, shelled and deveined
1	1-inch piece fresh ginger,* crushed
1	scallion, green part included, cut into 2-inch lengths and crushed
3	tablespoons water, approximately
2 to 3	ounces fresh pork fat
	Salt to taste
1	teaspoon sugar
	Cornstarch
1½	tablespoons dry sherry or shao hsing wine *
1	egg white
10 to 12	crab claws from a 1-pound can (a fresh pasteurized product available in many fish stores in America)
	Peanut, vegetable, or corn oil for deep-frying
	Seasoned Salt (see recipe)

* Available in Chinese markets and by mail order. For more information see Chapter XI.

1. Shell and devein the shrimps and cut into cubes, about 1½ cups. Put them into the container of an electric blender.

2. Put the crushed ginger and scallion into a small bowl and add about 3 tablespoons water. Set aside.

3. Drop the pork fat into boiling water and simmer about 5 minutes. Drain, and when cool enough to handle, chop. There should be about ⅓ cup. Add to the blender.

4. Add the salt, sugar, 2 tablespoons cornstarch, wine, and egg white to the blender. Spoon out 2 tablespoons of the ginger-scallion water and add it. Blend until smooth, then spoon the mixture out into a mixing bowl.

5. Measure about ¼ cup of the shrimp mixture for each crab claw. Using dampened fingers, shape the shrimp mixture smoothly around the meaty part of each crab claw, leaving the claw itself extending as a handle. Dredge the thus-wrapped shrimp mixture lightly in cornstarch to seal when cooking.

6. Heat oil for deep frying over low heat, and when it is only moderately hot add the crab claws. Do not let them brown too quickly, for they must cook about 15 minutes to cook thoroughly. (If they start to brown too fast, turn off the fire.) As the claws cook over low heat, turn them occasionally. Drain well. Serve with seasoned salt for dipping.

YIELD: 10 to 12 crab claws

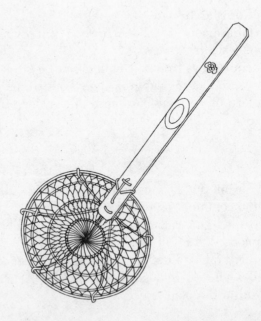

Fermented salted black beans, widely available in Chinese markets and by mail order, greatly complement foods otherwise neutral in flavor—frogs' legs, for example.

FROGS' LEGS WITH BLACK BEANS

6 pairs frogs' legs
4 tablespoons dry sherry or shao hsing wine *
1 tablespoon cornstarch
⅓ cup fermented salted black beans *
   Peanut, vegetable, or corn oil
4 small hot, fresh or dried red peppers *
2 tablespoons chopped garlic
¼ teaspoon monosodium glutamate (optional)
   Salt to taste
½ teaspoon sugar

* Available in Chinese markets and by mail order. For more information see Chapter XI.

1. Split the frogs' legs in half, then cut the legs into pieces at the joints. Place the pieces in a bowl and add 1 tablespoon of the wine. Using a sieve, sprinkle the pieces with the cornstarch. Stir to coat, then set aside.

2. Combine the beans with 2 tablespoons of the wine and mash lightly. Set aside.

3. In a wok or skillet heat 2 cups of oil, and, when it is smoking, turn off the heat. Add the frogs' legs, stirring. Immediately turn on the heat and cook about 45 seconds, stirring. Add the hot peppers and cook, stirring, about 30 seconds. Drain well.

4. In a clean wok or skillet, add 2 tablespoons of oil, and when hot add the beans. Stir, mashing with a spoon until the beans are dry. Add the garlic and stir. Add the frogs' legs and hot peppers, then add the remaining tablespoon of wine, the monosodium glutamate, salt to taste, and sugar, cook briefly, and serve.

YIELD: 3 to 6 servings

There are many dishes in the world against which some people are unhappily—unfortunately for their own sake where taste is concerned—prejudiced. Such dishes would, of course, include liver and sweetbreads and tripe and snails. Another is squid, one of the most delectable forms of sea life. It is excellent when properly cooked, whether it be fresh or dried. Either fresh or dried squid may be used in the following recipe, and a combination of both, as indicated, is not amiss.

STIR-FRY SQUID WITH SCALLIONS AND GINGER

3   ounces dried squid,* 1 to 5 pieces depending on size
5   teaspoons baking soda
1   pound fresh squid *
¼   cup peanut, vegetable, or corn oil
3   scallions, green part included, trimmed and cut into 1-inch
      lengths and/or 2 or 3 fresh red long hot peppers,* cored,
      seeded, and cut into fine shreds
10   thin slices fresh ginger,* peeled
1   teaspoon sugar
    Salt to taste
¼   teaspoon monosodium glutamate (optional)
¼   teaspoon dry sherry or shao hsing wine *

* Available in Chinese markets and by mail order. For more information see Chapter XI.

1. Place the dried squid in a utensil large enough to hold them and cover with cold water. Add the soda and stir to dissolve. Let stand 24 hours, then drain.

2. Pick over the squid, which by now should be softened, and by rubbing and pulling with the fingers, remove the purplish thin layer of skin on top of each squid. Pull away and discard the cartilage-like "needles" if present. Clean the squid well of all but the firm white meat. Use or discard the tentacles, as you wish. Cover with cold water once more and let stand an hour or so. Drain.

3. Run the fresh squid under cold water and clean the same way as the dried squid, then split them open with a knife. Place the cleaned, white pieces of squid on a flat surface, skin side down. Score the upper surface of the squid in parallel lines ¼ inch apart, using a sharp knife. Turn and score in the opposite direction to make a small diamond pattern.

4. Repeat with the softened dried squid.

5. Place all the squid in a casserole. Bring a large quantity of water to a boil and pour it over the squid, stirring so that the water coats all pieces. Let stand about 30 seconds. Drain immediately and run under cold water.

6. Heat the oil in a wok or skillet, and when it is very hot add the squid. Stir quickly about 5 seconds, then stir in the scallions and/or peppers and the ginger. Blend the sugar, salt, and monosodium glutamate and add, stirring. Add the wine and cook over high heat, stirring, about 5 seconds. Spoon onto a hot platter and serve immediately.

YIELD: 4 to 6 servings

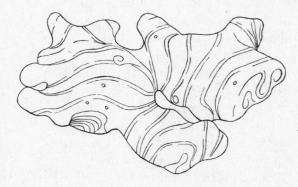

Of all the foods that grace the Chinese table, there is probably none that will appeal less to the Western palate than the one known in English as "sea slug" or "sea cucumber" and in French as *bêche de mer*. It is a black-colored sea creature with a horny or spiny exterior, and it is always cooked from the dried state. There are, generally speaking, two sorts of sea slugs available—one small, one large. When soaked and cooked, sea slugs have a gelatinous flesh that does not tempt to a fine degree most Western taste buds. It is, nonetheless, an important dish in Chinese cookery, and thus this recipe is included here. About four days should be allowed for the preparation of this dish—most of it soaking time, rather than preparation or cooking time.

SEA SLUGS WITH PORK SAUCE

1	large dried sea slug * (about 8 inches long)
	Water
8	scallions, tied in a bundle
2	pieces of ginger * (about 1 inch each), peeled
2	pounds fresh bacon, with bones and rind *
2 to 3	tablespoons dark soy sauce *
2	tablespoons sugar
	Salt to taste
½	teaspoon monosodium glutamate (optional)
6 to 8	dried black mushrooms *
1½	tablespoons shrimp eggs *
2	tablespoons dry sherry or shao hsing wine *
2	tablespoons peanut, vegetable, or corn oil
⅓	cup bamboo shoots,* thinly sliced
2	scallions, green part included, trimmed and cut into 2-inch lengths
5	thin slices fresh ginger,* peeled
1½	tablespoons cornstarch
2	tablespoons rendered chicken fat (see Chapter XI)

* Available in Chinese markets and by mail order. For more information see Chapter XI.

1. Hold the sea slug over a high gas flame or an electric burner heated to high, turning frequently, about 1 minute.

2. Place the sea slug in a very large mixing bowl or other large deep utensil and add lukewarm water to cover. Soak 12 hours, then drain.

3. Put the sea slug into a kettle large enough to hold it and add water to cover. Bring to a boil and simmer, covered, 1½ hours. Let cool, then drain and rinse. Add warm to hot water to cover and let stand 24 hours longer.

4. Drain and rinse in warm water. Carefully clean out the intestines on the inside of the sea slug, washing well.

5. Place the sea slug once more in the kettle and add 4 quarts warm water, the scallions, and the ginger. Bring to a boil, partially cover, and simmer 1 hour or until tender. Let cool in the cooking liquid.

6. Meanwhile, in a large saucepan combine the pork, 5 cups of water or enough to cover, 2 tablespoons soy sauce, the sugar, salt, and ¼ teaspoon monosodium glutamate and bring to a boil. Simmer, partially covered, 2 hours. Remove the pork, which can be chilled, sliced, and served cold as a separate dish. Set the broth aside.

7. Similarly, place the mushrooms in a bowl, add boiling water to cover, and let stand 15 to 30 minutes. Drain, and squeeze to extract most of the moisture. Cut off and discard the tough stems. Set the mushrooms aside.

8. Drain the sea slug thoroughly inside and out. Let stand to room temperature.

9. Combine the shrimp eggs and wine. Steam for 10 minutes.

10. Heat the oil in a wok or very large skillet over a high flame and add the sea slug. Cook 10 seconds, then add the shrimp eggs and bamboo shoots. Cook for 30 seconds. Add 2 cups of the pork broth and the mushrooms. Sprinkle with the remaining monosodium glutamate. If the color is not dark brown add more dark soy sauce, and salt to taste. As the sea slug cooks, spoon the sauce over it.

11. Transfer the sea slug to a large oval platter.

12. Put the scallions and ginger into the pan and thicken the sauce with the cornstarch mixed with 3 tablespoons water. Stir in the chicken fat and spoon the sauce over the sea slug.

YIELD: 95 Western servings, 12 Chinese servings

Shark's fin soup is to the Chinese meal what caviar and foie gras are to the Western menu. It is expensive, delicate, and coveted. It would be unthinkable to offer a dinner to honored guests without it. Unlike caviar (foie gras made from the start is another matter), shark's fin soup requires elaborate hours of preparation.

Shark's fin is, in truth, the fin of the shark. It is sold packaged with only the needlelike gelatinous protuberances that come from the main body of the fin; it is also sold in bulk with the main part and the needles intact. Both come in dried form, and either must be soaked and boiled to soften. The best shark's fin is the whole shark's fin (with body and needles together). We offer two recipes for the soup; one with the packaged "needles," the other with the main fin part plus its "needles." The quality of both kinds of shark's fin varies widely; the best quality is a pale ivory color—the paler the better—with a minimum of dark tough edge and foreign matter attached to it.

SHARK'S FIN SOUP I

1   ½-pound package of shark's fin "needles" * (consisting mostly of the needlelike gelatinous protuberances from the fin itself)
    Water
8   scallions, green part included, trimmed and tied in a package
4   ½-inch pieces fresh ginger,* peeled
8   chicken necks and/or chicken backs
8   wings or other bony parts of the chicken
1   whole raw chicken breast, skinned and boned
½   egg white (beat the egg white lightly, then divide in half)
2   tablespoons plus 1½ teaspoons cornstarch
6   cups Rich Chicken Broth (see recipe)
16   small thin slices cooked Smithfield ham

* Available in Chinese markets and by mail order. For more information see Chapter XI.

1. Empty the contents of the package of shark's fin needles into a mixing bowl. Add cold water to cover to a depth of about 2 inches above the shark's fin. Soak overnight, then drain in a colander.

2. Rinse the shark's fin in warm water and drain, then put into a kettle and add about 4 quarts of warm water. Add the scallions and ginger and simmer, partially covered, for 1 hour. Let cool.

3. Drain the shark's fin, discarding the water, scallions, and ginger. Pick the shark's fin over to retain the golden "needles" and other tender edible matter. Discard any tough or dark portions and foreign particles. If the quality of the "needles" is poor, this job will be tedious and time-consuming.

4. Rinse the shark's fin well once more, wrap in cheesecloth, and put it into a kettle. Add 10 cups of water and the chicken necks or backs and wings. Cover, bring to a boil, and simmer 1½ hours. Remove and discard the chicken pieces and drain well. Do not reserve the cooking liquid; it is fishy.

5. Cut the chicken breast into thin slices, then cut the slices into fine shreds. Put the meat into a bowl and add the egg white and 1½ teaspoons cornstarch. Blend with the fingers. Refrigerate for at least 30 minutes.

6. Heat the chicken broth in a kettle and add the shark's fin, after discarding the cheesecloth. Stir and bring to a boil. Turn off the heat and stir in the chicken shreds, stirring to separate well. Add the ham slices and stir again.

7. Bring to a boil. Blend the 2 tablespoons cornstarch with ¼ cup water and stir in. Simmer about 5 seconds, then turn off the heat.

YIELD: 6 to 10 servings

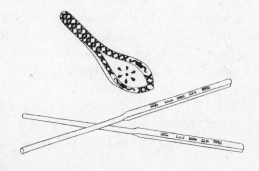

SHARK'S FIN SOUP II

         3   whole pieces of shark's fins * (pick the palest and
             cleanest pieces)
 15 to 18   scallions, tied in bundles of 5 each
    3 to 4   1-inch pieces fresh ginger,* crushed
         4   pounds chicken bones, including necks, wings, and
             backs
         1   pig's foot
         1   whole stewing chicken, split down the breast
         1   1-pound piece of ham, preferably Smithfield ham

* Available in Chinese markets and by mail order. For more information see Chapter XI.

1. Place the shark's fins in a large bowl and add water to cover. Soak 24 hours, then drain.

2. Place the shark's fins in a kettle and add water to cover to a depth of about 4 inches above them. Bring to a boil, cover, and simmer about 1½ hours. Let stand 24 hours.

3. Place the shark's fins in a basin and rinse well in warm water. Pick them over, taking away any foreign matter and pulling off and discarding any dark, tough pieces. Keep the fins intact as much as possible.

4. Place the picked-over shark's fins in a kettle and add about 4 quarts warm water. Add a bunch of scallions and a piece of ginger and cook 1 hour, until almost tender. Allow to cool in the liquid, then drain and discard the liquid. Repeat this process until the shark's fins are soft—2 or 3 times—using fresh scallions and ginger each time.

5. Wrap the shark's fins in cheesecloth doubled over into a 12- x 12-inch square, including all bits and pieces. Put into the bottom of a kettle, and add the chicken bones and pig's foot. Add water to cover and simmer 1½ to 2 hours, or until the shark's fins are very soft. Allow to cool. Discard the bones and cooking liquid and set the shark's fins aside.

6. Meanwhile, crack the inside of the chicken's backbone and wing joints so that the chicken lies flat when opened up.

7. Place the chicken and ham in a kettle with cold water to cover.

Bring to a boil, simmer about 1 minute, and drain immediately. Run under cold running water.

8. Lay the chicken, opened up and skin side down, in a heatproof casserole or large soup bowl that will fit the top of a steamer and cover this with the ham. Add water to cover, about 5 cups or more, and place in the top of a large steamer. Cover and steam over boiling water 4 to 6 hours. Remove the ham when it is cooked, in about 2 hours. Continue cooking until the chicken is tender.

9. Remove the casserole of chicken from the steamer and cool slightly. Strain and reserve the broth. Pull out as many as possible of the large bones from the chicken to make room in the bowl for the shark's fins. If necessary, also remove some meat and skin. Replace in the casserole, skin side down. Slice the ham thin and arrange the pieces in the soup bowl. Add enough of the reserved stock to cover. Place in the top of a steamer, cover with the steamer lid, and steam about 30 minutes, or until fiery hot.

10. Meanwhile, remove the shark's fins from the cheesecloth, place them in a saucepan, and add stock to cover. Simmer about 15 minutes. Remove the shark's fins, discarding the stock (it has a fishy flavor), transfer it to the soup bowl on top of the chicken and ham, and serve.

YIELD: 12 to 16 servings

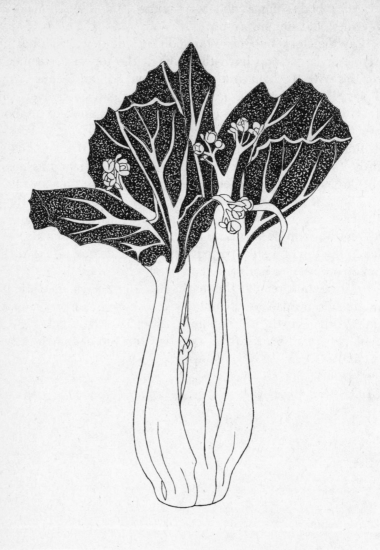

VII

Vegetables

Watercress is one of the more elegant and—in recent years—one of the most abundant of salad greens. It is very good when cooked, Chinese fashion, with bamboo shoots and mushrooms.

STIR-FRY WATERCRESS

2   bunches fresh emerald-green watercress
6   dried black mushrooms *
⅓   cup shredded bamboo shoots *
3   tablespoons peanut, vegetable, or corn oil
    Salt to taste
1   teaspoon sugar
¼   teaspoon monosodium glutamate (optional)
1   tablespoon kao liang Chinese liqueur * (optional)

* Available in Chinese markets and by mail order. For more information see Chapter XI.

1. Trim off and discard the tougher parts of the watercress stems, leaving those that are tender. Rinse the watercress well and shake or

269

pat dry. There should be about 7 or 8 cups of loosely packed leaves with tender stems.

2. Place the mushrooms in a mixing bowl, add boiling water to cover, and let stand 15 to 30 minutes. Drain, then squeeze to remove excess moisture. Cut off and discard the tough stems. Shred the caps. There should be about ⅓ cup.

3. In a wok or skillet heat the oil and add the bamboo shoots and mushrooms. Cook, stirring, over high heat about 1 minute. Add the watercress, stirring.

4. Add the salt, sugar, and monosodium glutamate and cook 1 minute, stirring.

5. Add the kao liang, if used, and cook about 5 seconds.

6. Spoon the vegetables onto a serving dish, leaving any liquid in the pan. Reduce it over high heat and pour in the liquid that will have accumulated in the serving dish (it accumulates rather quickly). Reduce briefly once more and pour the remaining liquid over the vegetables.

YIELD: 4 to 8 servings

Cream sauces in Chinese cookery are relatively rare, but they do exist. This is a delicate creation of romaine or other lettuce in cream sauce.

ROMAINE LETTUCE IN CREAM SAUCE

1   head romaine lettuce
½   cup milk
½   cup chicken broth
     Salt to taste
1   tablespoon cornstarch
¼   cup peanut, vegetable, or corn oil
½   teaspoon sugar
¼   teaspoon monosodium glutamate (optional)
1   tablespoon rendered chicken fat (see Chapter XI)

1. Cut out and discard the core of the romaine. Separate the lettuce leaves. Leave the small leaves whole and cut the large leaves into 4-inch lengths. Rinse and drain very well, then pat dry.

2. Combine the milk with the chicken broth and salt and set aside.

3. Spoon the cornstarch into a small bowl and add about 3 tablespoons of the milk and chicken-broth mixture. Set aside.

4. In a wok or skillet heat 3 tablespoons of the oil, and when it is hot turn the heat off. Add the romaine and turn on the heat to high. Cook over high heat, turning and stirring the lettuce, about 1 minute. Add the sugar, salt to taste, and monosodium glutamate. Cook about 3 minutes, stirring, then quickly remove the lettuce to a serving dish, using a slotted spoon or chopsticks. Wipe out the pan.

5. Add the remaining tablespoon of oil. When hot, add the milk and chicken-broth mixtures. Bring to a boil, stirring. Stir the cornstarch mixture and add it. When thickened, turn off the heat and stir in the chicken fat. Add salt to taste. Spoon the sauce over the vegetable and serve immediately.

YIELD: 3 to 6 servings

No one, perhaps, knows how to cook spinach with more finesse than the Chinese. Here is a recipe for spinach with bamboo shoots.

SPINACH WITH BAMBOO SHOOTS

1 pound fresh spinach (do not use frozen spinach for this recipe)
½ cup peanut, vegetable, or corn oil
¼ cup finely shredded bamboo shoots *
   Salt to taste
¼ teaspoon monosodium glutamate (optional)
2 teaspoons sugar

* Available in Chinese markets and by mail order. For more information see Chapter XI.

1. Wash the spinach leaves thoroughly under cold running water. Drain well.

2. Heat the oil in a wok or skillet and add the bamboo shoots. Cook briefly, stirring, and add the spinach. Cook about 1 minute, stirring.

3. Add salt, the monosodium glutamate, and sugar and cook, stirring, about 1½ to 2 minutes longer. Transfer to a hot platter, but do not add the liquid in the pan.

YIELD: 4 servings

Among the more interesting vegetables in Chinese markets are long string beans, which resemble in flavor Western-style string beans. They differ slightly in texture, however, and are about fourteen inches in length. Here is a quick, simple, and good way to cook them. Fresh Western-style string beans may be substituted in this dish.

STIR-FRY LONG BEANS

1   pound long beans *
3   tablespoons peanut, vegetable, or corn oil
     Salt to taste
1   teaspoon sugar
1   tablespoon dry sherry or shao hsing wine *
¼   teaspoon monosodium glutamate (optional)
½   cup water

* Available in Chinese markets and by mail order. For more information see Chapter XI.

1. Trim off and discard the tips of the beans. Cut the beans into 2-inch lengths.

2. Heat the oil in a wok or skillet and add the beans. Cook, stirring, over high heat about 15 seconds, then add the salt, sugar, wine, and monosodium glutamate. Cook, stirring, about 2 minutes.

3. Add the water, cover, and cook about 3 or 4 minutes. Serve hot.

YIELD: 4 to 8 servings

In Chinese cookery, even the lowly string bean can achieve glory with a bit of wine and mushrooms and bamboo shoots.

STIR-FRY STRING BEANS WITH VEGETABLES

1   pound string beans
8   dried black mushrooms *
½   cup thinly sliced bamboo shoots *
     Peanut, vegetable, or corn oil
     Salt to taste
½   teaspoon sugar
¼   teaspoon monosodium glutamate (optional)
1   tablespoon dry sherry or shao hsing wine *
1   tablespoon water

* Available in Chinese markets and by mail order. For more information see Chapter XI.

1. Trim the beans at the end and "string," if necessary.

2. Place the mushrooms in a bowl and add boiling water to cover. Let stand 15 to 30 minutes, then drain and squeeze to extract most of the moisture. Cut off and discard the tough stems. Cut the mushrooms into thin slices and combine them with the bamboo shoots.

3. In a wok or deep-fryer heat oil for deep frying and add the beans. Cook, stirring, about 2 minutes if the beans are young and tender and slightly longer if not. Drain in a sieve-lined bowl to catch the drippings.

4. Heat 2 tablespoons of oil in a wok or skillet, and when hot add the mushrooms and bamboo shoots. Cook about 1 minute, stirring, and add the beans. Add salt and the sugar and cook about 30 seconds.

5. Add the monosodium glutamate and wine and stir. Cook about 1 minute, then add the water and cook about 1 minute longer, stirring. Serve immediately.

YIELD: 4 to 6 servings

This is a simply made and very tasty dish, whether or not the optional peppers are used.

DRY-FRIED STRING BEANS

1½   pounds string beans
1   cup peanut, vegetable, or corn oil
½   pound ground lean pork
10   hot dried red peppers * (optional), crumbled or chopped
     fine
1   tablespoon dark soy sauce *
1   teaspoon sugar
¼   teaspoon monosodium glutamate (optional)
½   teaspoon salt or to taste
1   tablespoon dry sherry or shao hsing wine *

* Available in Chinese markets and by mail order. For more information see Chapter XI.

1. Wash the beans under running water and cut or pinch off the tips of the beans from both ends. Leave them whole unless they are very long. Dry the beans well on paper toweling.

2. Heat the oil in a wok or skillet until it smokes. Add the beans, standing back to avoid being spattered. Cook them over high heat,

stirring and turning frequently, until they are wrinkled and lightly browned through, about 8 to 10 minutes. Drain them in a colander and set aside.

3. Pour off all but about 2 tablespoons of oil from the pan. Add the ground pork and the peppers and stir about over high heat, breaking up the lumps, until the pork is cooked and no pink shows, about 2 to 3 minutes. Add the soy sauce and stir in until well mixed.

4. Put the string beans back into the pan, add the sugar, monosodium glutamate, salt, and wine, and stir until well mixed, about 1 minute.

YIELD: 4 to 8 servings

This is a very simple, basic, and gratifying dish made, as the name implies, with bean sprouts, pork, and hot peppers.

BEAN SPROUTS WITH PORK AND PEPPERS

4 cups bean sprouts *
1 cup shredded, seeded, fresh red or green long hot peppers *
¾ cup peanut, vegetable, or corn oil
½ cup finely shredded pork (about ¼ pound)
½ tablespoon light soy sauce *
Salt to taste
1 teaspoon sugar
¼ teaspoon monosodium glutamate (optional)
1 tablespoon dry sherry or shao hsing wine * (optional)

* Available in Chinese markets and by mail order. For more information see Chapter XI.

1. Place the bean sprouts in a basin of cold water and let stand. Drain well and set aside.

2. Rinse the hot peppers and drain well. Set aside.

3. Heat ¼ cup of the oil in a wok or skillet and add the shredded

pork and the soy sauce. Cook, stirring, about 30 seconds, just to separate the pieces of pork. Do not cook longer. Remove the pork and set aside.

4. Put another ¼ cup oil into the pan and add the bean sprouts. Cook, stirring, about 30 seconds, then drain in a sieve-lined bowl. Discard the liquid in the pan and wipe out.

5. Blend salt, sugar, monosodium glutamate, and wine and set aside.

6. Add the last ¼ cup of oil to the pan and heat over a high flame. Add the pork, stirring. Add the peppers and cook 30 seconds, stirring. Add the bean sprouts and stir in the wine mixture. Stir quickly and serve immediately.

YIELD: 4 to 8 servings

This is a delicate dish made with celery cabbage, one of the best known or at least most widely available Chinese vegetables, steamed and served with a lightly thickened chicken sauce. If you do not have rich chicken broth on hand, use canned chicken broth, but add 2 or 3 tablespoons of rendered chicken fat to the broth before steaming the cabbage.

CELERY CABBAGE WITH CHICKEN SAUCE

1½	pounds celery cabbage *
1½	cups Rich Chicken Broth (see recipe)
	Salt to taste
3	tablespoons rendered chicken fat * (see Chapter XI)
1½	tablespoons cornstarch
¼	cup cold water
1	teaspoon sugar
½	teaspoon monosodium glutamate (optional)

* Available in Chinese markets and by mail order. For more information see Chapter XI.

1. Separate the leaves of the cabbage. Trim off a small piece of the bottom and slice off the tender tips of each leaf, about 1 or 2 inches from the top, and discard or reserve for another purpose. Cut each leaf into thirds, cutting on either side of the center rib. Cut the center ribs in halves or thirds widthwise, depending on the length. Arrange the pieces in a deep dish that can be fitted in the top of a steamer. (An 8½-x-3-inch soufflé dish works well.)

2. Add ½ cup of the chicken broth and salt to taste. Steam over boiling water 40 minutes.

3. Transfer the vegetable to a serving dish, discarding the accumulated liquid.

4. Heat the chicken fat, and when it is melted add the remaining chicken broth. Stir in the cornstarch blended with the water. Add the sugar, monosodium glutamate, and salt to taste. When the sauce is thickened, pour over the cabbage and serve.

YIELD: 6 to 8 servings

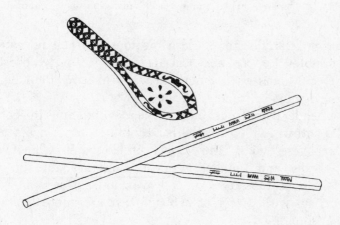

It is always fascinating to consider an overlapping of the world's cultures where food is concerned. Such an overlapping occurs, of course, with such filled dumplings as won ton and ravioli, Siberian pelmeny and kreplach. It also occurs in sweet and sour red cabbage with chestnuts, and, in the recipe below, lightly sugared Celery Cabbage with Chestnuts.

CELERY CABBAGE WITH CHESTNUTS

20 to 30 fresh or dried peeled chestnuts *
    1 head celery cabbage * (2 pounds)
    ½ cup peanut, vegetable, or corn oil
    1 tablespoon dark soy sauce *
    ⅔ cup water
    2 teaspoons sugar
      Salt to taste
    ½ teaspoon monosodium glutamate (optional)

* Available in Chinese markets and by mail order. For more information see Chapter XI.

1. If using fresh chestnuts, slash the tops and boil in water for 25 to 30 minutes. Let cool and peel. If using dried peeled chestnuts, soak for 2 to 3 hours, then simmer in water to cover for 1 hour, or until the chestnuts are tender. Drain.

2. Meanwhile, trim the cabbage at the root end. Split the cabbage into half lengthwise, then cut the halves into 1½- or 2-inch sections. If the cabbage is wide (the variety purchased in Chinatown is generally wider and rounder than the kind available in supermarkets), remove the larger outer leaves and cut separately. You should end up with pieces of cabbage that are approximately 1½ or 2 inches square.

3. In a wok or very large skillet heat the oil until hot and add the cabbage. Cook over high heat, stirring frequently, about 10 minutes.

4. Add the soy sauce, water, sugar, salt, and monosodium glutamate. Cover and cook 8 to 10 minutes. Add the chestnuts, cover, and turn the heat to low. Cook about 5 minutes, then uncover and

turn the heat to high. Cook briefly, stirring, until most of the liquid in the pan has been reduced.

YIELD: 6 to 8 servings

Although sweet and sour dishes are well known in the Western world, the best-known are made with pork or fish. Vegetables, too, take well to such seasoning, including celery cabbage.

SPICY SWEET AND SOUR CABBAGE

3 pounds celery cabbage *
   Salt
¾ cup sugar
½ cup red wine vinegar
⅓ cup peanut, vegetable, or corn oil
1 tablespoon Szechwan peppercorns *
½ cup finely shredded fresh ginger *
½ cup slivered, seeded fresh long hot red peppers *
6 hot dried red peppers *

* Available in Chinese markets and by mail order. For more information see Chapter XI.

1. Remove and discard the core of the cabbage. Cut the leaves into shreds. Place in a bowl and add about 2 tablespoons salt, stirring to distribute it. Let stand 1 hour, then squeeze between the hands to extract much of the moisture. Arrange the cabbage on a serving dish.

2. In a saucepan, combine the sugar and vinegar and heat briefly, just until the sugar dissolves. Add a little salt to taste.

3. Heat the oil in a wok or skillet and add the peppercorns. Cook, stirring, just until the oil starts to smoke. Turn off the heat. Spoon out and discard the peppercorns and add the ginger, slivered fresh red peppers, and hot dried peppers. Cook, stirring, about 30 seconds.

Pour the sauce, including the oil, over the cabbage and cover closely. Let stand to room temperature, stirring occasionally. Serve at room temperature or chilled.

YIELD: 4 to 6 servings

The following is an intriguing combination of Chinese cabbage made in layers with something that vaguely resembles a fish and chicken omelet.

CHINESE CABBAGE LAYERS

The dish:

1   large head celery cabbage *
¾   cup chopped raw shrimp (about ½ pound)
¾   cup chopped boneless, skinless chicken breast (about 1 whole chicken breast)
¾   cup chopped flounder fillet (about ½ pound)
¼   cup chicken broth
Small piece of nonsalted, nonsmoked pork fat (about ¼ pound)
2   tablespoons sherry or shao hsing wine *
Salt to taste (about 2 teaspoons)
½   teaspoon monosodium glutamate (optional)
¼   cup cornstarch
2   tablespoons water
1   teaspoon sugar
2   eggs
1   tablespoon all-purpose flour

The sauce:

3   tablespoons peanut, vegetable, or corn oil
2   cups chicken broth
Salt to taste

½   teaspoon monosodium glutamate (optional)
½   teaspoon sugar
2   tablespoons cornstarch
¼   cup water
½   cup finely minced Smithfield ham or other cured ham

* Available in Chinese markets and by mail order. For more information see Chapter XI.

1. Use one large head of celery cabbage and remove 8 to 10 of the larger leaves. Slice off and discard the bottom ends, leaving the tender tops. Trim slightly so that the leaves are about the same size (the reserved tops should be about 7 inches in length).

2. Bring about 3 quarts of water to a boil and add the tender tops. Blanch about 2 minutes and drain immediately. Run under cold water to chill and drain again. Set aside.

3. Place the chopped shrimp, chicken breast, and flounder in the container of an electric blender. Add the chicken broth and blend, stirring down with a plastic spatula as necessary, taking care not to get the spatula in the blender blade.

4. Drop the pork fat into boiling water, and when it is cooked drain it. Cut it into tiny cubes (there should be about 2 tablespoons of fat). Add this to the blended mixture. Add half the wine, salt, ¼ teaspoon monosodium glutamate, 1 tablespoon of the cornstarch blended with the 2 tablespoons water, and half the sugar. Blend well.

5. In a bowl combine the eggs, the remaining 3 tablespoons of cornstarch, the flour, salt, the remaining sugar, the remaining wine, and ¼ teaspoon monosodium glutamate.

6. This dish will be steamed, and for that purpose it will require stacking the cabbage and filling on 2 dinner plates. First bring water to boil in the bottom of a steamer and preheat the oven to 275°. Then place a large cabbage leaf flat on one plate and add 2 tablespoons of the egg mixture, spreading it all over with the fingers. Add about 4 to 6 tablespoons of the filling and smooth it over. Top with a cabbage leaf, more of the egg mixture, and more of the filling. As you work, keep the outside edges and surface of the stacks neat by saving the largest leaves for the top and by putting the smaller leaves (overlapping two if necessary) in the center of the stack. When half the ingredients are used, finish with a cabbage leaf and

place the dish in the steamer. Cover and steam over boiling water for about 10 minutes, or slightly longer. While the first dish is steaming, start filling the second dish in the same way you did the first.

7. When the first dish is steamed, remove and cool slightly while repeating the steaming process with the second dish. As soon as the contents of both dishes are just cool enough to handle, cut the stacks into squares or wedges and remove to a serving dish. Cover the serving dish with foil and place it in the warm oven.

8. To make the sauce, heat the oil in a wok or saucepan, and when very hot add the chicken broth. Add salt to taste, the monosodium glutamate, and the sugar. Blend the cornstarch with the water and stir it in. Cook briefly.

9. Remove the cabbage layers from the oven, uncover, and pour the sauce over the wedges or squares. Sprinkle with the finely minced ham and serve.

YIELD: 4 to 8 servings

Cabbage with shredded pork is a hearty dish, particularly good in winter. As noted below, it may be made in advance and reheated —or kept warm over very low heat.

STIR-FRY CABBAGE AND SHREDDED PORK ❖

1½   pounds celery cabbage *
1   12-ounce can bamboo shoots *
½   pound lean pork
2   tablespoons dark soy sauce *
8   tablespoons peanut, vegetable, or corn oil
    Salt to taste
1   teaspoon sugar
½   teaspoon monosodium glutamate, or to taste (optional)

* Available in Chinese markets and by mail order. For more information see Chapter XI.

1. Separate the leaves of the cabbage and cut one leaf at a time into thirds. Pile the thirds, one atop the other, and slice lengthwise (the direction in which the leaf grew) into fine shreds about 2 inches long.

2. Drain the bamboo shoots, drop the pieces into boiling water, and simmer about 5 minutes. This will remove the canned flavor. Drain and cool. Thinly slice the bamboo shoots, then cut the slices into thin strips the same length as the cabbage. There should be about 1 cup loosely packed.

3. Thinly slice the pork and then cut the slices into fine shreds the same length as the cabbage and bamboo shoots. Place the pork in a bowl and add the soy sauce, stirring to coat the pieces.

4. Line a mixing bowl with a sieve or colander.

5. Heat half the oil in a wok or skillet, and when it is almost smoking add the pork, stirring quickly to cook. When the meat starts to brown, about 2 minutes, drain it in the sieve. Reserve both the pork and juices that drain from it.

6. Wipe out the pan and add the remaining oil. Add the bamboo shoots and cook, stirring, about 30 seconds. Add the cabbage and cook, stirring almost constantly, until the cabbage is quite wilted. Add the pork juices, the salt, sugar, and monosodium glutamate. Continue cooking and stirring 3 to 4 minutes. Cover and cook 3 minutes longer, or until the cabbage is tender. Add the pork and toss quickly until hot and well blended, about 2 minutes. Turn into a heatproof casserole and cover. Keep warm over a very low fire until ready to serve. (The dish may be cooked in advance and reheated.)

YIELD: 8 or more servings

This is an original creation that came about after Virginia Lee came to America and dined on beef Wellington. She decided to make a Chinese dish made of something wrapped in pastry, and it was greeted with such pleasure by those she served it to that she named it in honor of her friend, Dr. Wellington Koo, the distinguished Chinese statesman, former ambassador from China to the Court of St. James and to the United States.

CABBAGE WELLINGTON ❖

The pastry:

        5 cups unsifted all-purpose flour
        1 cup lard
        1 tablespoon salt
        1¼ cups cold water
        1 egg yolk mixed with 1 tablespoon water for glaze (optional)

The filling:

        1 head celery cabbage * (3¼ to 3½ pounds)
        2 large sheets of caul fat (lace fat) *
        1 tablespoon salt

* Available in Chinese markets and by mail order. For more information see Chapter XI.

1. Place the flour in a large bowl and add the lard and salt. Blend with the fingers until it has the texture of coarse cornmeal. Gradually add the water and knead the dough until tender, about 10 minutes.
2. Shape the dough into a ball and put it into a bowl. Cover with a cloth and let stand 30 minutes.
3. Preheat the oven to 400 degrees.
4. Pull off and discard the tough outer leaves of the cabbage. Trim off a thin slice of the base. Use a sharp knife to make 2 cross-shaped incisions, each about 2 inches deep, in the bottom of the cabbage. This will facilitate cooking.
5. Flatten the pastry into a square and roll it out with a rolling

pin into a rectangle large enough to cover the cabbage completely. It can be slightly thicker in the center than on the sides.

6. Cover the pastry with 1 layer of caul fat and place the cabbage in the center. Sprinkle the top of the cabbage with the tablespoon salt. Bring up the edges of the caul fat to totally enclose the cabbage, wrapping it firmly, then bring up the edges of the pastry. Fold one edge over the other from each direction to totally enclose the cabbage. Pinch the edges together with the fingers to seal well, as tightly and closely as possible. The finished product should look like a very fat, smooth sausage. Prick 6 holes along the length of the pastry with a skewer. (You may decorate the pastry with cutout dough if you wish.)

7. Line a jelly-roll pan with another layer of caul fat and place the cabbage-filled pastry on top. Bake for one hour, then reduce the heat to 300 degrees and bake 2 hours longer. The pastry may be brushed with the egg-yolk mixture during the last hour of baking.

8. Crack open the top of the pastry and serve the cabbage while hot, spooning a little Cabbage Wellington Sauce (see recipe below) over the cabbage. The pastry is edible but secondary to the dish.

YIELD: 6 to 8 servings

CABBAGE WELLINGTON SAUCE

6   tablespoons light soy sauce *
3   tablespoons red wine vinegar
¾   teaspoon sugar
½   teaspoon monosodium glutamate (optional)
3   teaspoons sesame oil *
     Hot oil * to taste (optional)
3 to 6   tablespoons thinly sliced fresh green long hot peppers *
          (optional)

* Available in Chinese markets and by mail order. For more information see Chapter XI.

Put all the ingredients into a bowl and stir to blend well.

YIELD: About ¾ cup

This is an interesting, piquant, cold salad dish that is like a sweet and sour relish. It is eaten with other dishes on a Chinese menu as though it were a vegetable.

SPICY CUCUMBER SALAD ❖

3   pounds whole, very fresh young new cucumbers
     Salt
3   dried black mushrooms *
1½   tablespoons shredded fresh ginger *
⅓   cup shredded, seeded, hot or sweet, red or green peppers
6   hot dried red peppers * (optional)
4 or 5   tablespoons red wine vinegar
5   tablespoons sugar
1   tablespoon light soy sauce *

¼   teaspoon monosodium glutamate (optional)
3   tablespoons sesame oil *
1   tablespoon Szechwan peppercorns *

* Available in Chinese markets and by mail order. For more information see Chapter XI.

1. Trim off the ends of the cucumbers and discard. Cut the cucumbers in half, then in quarters or eighths depending on size. Using a melon ball cutter, scoop out the seeds and some of the meat and discard, leaving a shell ⅛ inch thick.

2. Use a paring knife to cut the cucumber shells into rectangles, leaving on about ⅛ inch of the firm white cucumber flesh. The rectangles should measure about 2 inches by ¾ inch. There should be about 2 cups of the prepared cucumber pieces. Put the pieces into a mixing bowl and add salt, about 2½ teaspoons. Stir to distribute. Let stand 1 hour.

3. Meanwhile, put the mushrooms into a small bowl and add very hot or boiling water to cover. Let stand 15 to 30 minutes, then drain and squeeze the mushrooms to extract much of the moisture. Cut off the stems and discard. Slice the mushroom caps into thin strips (julienne). Place in a small bowl.

4. To the mushrooms add the ginger, shredded peppers, and hot dried red peppers. Set aside.

5. Combine the vinegar, 3 tablespoons of the sugar, the soy sauce, monosodium glutamate, and salt to taste and stir to dissolve the sugar. Set aside.

6. When the cucumber pieces are ready, drain and rinse under cold water. Drain well.

7. Bring enough water to cover the cucumber pieces to a boil. Turn off the heat and add the cucumber pieces. Let stand 15 seconds, no longer. Drain. Return the pieces to a bowl and add ½ teaspoon salt and the remaining 2 tablespoons of sugar and cover.

8. Heat the sesame oil in a small saucepan and add the peppercorns. Cook, stirring, until the oil starts to smoke. Immediately remove from the heat and strain the oil into a wok or skillet. Add the mushroom mixture and cook, stirring, about 30 seconds. Add the vinegar mixture and cook, stirring, about 1 minute. Turn off the heat.

9. Spoon the vegetables and sauce over the cucumber pieces. Cover immediately and let cool, then chill.

10. When ready to serve, drain. Serve the cucumber salad in a small dish.

YIELD: 4 to 6 servings

Eggplant occupies an unusual place in the world's hierarchy of vegetables. It is not a commonplace vegetable like tomatoes and corn and the lowly string bean. It has a character all its own and dominates almost any dish in which it is used, be it the *baba ghanouj* of the Middle East; *ratatouille* of the French Riviera; or the Spicy Braised Eggplant below. The last is Chinese, of course, and it is an admirable side dish or appetizer.

SPICY BRAISED EGGPLANT

¼ cup small dried shrimps * (optional)
6 small dried black mushrooms *
4 fresh green long hot or sweet peppers * or 2 green bell peppers
3 to 4 tablespoons chili paste with garlic (Szechwan paste) *
½ tablespoon dark soy sauce *
½ tablespoon light soy sauce *
2 tablespoons dry sherry or shao hsing wine *
1 to 1½ tablespoons red wine vinegar, or according to taste
¼ teaspoon monosodium glutamate (optional)
1 teaspoon sugar
 Salt to taste
1 medium eggplant (about 1 to 1¼ pounds)
 Peanut, vegetable, or corn oil
½ cup water

* Available in Chinese markets and by mail order. For more information see Chapter XI.

1. Soak the shrimps, if used, in cold water to cover for 1 hour, then drain and set aside.

2. Soak the mushrooms in boiling water to cover for 15 to 30 minutes, then drain and squeeze to extract most of the moisture. Cut off and discard the tough stems. Set aside.

3. Trim the peppers and split them in half. Remove the seeds and white fibers, then cut the peppers into bite-size pieces. Set aside.

4. Blend together the chili paste with garlic, soy sauces, wine, vinegar, monosodium glutamate, sugar, and salt. Set aside.

5. Trim off the ends of the eggplant and discard. Cut the eggplant into eighths, lengthwise. Cut the slices into 1½- to 2-inch cubes. Place in a colander and rinse under cold water. Drain well.

6. Heat ½ cup of oil in a wok or skillet, and when it is hot add the eggplant cubes, stirring and pressing, and cook until lightly browned, about 5 minutes.

7. Add the drained shrimps, if used, and cook about 30 seconds.

8. Remove the eggplant and drain well in a sieve-lined bowl.

9. Heat 2 tablespoons of oil in the pan and add the mushrooms and peppers. Stir until tender, about 1 or 2 minutes. Return the eggplant to the pan and cook, stirring, about 5 minutes. Add the water. Cook, stirring, about 5 seconds, then add the soy sauce mixture. Cook and stir about 5 minutes. Serve hot or warm.

YIELD: 4 to 8 servings

Doubtless, to paraphrase a Western adage, destiny could have made a better way to cook string beans and mushrooms and corn, but doubtless destiny never did. The corn here is miniature ears of baby corn. It comes in fifteen-ounce cans and is available at some supermarkets and in almost any Chinese grocery. The corn used in this recipe is not the pickled kind that can be found in some stores.

VEGETABLES IN CHICKEN SAUCE

12　dried black mushrooms * (or use 1 cup drained, canned Western-style button mushrooms)
 1　pound fresh string beans
10　large celery cabbage * leaves
 1　teaspoon baking soda
 ¼　cup peanut, vegetable, or corn oil
 1　15-ounce can miniature ears of baby corn on the cob,* drained
 3　cups chicken broth
   Salt to taste
 1　teaspoon sugar
 ½　teaspoon monosodium glutamate (optional)
 1　tablespoon dry sherry or shao hsing wine *
1½　tablespoons cornstarch
 ¼　cup water
 ¼　cup rendered chicken fat (see Chapter XI)

* Available in Chinese markets and by mail order. For more information see Chapter XI.

1. Place the dried mushrooms in a bowl and add boiling water to cover. Let stand for 15 to 30 minutes, then drain. Squeeze to extract most of the moisture and cut off and discard the stems. If the canned button mushrooms are used, drain, and leave them whole.

2. Trim off the ends of the string beans and cut the beans into uniform, 2-inch lengths (there should be about 1 quart when cut).

3. Only the center stem section of each cabbage leaf will be used, since the leafy part will cook too fast and make the dish mushy. Trim

the leaves, one at a time, by making 2 parallel cuts on each side of the stem, then cut off a small part of the bottom and top. Discard the trimmings or save for another use. Cut the stems into pieces about ¾ inch wide and 4 inches long.

4. Bring about a quart of water to a boil and add the cabbage pieces. Cook about 1 minute, then drain under cold running water. Set aside.

5. Bring another quart of water to a boil and add the soda. Add the beans and cook until crisp tender, 1 minute or longer. Drain well and rinse under cold water. Set aside.

6. Heat the oil in a wok or skillet, and when it is hot add the beans. Stir about 1 minute over high heat, then add the corn, mushrooms, and cabbage. Stir until the moisture that naturally clings to the vegetables dissipates. When very hot, add the chicken broth and bring to a boil. Add the salt, sugar, monosodium glutamate, and wine and bring to a boil.

7. Using a slotted spoon, scoop the vegetables onto a hot serving dish.

8. Immediately combine the cornstarch and water and stir it into the sauce. When the sauce boils and thickens, pour it over the vegetables. Pour the melted chicken fat over all and serve.

YIELD: 6 to 8 servings

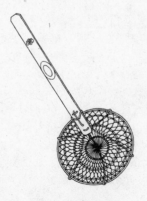

Turnips enjoy a contrasting esteem in the Western world. They are, by and large, thought of as a dish of the poor, although they contribute much to boiled beef dishes and they are the basis for an elegant French cream soup. There is one dish in Far Eastern cooking that is particularly admired by the Chinese, and it is a Chinese turnip cake. It is a dish as "rich as Croesus," to alter the original meaning of that phrase a bit. The "cake" is a savory dish that serves as a main course, and it is made with turnips, mushrooms, and pork. The long white Chinese turnips found in Chinese groceries must be used; ordinary turnips cannot be substituted.

TURNIP CAKE

3   long white Chinese turnips * (about 3 to 3½ pounds)
24 small black dried mushrooms *
1   cup small dried shrimps *
1   strip Chinese winter-cured pork *
4   small Chinese pork sausages *
    Peanut, vegetable, or corn oil
    Salt to taste (about 2 to 4 tablespoons)
1   teaspoon sugar
¼   teaspoon ground pepper
1¾ cups water
1   pound rice powder *
    Sprigs of fresh coriander * for garnish
    Oyster sauce *

* Available in Chinese markets and by mail order. For more information see Chapter XI.

1. Peel the turnips and cut them into thin rounds about ¼ inch thick or slightly thicker. Stack the slices, a few at a time, and cut them into ¼-inch strips. There should be about 3 quarts.

2. Place the mushrooms in a mixing bowl and add boiling water to cover. Let stand 15 to 30 minutes, then drain, but save the mushroom liquid. Cut off and discard the tough stems from the mushrooms. Shred the mushrooms into ¼-inch strips.

3. Place the dried shrimps in a mixing bowl and add the mushroom liquid. Soak about 5 minutes, then drain and discard the liquid.

4. Trim away the rind from the winter-cured pork and discard it. Cut the pork into ½-inch cubes. There should be about 2 cups.

5. Cut the Chinese sausages into ½-inch-thick slices. There should be about 1 cup.

6. Heat ¼ cup oil in a large wok or skillet and add the winter-cured pork and sausage rounds. Cook, stirring, about 15 seconds. Add the shrimps and the mushrooms and cook, stirring, about 30 seconds, then add the turnips.

7. Add salt to taste, the sugar, and the pepper. Cook, stirring, 8 to 10 minutes, or until the shreds of turnips lose their natural crisp whiteness and are limp. When ready, they will look more or less like wilted cooked onions.

8. Add the water, then stir in the rice powder, stirring constantly. The mixture should be thick and pasty. Remove from the heat.

9. Lightly oil a large round cake pan, about 10 inches in diameter and about 3 inches deep. Spoon in the turnip mixture and pat down. Smooth the top. Decorate with a few sprigs of fresh coriander.

10. Place the pan in the top of a steamer. Cover and place over a large quantity of boiling water and steam 1½ hours, or until a chopstick inserted in the cake comes out clean.

11. Let the cake cool. Cut it into slices about ¼ inch thick. Slice only as much as necessary. (The remainder will keep for several days in the refrigerator, or it may be frozen.)

12. When ready to serve, cut the slices into rectangles about 3 inches long.

13. Heat about 2 tablespoons of oil in a wok or skillet and cook the slices until golden on one side, then turn and cook until golden on the other. Serve hot, with oyster sauce as a dip.

YIELD: 30 to 40 or more servings

There are thousands of Chinese recipes that call for egg white, thus leaving the query as to what to do with the yolk. One solution is the following recipe, which calls for numerous yolks as a principal ingredient. The simplest way to conserve a yolk when a white is called for is to drop the yolk into a freezer container and to keep adding yolks as they become available, freezing after each addition. One-cup glass jars with screw tops are very good for this. This stir-fry dish is from North China. It is, of course, devastatingly rich, and in its own way quite extraordinary to the palate.

STIR-FRY EGG YOLKS WITH WATER CHESTNUTS

¾   cup egg yolks (about 9)
1½   cups chicken broth
1½   tablespoons cornstarch
1   cup finely diced water chestnuts *
½   teaspoon sugar
¼   teaspoon monosodium glutamate (optional)
     Salt to taste
     Peanut, vegetable, or corn oil
¼   cup ham, preferably Smithfield, so finely minced as to be almost pulverized

* Available in Chinese markets and by mail order. For more information see Chapter XI.

1. Place the yolks in a mixing bowl and beat them. Beat in the chicken broth and cornstarch and stir in the water chestnuts. Add the sugar, monosodium glutamate, and salt.

2. Heat ½ cup of oil in a wok or skillet, and when it is moderately hot add the egg mixture. Stir by gently bringing the egg mixture from the bottom of the pan to the top in a folding motion. Stir until set, then pour 1 tablespoon of oil over it. Spoon into a serving dish, sprinkle with the ham, and serve.

YIELD: 4 to 8 servings

Snow peas, because of their elegance and cost, are rather the caviar among the world's vegetables. They are incredibly delicious quickly and simply cooked but, if you happen to have a good harvest (and more and more people in the Western world are growing their own), they are fascinating when cooked with Szechwan preserved vegetable.

STIR-FRY SNOW PEAS WITH SZECHWAN PRESERVED VEGETABLE

1	pound snow peas *
2 to 3	pieces Szechwan preserved vegetable *
¼	cup peanut, vegetable, or corn oil
	Salt to taste
1	teaspoon sugar
1	tablespoon dry sherry or shao hsing wine *
¼	teaspoon monosodium glutamate (optional)

* Available in Chinese markets and by mail order. For more information see Chapter XI.

1. "String" the snow peas if they are not baby peas. Trim off the ends.
2. Slice the Szechwan vegetable very thin, shred it, and chop it fine. There should be about ½ cup in all.
3. Heat the oil and add salt to taste. Immediately add the Szechwan vegetable and toss about 5 seconds, then add the snow peas, tossing.
4. Cook, stirring, about 5 seconds, then add the sugar, wine, and monosodium glutamate. Cook, stirring and tossing, about 1 minute over high heat. Do not overcook, or the peas will lose their crispness.

YIELD: 4 to 8 servings

SNOW PEAS AND STRAW MUSHROOMS

1   pound snow peas *
¼   teaspoon monosodium glutamate (optional)
2   tablespoons dry sherry or shao hsing wine *
    Salt to taste
1   teaspoon sugar
¼   cup peanut, vegetable, or corn oil
1   15-ounce can straw mushrooms * (the 15-ounce can specifies
    that it offers 8 ounces drained weight), drained

* Available in Chinese markets and by mail order. For more information see Chapter XI.

1. Pick over the snow peas and "string" them by pulling off stems from one side to the other.

2. Combine the monosodium glutamate, wine, salt, and sugar and stir to blend. Set aside.

3. Put the oil into a wok or skillet, and when it is very hot add the straw mushrooms, stirring constantly. Cook about 1½ minutes, stirring, then add the snow peas. Cook, stirring briskly, about 1 minute. Add the wine mixture and cook, stirring, about 30 seconds. The snow peas are done when they are still crisp but have lost their raw taste. They must remain emerald green; if they overcook, they will lose their texture and color.

YIELD: 4 to 8 or more servings

SWEET AND SOUR CABBAGE

1½   pounds cabbage
½   cup water
½   cup sugar
3½   tablespoons red wine vinegar
1   tablespoon dark soy sauce *
1½   tablespoons cornstarch
¼   teaspoon monosodium glutamate (optional)
   Salt to taste
5   tablespoons peanut, vegetable, or corn oil

* Available in Chinese markets and by mail order. For more information see Chapter XI.

1. Cut out the core of the cabbage and cut the cabbage into eighths. Then cut the leaves into bite-size morsels, 1½ inches square, more or less.

2. Combine the water, sugar, vinegar, soy sauce, cornstarch, monosodium glutamate, and salt. Blend well, then set aside.

3. Heat ¼ cup of the oil in a wok or skillet, and when it is very hot add the cabbage. Cook, stirring, over high heat 2 to 3 minutes. Remove the cabbage.

4. Add the remaining tablespoon of oil to the pan and add the sauce. Stir about 1 minute, until it thickens. Add the cabbage and toss it about in the sauce 45 seconds to 1 minute. The cabbage must remain crisp-tender, and more on the crisp than tender side. The sauce clings loosely but does not thoroughly coat the pieces.

YIELD: 6 to 8 servings

Straw mushrooms, available in cans in any Chinatown, are a delectable item with a most agreeable texture. They can be cooked with many vegetables, including broccoli or broccoli rape. And they are excellent with Chinese mustard greens, which are also available in Chinese markets in this country.

MUSTARD GREENS WITH STRAW MUSHROOMS

3 or 4   heads Chinese mustard greens *
1   teaspoon baking soda
3   tablespoons peanut, vegetable, or corn oil
      Salt to taste
1½   teaspoons sugar
¼   teaspoon monosodium glutamate (optional)
1   15-ounce can straw mushrooms * (the 15-ounce can specifies that it offers 8 ounces drained weight), drained
2¾   cups chicken broth
2   tablespoons cornstarch
¼   cup rendered chicken fat (see Chapter XI)

* Available in Chinese markets and by mail order. For more information see Chapter XI.

1. Peel away and discard the tough or wilted dark outer leaves from the mustard greens. Cut off and discard the tough base end of each set of mustard greens. Pull off the tender light green leaves, but cut off and discard the soft leafy portion, leaving only the firm center portion of each leaf. Cut those firm center pieces into 1½-inch lengths. Wash and drain well.

2. Put enough water into a saucepan to cover the greens when they are added. Bring this water to a boil and add the soda and the greens. Let the water return almost but not quite to a boil, then drain the greens and drop them immediately into a basin of cold water. When chilled, drain the greens well.

3. Heat the oil in a wok or skillet, and when it is hot and almost to the smoking point add salt to taste. Add the greens and cook, stir-

ring, 10 seconds. Add the sugar and monosodium glutamate and cook, stirring, about 20 seconds longer.

4. Add the drained mushrooms and cook, stirring, about 2 minutes. Add 2½ cups of chicken broth, bring to a boil, and cook about 1 minute. Blend the cornstarch with the remaining broth and stir it into the simmering sauce. Cook, stirring, until thickened. Transfer to a platter and dot with chicken fat.

YIELD: 4 to 8 servings

It is odd that fava beans in this country are associated primarily with the Italian kitchen. They are, however, and they are quite generally known as Italian beans. They are rich, meaty green beans that look something like lima beans and come in a bumpy green shell, and when available fresh they are a great delicacy. Their prime time is in April and May, and they can be bought in fruit and vegetable stores, particularly those in Italian neighborhoods.

BRAISED FRESH FAVA BEANS CHINESE STYLE

    2   pounds fava (Italian) beans
    3   tablespoons peanut, vegetable, or corn oil
    ½   cup shredded bamboo shoots *
    1   cup water
 2 to 3 tablespoons sugar
         Salt to taste
    ¼   teaspoon monosodium glutamate (optional)
    3   scallions, green part included, finely chopped

* Available in Chinese markets and by mail order. For more information see Chapter XI.

1. Shell the beans and, if you really want to be refined, remove the outer coating or membrane that surrounds each bean.

2. Heat the oil, and when it is almost smoking turn off the heat. Add the favas and turn on the heat. Cook briefly, stirring, then add

the bamboo shoots. Cook, stirring, about 30 seconds. Add the water and cook until the water is reduced to half. Add the sugar, salt, and monosodium glutamate. Cook, stirring, about 2½ minutes, then add the scallions. Cook 5 to 10 minutes longer, tasting a bean to determine when tender.

YIELD: 4 to 8 servings

There is a definite place, the Chinese feel, for tinned mushrooms, even the ordinary button mushrooms, produced in America and found on most supermarket shelves. This is the case with the following recipe for fava beans (Italian beans) with mushrooms in a light chicken sauce.

FAVA BEANS WITH BUTTON MUSHROOMS

    4   pounds fava (Italian) beans, in the shell
    2   tablespoons peanut, vegetable, or corn oil
    ½   cup plus 3 tablespoons water
        Salt to taste
   1½   teaspoons sugar
    ½   teaspoon monosodium glutamate (optional)
    1   cup drained, canned button mushrooms
    1   cup chicken broth
    1   tablespoon cornstarch
    1   tablespoon rendered chicken fat (see Chapter XI)

1. Shell the fava beans, then peel off the outer coating or membrane that surrounds each bean.
2. Heat the oil in a wok or skillet and add the beans. Cook, stirring, about 1 minute. Add the ½ cup water, salt, 1 teaspoon of the sugar, and half the monosodium glutamate. Cook, stirring, 2 minutes over high heat.
3. Remove the solids with a slotted spoon and drain.

4. Add the mushrooms to the pan and cook about 1 minute, stirring. Drain, including the liquid in the pan.

5. Wipe out the pan or use a clean one and add the chicken broth, salt to taste, the remaining ½ teaspoon of sugar, and the remaining monosodium glutamate. Blend the cornstarch with the 3 tablespoons water and stir it into the sauce. Add the beans, mushrooms, and chicken fat and serve hot.

YIELD: 6 to 8 servings

In Chinese markets, there is a splendid vegetable related to the garden-variety chrysanthemum plant. The leaves resemble those of the chrysanthemum plant, and the taste is similar. We point this out because we do not recommend using the garden variety for cooking. The chrysanthemum leaves found on the market in any Chinatown, however, are delectable—and seasonal. They come in the spring of the year. Edible chrysanthemum leaves must be trimmed well at the ends, and they must be washed as thoroughly as spinach in many cold waters, for they have a great deal of sand. Here is one use for the chrysanthemum leaves.

STIR-FRY CHRYSANTHEMUM LEAVES

1 bunch fresh chrysanthemum leaves * (1 to 1½ pounds)
3 tablespoons peanut, vegetable, or corn oil
2 teaspoons salt
½ teaspoon sugar
1 tablespoon dry sherry or shao hsing wine *

* Available in Chinese markets and by mail order. For more information see Chapter XI.

1. Pick over the chrysanthemum leaves very well, cutting off and discarding the tough stem ends. Rinse the leaves in several changes of cold water to rid them of any trace of soil or sand. When picked

over, there should be enough greens to fill, when loosely packed, a French salad basket. Drain the leaves well and pat them quite dry with paper toweling.

2. Heat the oil in a wok or skillet and add 1 teaspoon of the salt. When the oil is very hot, add the chrysanthemum leaves. Cook over high heat, stirring rapidly, about 1 minute, or until wilted. Add the sugar and remaining salt and cook about 2 seconds. Add the wine and stir, then cook about 30 seconds and drain. Serve as a vegetable or as a garnish.

YIELD: 4 to 8 servings

This dish uses dried bean curd to produce an eminently edible creation that tastes remarkably like roast duck. The mock duck is eaten in exactly the same manner as Peking Duck, with the same sauces. Chinese pancakes can also accompany it, if you wish.

MOCK PEKING DUCK

 6   sheets dried bean curd *
     Cold water
 4½ tablespoons all-purpose flour
     Water
 2   teaspoons sesame oil *
 4   tablespoons finely chopped ham
 6   tablespoons finely chopped scallions, green part included
     Light soy sauce *
 ½   cup peanut, vegetable, or corn oil, approximately
     Peking Duck Sauce I or II (see recipes)

 * Available in Chinese markets and by mail order. For more information see Chapter XI.

1. Bean curd comes in large, semicircular thin sheets as well as in squares. Because the sheets are notably fragile, they are frequently

broken. Broken pieces may be used to make this dish by slightly overlapping them and patching them.

2. Place the sheets, one at a time, on a flat surface and sprinkle the whole sheet with water, not forgetting the edges, until the entire surface is wet. The sheet will become wrinkled and soft almost immediately.

3. Blend the flour with ¾ cup cold water and the sesame oil. Spread the sheet generously with part of the mixture.

4. Blend the ham and scallions together and sprinkle the sheet lightly with the mixture, using 2 teaspoonfuls, more or less.

5. Fold the sheet over in half from left to right, enclosing the ham-scallion mixture. Fold in and press down any dried edges. Spread the top with the flour mixture and sprinkle with the ham and scallion mixture. Fold over in half once more from right to left. You should now have a rough rectangle about 9 inches long and 5 inches wide. Spread the surface with more of the flour mixture and sprinkle with a little of the ham-scallion mixture. Fold over again in half from left to right.

6. Repeat the process with the rest of the sheets, placing the finished rolls on plates that will fit into the top of a steamer.

7. Bring water in the bottom of the steamer to a boil. Meanwhile, brush the tops of the layers with soy sauce.

8. Steam each plateful of mock duck, covered, over boiling water for 10 minutes. Cool. (At this point the dishes may be covered lightly with foil and refrigerated overnight or longer.)

9. When ready to cook, slice each strip crosswise into 1½- or 2-inch pieces; the pieces are supposed to resemble pieces of roast duck skin.

10. Heat the oil, ½ cup or enough to cover the bottom of a wok or skillet, and when hot cook the strips, a few at a time, until brown, the color of potato pancakes. Drain on paper toweling. The strips should be quite crisp. Serve with Peking Duck Sauce.

YIELD: 6 to 8 servings

VIII

Soups and Hot Pots

A canned clear chicken broth is acceptable for all the recipes in this book, but in many cases, particularly in the soup recipes that follow, a rich homemade chicken broth will improve the dish. Here is a recipe for such a broth. It will keep in the refrigerator for about three days; if you wish to keep it longer, bring the broth to a boil once more, then cool and re-store—or freeze it indefinitely.

RICH CHICKEN BROTH ❖

1   chicken (3 pounds), cut into quarters
3   quarts water

1. In a kettle bring the chicken to a boil in water to cover. Discard the water and rinse the chicken in cold water.
2. Bring 3 quarts of fresh water to a boil and add the blanched chicken. As soon as it comes to a boil again, turn down the fire to maintain the lowest possible simmer (a few bubbles at a time) and cook for 4 to 5 hours.
3. Cool the chicken in the broth and then discard the chicken; all its flavor will have cooked out.

YIELD: About 1½ quarts

Note: Up to half the fat may be removed from the broth if desired, but if more is taken off, the broth will lose flavor.

Egg drop soup, like won ton, is a great Western favorite. Rich Chicken Broth is recommended: the better the stock, the better the soup.

EGG DROP SOUP

1   quart Rich Chicken Broth (see recipe)
¼   cup cornstarch
      Salt to taste
¼   teaspoon monosodium glutamate (optional)
1   egg, thoroughly beaten but not frothy
2   tablespoons chopped scallions, green part included
      Freshly ground pepper

1. Remove about ¼ cup of the cold chicken broth and blend it in a small bowl or cup with the cornstarch.
2. Bring the remaining chicken broth to a boil, and when it is simmering, stir in salt to taste, the monosodium glutamate, and the well-blended cornstarch mixture. When the soup has thickened and cooked for about 1 minute, turn off the heat.
3. Immediately but slowly start adding the egg in a thin stream, stirring constantly in a circular fashion so that the egg forms thin shreds in the hot broth.
4. Serve in individual bowls sprinkled with the chopped scallions, and with freshly ground pepper on the side.

YIELD: 4 to 6 servings

Winter melon is a curious thing. Dictionaries tell us that it is a member of the muskmelon family, and yet the flesh doesn't have the sweet fleshiness of any of the breakfast or dessert melons of the world. It has a frosty but dark green exterior and an interesting texture, and it resembles, as much as anything, the common pumpkin in shape. It may be purchased whole or by the slice. This recipe for winter melon soup calls for it by the slice.

WINTER MELON AND HAM SOUP

1   small uncooked ham hock or one small cooked Smithfield
     ham slice (about ½ pound)
1   slice winter melon * (2 pounds)
½   teaspoon ground white pepper
5   cups Rich Chicken Broth (see recipe)

* Available in Chinese markets and by mail order. For more information see
Chapter XI.

1. If the ham hock is to be used, soak in cold water to cover overnight. No advance preparation is needed for the ham slice.

2. Put the ham hock or ham slice on to cook in cold water to cover.
Simmer 1 hour, or until tender.

3. Cut off and discard the rind of the winter melon, and also the
soft center part with seeds. Put the flesh of the melon into a saucepan with cold water to cover, bring to a boil, and simmer 15 to 30
minutes, depending on the age of the melon. Cook only until crisp
tender and not mushy, then drain and run under cold water. Cut it
into slices about ¼ inch thick. There should be about 20 slices.

4. Cut the best part of the ham hock or of the ham slice into the
same size rectangles as the melon, but thinner, about ⅛ inch thick.
There should be about the same amount of ham as melon. The remainder of the ham may be put to another use.

5. Put the pepper into the bottom of a soup bowl. Lay the ham
and melon neatly in the bottom of the bowl, overlapping and alter-
nating the slices.

6. Bring the chicken broth to a boil, then pour carefully into the
soup bowl and serve piping hot.

YIELD: 6 to 8 servings

Here is another way to make beef balls (see Steamed Beef Balls in Chapter V).

BOILED BEEF BALLS IN SOUP

½   pound ground sirloin
    Salt to taste
¼   teaspoon monosodium glutamate (optional)
1   tablespoon cornstarch
½   tablespoon dry sherry or shao hsing wine *
¼   cup cold water
5   cups Rich Chicken Broth (see recipe)
½   teaspoon ground white pepper
2   scallions, green part included, trimmed and cut into 2-inch
      lengths
¼   cup finely chopped fresh coriander leaves *

* Available in Chinese markets and by mail order. For more information see Chapter XI.

1. In a mixing bowl combine the beef with salt, the monosodium glutamate, cornstarch, and wine. Blend, stirring with one hand in a circular motion. Gradually add the water, always stirring in one direction.

2. Shape the mixture into 20 meat balls and drop them into cold water. Let stand 10 minutes.

3. Bring the chicken broth to a boil. Add the meat balls and simmer 10 minutes.

4. Sprinkle the bottom of a soup bowl with the ground white pepper. Add the scallions and the soup with the meat balls. Serve sprinkled with the fresh coriander.

YIELD: 6 to 8 servings

If the French are proud of their quenelles or fish balls of pike and other fish, the Chinese can take justifiable joy in their fish balls. These are splendid and easy to make.

FISH BALL SOUP ❖

    1   tablespoon coarsely chopped fresh ginger *
    1   scallion, green part included, trimmed and chopped
    ¼   cup plus 5 tablespoons water
    ½   pound flounder fillets, cubed
    1   tablespoon dry sherry or shao hsing wine *
    1   egg white
    1   tablespoon cornstarch
        Salt to taste
    ¼   teaspoon monosodium glutamate (optional)
    1   tablespoon lard, preferably rendered leaf lard (see Chapter
        XI)
    5   cups Rich Chicken Broth (see recipe)
        Minced scallions or fresh coriander * for garnish

* Available in Chinese markets and by mail order. For more information see Chapter XI.

1. Put the ginger, scallion, and ¼ cup water into the container of an electric blender and blend on high speed. Strain the liquid into a bowl through fine cheesecloth and discard the solids. Rinse out the blender.

2. Place the cubes of fish in the container of the blender and add the 5 tablespoons of water, wine, and egg white. Blend until a smooth puree, stirring down.

3. Scoop out the fish mixture into a mixing bowl. Add one tablespoon of the ginger-scallion juice (the rest may be reserved for another use). Add the cornstarch, salt, monosodium glutamate, and lard and mix thoroughly.

4. Have a heatproof casserole of cold water ready. Do not put it on the stove.

5. To shape the fish balls, wet your hand and spoon some of the

fish mixture into your palm. Close your fist, allowing the mixture to emerge from the hole formed by your thumb and index finger. In other words, use your hand and fist like a pastry tube. As the balls emerge, one by one, let them fall into a spoon and drop each ball from the spoon into the cold water. Wet the spoon with cold water each time.

6. When all the balls have been formed, place the casserole on the stove and bring the water slowly to a boil. Let cook just until the fish balls rise to the surface and float, then remove and transfer immediately to cold water. Drain and put into a jar of cold water, seal, and store in the refrigerator until ready to use.

7. When ready to use, drain the fish balls and put them into cold water to barely cover. Bring slowly to a boil and cook just long enough to heat through.

8. Drop the balls into the hot chicken broth, garnish with the minced scallion or coriander, and serve.

YIELD: 6 to 8 servings

Some of the world's simplest soups have an exemplary appeal, and the roster would include the following fish soup made with bony pieces of fish.

FISH SOUP

¾   pound cod cheek or the head of any non-oily fish, gill removed
1   whole raw chicken liver
2   tablespoons tree ear mushrooms *
10   spinach leaves, tough stems removed
½   cup snow peas *
½   cup bamboo shoots,* cut into ⅜-inch dice
5   cups Rich Chicken Broth (see recipe)
2   tablespoons cornstarch
¼   cup water
2   egg whites

* Available in Chinese markets and by mail order. For more information see Chapter XI.

1. Bring enough water to a boil to cover the fish and chicken liver when added. Add the cod cheek or fish head and the chicken liver. Return to a boil and remove from the heat. Drain and rinse under cold running water, then set aside.

2. Place the tree ears in a mixing bowl and add hot water to cover. Let stand 10 minutes or longer, until they expand, then drain. Cut and discard any toughened portion. Cut in half.

3. Remove the flesh from the fish bones and set aside. Discard the bones. Cut the liver into ⅜-inch dice and set aside.

4. Drop the spinach leaves into boiling water, let stand about 10 seconds, and drain. Run under cold water, then squeeze to extract excess moisture.

5. Drop the snow peas into boiling water and let stand about 15 seconds. Drain, then run under cold water and drain well.

6. Bring the broth to a boil and add the bamboo shoots, chicken liver slices, tree ears, and flesh of the fish. Simmer very gently, just until the fish flakes easily.

7. Blend the cornstarch with the ¼ cup water and stir it into the soup. Heat to thicken and add the spinach. Remove from the heat and, while piping hot, pour into a soup bowl. Immediately but gradually add the egg whites, stirring constantly.

YIELD: 6 to 8 servings

As we have noted, shrimp noodles have a multitude of uses. When first made, the noodles may be drained and run under cold water, then maintained for 3 days in the refrigerator, provided they are covered with cold water and sealed tightly.

SOUP WITH SHRIMP NOODLES

5   cups Rich Chicken Broth (see recipe)
4   cups Shrimp Noodles (see recipe)
3   scallions, green part included, finely chopped
     Salt to taste
¼   teaspoon ground white pepper

1. Heat the broth until it is piping hot, add the noodles, and heat them to the boiling point.
2. Scatter the scallions, salt, and pepper over the bottom of a soup bowl and pour in the broth with the noodles. Stir lightly and serve.

YIELD: 6 to 8 servings

One of the most appetizing soups in the Chinese repertoire—and one that creates appetite with its seductive blend of the hot and sour—is called simply Hot and Sour Soup. It contains two kinds of mushrooms (fungi, if you will), shredded pork, and bean curd. The hot comes from white pepper, incidentally—not hot oil—and the sour comes from vinegar.

HOT AND SOUR SOUP

2	large dried black mushrooms *
6	tree ear mushrooms *
4	dried tiger lily stems *
1	tablespoon peanut, vegetable, or corn oil
¼	cup finely shredded pork
1	tablespoon light soy sauce *
½	cup finely shredded bamboo shoots *
5	cups Rich Chicken Broth (see recipe)
	Salt to taste
2 to 3	tablespoons red wine vinegar, according to taste
1	teaspoon dark soy sauce *
2	tablespoons cornstarch
3	tablespoons water
1½	pads fresh white bean curd,* cut into thin strips
2	eggs, lightly beaten
1	tablespoon sesame oil *
1	teaspoon freshly ground white or black pepper
2	tablespoons chopped scallions, green part included, for garnish
	Minced fresh coriander * for garnish (optional)

* Available in Chinese markets and by mail order. For more information see Chapter XI.

1. Place the mushrooms, tree ears, and tiger lily stems in a mixing bowl. Pour very hot or boiling water over them and let stand 15 to 30 minutes, then drain.
2. Cut off and discard the stems of the mushrooms and the harder

part of the tree ears. Cut both the mushrooms and tree ears into thin slices. With the fingers, shred the tiger lily stems, and if they are very long cut them in half.

3. Heat a wok or skillet, and when it is hot add the peanut, vegetable, or corn oil and shredded pork. Stir to separate the strands of pork and add the light soy sauce. Add the mushrooms, tree ears, tiger lily stems, and bamboo shoots. Stir quickly about 1 minute and add the chicken broth and salt. Stir in the vinegar and dark soy sauce.

4. Combine the cornstarch and water and stir into the simmering broth. When slightly thickened, add the bean curd, bring to a boil, and turn off the heat for about 30 seconds, to let the broth cool a bit so the eggs won't overcook when they are added.

5. Add the sesame oil and pepper and stir to blend. Pour the soup into a hot soup tureen and gradually add the eggs in a thin stream, stirring in a circular motion. Sprinkle with the chopped scallion and the minced fresh coriander, if desired. Serve immediately.

YIELD: About 6 to 8 servings

Abalone, that incredibly good and tender mollusk when properly cooked, has by and large a regional following in the Western world, owing, no doubt, to its rarity. It is highly prized on America's West Coast and in Hawaii, and it is one of the joys of the Chinese table. In the following soup it is complemented with chicken. Tinned abalone is used, for fresh abalone is practically unavailable outside the West Coast and Hawaii.

CHICKEN AND ABALONE SOUP

1   15-ounce can abalone *
½   chicken breast, skinned and boned
½   egg white (beat the egg white lightly, then divide in half)
2   teapoons cornstarch

    1   tablespoon dry sherry or shao hsing wine,* or more, if
           desired
2 to 3 cups water
    1   quart Rich Chicken Broth (see recipe)
        Salt and freshly ground pepper to taste

* Available in Chinese markets and by mail order. For more information see Chapter XI.

1. Place the can of abalone in a kettle and add water to cover. Bring to a boil and let boil 1 hour. Let cool before opening.

2. Place the skinned and boned chicken breast half on a flat surface and, holding the knife at an angle, slice as thin as possible. (This is easier to do if the meat is partially frozen.) Flatten each slice lightly with the side of a knife. There should be about ½ cup of slices.

3. Beat the egg white lightly. Blend the cornstarch and wine and stir into the egg white to make a light paste. Add the chicken slices and stir to coat. Refrigerate 30 minutes or longer.

4. Open the can of abalone and reserve the liquid. Remove 5 of the abalone to be used in the soup and reserve the rest for another use. (To store, place the leftover abalone in a glass jar and add the reserved liquid.)

5. Slice the 5 abalone into very thin round slices. There should be about ½ cup. Set aside.

6. Bring the 2 to 3 cups of water to a boil. Turn off the heat and add the chicken slices. Stir just until the pieces are separated. Let stand 10 seconds, no longer, then drain immediately and drop into cold water. Drain once more.

7. Bring the chicken broth to a boil. Add the abalone and chicken and return to a boil. Add salt to taste and, if desired, a little more wine to taste. Sprinkle with pepper and serve.

YIELD: 4 to 8 servings

This is an altogether uncommon meat ball dish to Western palates. The beef balls here contain bean curd as an essential ingredient.

BEAN CURD AND BEEF BALL SOUP

½　cup chopped scallions, green part included
½　pound ground beef
2　teaspoons cornstarch
　　Salt to taste
¼　teaspoon monosodium glutamate (optional)
1　pad fresh white bean curd *
4 to 5　cups Rich Chicken Broth (see recipe)
2 or 3　leaves iceberg lettuce, quartered
　　Freshly ground pepper to taste

* Available in Chinese markets and by mail order. For more information see Chapter XI.

1. Place the scallions in a cup and add boiling water to barely cover. Let stand.
2. Place the beef in a mixing bowl and add the cornstarch, salt, and monosodium glutamate. Strain out 1 tablespoon of water from the scallions and add it, discarding the rest of the scallion liquid and the scallions. Mix well with the fingers.
3. Squeeze the pad of bean curd with your hand and add it to the beef. Continue to knead the beef with the bean curd until thoroughly homogenized. Shape into 16 or 18 balls, each measuring about 1½ inches.
4. Heat the chicken broth, and when it is almost boiling drop in the meat balls. Let simmer until they rise to the surface, 15 to 20 minutes. Add salt to taste to the soup.
5. Put the iceberg lettuce into a soup bowl and sprinkle liberally with pepper. Pour in the soup and the meat balls and serve piping hot.

YIELD: 6 to 8 servings

This is an uncommon and an uncommonly good soup made with a mousselike liver mixture steamed with chicken broth. The liver is delicately seasoned with ginger and scallion juice.

LIVER SOUP

1   pound chicken livers, picked over well to remove tough connective tissue
2   tablespoons finely minced fresh ginger *
3   tablespoons chopped scallions, green part included
6   tablespoons water
3   eggs
     Salt to taste
¼   teaspoon monosodium glutamate (optional)
½   teaspoon finely ground pepper, preferably white
½   teaspoon sugar
6   cups Rich Chicken Broth (see recipe)
1   tablespoon dry sherry or shao hsing wine *
¼   cup finely minced fresh coriander *

* Available in Chinese markets and by mail order. For more information see Chapter XI.

1. Cut the livers into small pieces and put into the container of an electric blender. Blend on high speed from 1 to 2 minutes, or until finely pureed.
2. Line a heatproof bowl with a clean linen or cotton cloth and pour in the liver puree. Gather up the edges of the cloth to form a bag and, holding the bag over the bowl, carefully squeeze the sides to gently force the liver through.
3. Combine the ginger, scallions, and water in the blender container. Blend well about 2 minutes. Strain this juice through a clean cloth into a small bowl. Add 3½ tablespoons of the ginger-scallion liquid to the liver.
4. Break the eggs into a bowl and add the salt, monosodium glutamate, pepper, and sugar. Beat to blend thoroughly, then beat

this mixture into the liver mixture. Stir in ¾ cup of the chicken broth, then stir in the wine. Place the bowl in the top of a steamer and steam, covered, over low boiling water 15 minutes, or until set.

5. Bring the remaining chicken broth to a boil, and when ready to serve pour the chicken broth gently over the liver and sprinkle the minced coriander over the soup. Serve spoonfuls of the liver and the broth in individual bowls.

YIELD: 6 to 8 servings

The following soup made with dried mushrooms and chicken wings is the essence of simplicity. The soup is steamed and the broth comes out clean and pure. In China, a similar soup is made with the mushrooms and chicken feet, rather than wings.

CHICKEN WING AND MUSHROOM SOUP *

16 to 20	medium dried black mushrooms *
2	cups boiling water, approximately
10	chicken wings
2	teaspoons rendered chicken fat (see Chapter XI)
	Salt to taste
2	tablespoons dry sherry or shao hsing wine *
¼	teaspoon monosodium glutamate (optional)

* Available in Chinese markets and by mail order. For more information see Chapter XI.

1. Place the mushrooms in a bowl and add about 2 cups of boiling water. Let stand 15 to 30 minutes.

2. Remove the mushrooms, but reserve the soaking liquid. Squeeze the mushrooms to remove most of the moisture, then cut off and discard the stems. Leave the caps whole.

3. Divide the wings at the joints. Discard the wing tips. Arrange the main wing bones and second joints over the bottom of a soup dish or other bowl that may be used for steaming. (A 7- or 8-cup soufflé dish would be good for this.)

4. Rub the mushroom caps with the chicken fat, then arrange the caps, stem side down, over the chicken pieces.

5. Measure the reserved mushroom liquid (discarding any sediment) and add enough water to make 5 cups in all. Pour over the chicken and mushrooms and add the remaining ingredients. Set the bowl in the top of a steamer, cover, and steam over boiling water 2½ hours.

YIELD: 6 to 8 servings

Some foods have a natural affinity for each other, and they include the pork balls that complement the watercress in this excellent soup. It has cellophane noodles (sometimes called "bean thread") as an added fillip.

WATERCRESS AND PORK BALL SOUP

½ pound ground pork
    Minced fresh ginger * squeezed through cheesecloth to produce 1 teaspoon of fresh ginger juice (if fresh ginger is not available, soak whole dried ginger overnight and grate it)
½ teaspoon sugar
4 teaspoons cornstarch
    Salt to taste
2 teaspoons dry sherry or shao hsing wine *
¼ teaspoon monosodium glutamate (optional)
4 teaspoons beaten egg (beat 1 whole egg and measure out the correct amount)
5 cups Rich Chicken Broth (see recipe)
¼ pound watercress, rinsed and trimmed of tough stems
2 ounces cellophane noodles (bean thread, transparent noodles),* soaked in warm water 30 minutes
    Freshly ground pepper to taste

* Available in Chinese markets and by mail order. For more information see Chapter XI.

1. Place the pork, ginger juice, sugar, cornstarch, salt, wine, monosodium glutamate, and egg in a mixing bowl and blend with your fingers.

2. Lightly oil a plate that will fit in the top of a steamer. Shape the pork into 16 to 18 balls with oiled fingers and arrange them on the plate. Place the plate in the top of the steamer, cover, and steam the balls over boiling water for 20 minutes.

3. Meanwhile, bring the chicken broth to a boil.

4. Similarly, bring enough water to a boil to cover the watercress when it is added. Add the watercress, immediately turn off the heat, and let stand about 2 minutes. Drain and drop at once into a basin of cold water.

5. Put the cellophane noodles into a saucepan, cover with cold water, and bring to a boil. Boil for 10 minutes, add watercress and bring to a boil, then drain and place in the bottom of a soup tureen.

6. Put the piping hot soup and meat balls into the tureen. Sprinkle with pepper and serve.

YIELD: 6 to 8 servings

This is a very simple soup that makes use of leftover raw chicken giblets.

WATERCRESS AND CHICKEN GIBLET SOUP

3   chicken necks
3   chicken gizzards
3   chicken hearts
     Any available spare chicken bones
1   quart water
3   chicken livers
1   bunch fresh watercress, picked over and any tough stems
         removed
     Salt to taste
¼   teaspoon monosodium glutamate (optional)

1. Place the chicken necks, gizzards, hearts, and bones in a low 1½-quart dish that will fit in the top of a steamer. Add the 1 quart water and place, uncovered, in the top of the steamer. Do not add salt. Steam over boiling water for 1 hour or longer, until the meat is tender.

2. Cover the chicken livers with boiling water and let stand 15 minutes, until half cooked. Drain.

3. Meanwhile, drop the watercress into boiling water and immediately turn off the heat. Let stand about 1½ minutes. Drain and immediately run under cold water, then drain again. Gather the stems together neatly to reconstitute a bunch and cut the bunch a little bit on both sides to make it neat. Set aside.

4. Remove the hearts, gizzards, necks, and bones from the broth in the steamer. Discard the hearts, necks, and bones and sieve the broth into another container. Cut the gizzards lengthwise into thin slices and return these to the broth. Add the chicken livers, cut into pieces, salt to taste, and the monosodium glutamate. Add the blanched watercress, bring to a boil, and serve.

YIELD: 4 to 6 servings

There is one Chinese dish that Americans "discovered" during the past decade, and it became uncommonly popular as time progressed. This was mo-shu-ro, a blend of tree ear mushrooms, tiger lily stems, and shredded pork, all cooked and scrambled with egg and various seasonings. Mo-shu in that form is served with rice or rolled in pancakes. The following is also a mo-shu dish, similar in ingredients, but this time a soup.

MO-SHU SOUP

16	tree ear mushrooms *
⅛	pound finely shredded pork (about ¼ cup)
1	teaspoon light soy sauce *
1	teaspoon plus 3 tablespoons cornstarch
20	tiger lily stems *
10	spinach leaves, tough stems removed
2	eggs
¼	cup water
1	quart Rich Chicken Broth (see recipe)
	Salt to taste
¼	teaspoon or more ground white pepper

* Available in Chinese markets and by mail order. For more information see Chapter XI.

1. Place the tree ears in a mixing bowl and pour boiling water over them. Let stand 15 to 30 minutes or longer, then drain. Cut off and discard the small hard base, if necessary.

2. Place the pork in a bowl and add the soy sauce and the teaspoon cornstarch. Blend well and let stand.

3. Soak the tiger lily stems in boiling water for 10 to 15 minutes, until they expand. Cut off the tough dark ends and shred the stems into fibers with your fingers.

4. Drop the spinach leaves into boiling water to cover. When the water boils again, drain immediately. Run cold water over the leaves and set aside.

5. Beat the eggs and set them aside. Blend the 3 tablespoons cornstarch with the ¼ cup water and set aside.

6. Bring about 3 cups of water to a boil and turn off the heat. Immediately add the pork and stir around to separate the shreds. Let stand 1 minute, then drain.

7. Bring the broth to a simmer and add the tree ears and tiger lily stems. Add salt to taste, the spinach, and the pork. When the broth resumes a boil, add the cornstarch-water mixture, stirring constantly.

8. Pour the soup into a soup bowl and immediately but gradually add the egg in a steady stream, stirring constantly. Serve sprinkled with ground pepper.

YIELD: 4 to 6 servings

The vegetable commonly called "Szechwan cabbage" in English is not really cabbage at all but a form of radish preserved with hot chilies. It is available in tins imported from the Orient, and on most cans it is labeled "Szechwan preserved vegetable." It is a spicy, intriguing food, and it goes well with pork in soup.

SZECHWAN CABBAGE AND PORK SOUP

¼   pound shredded pork
½   teaspoon cornstarch
1   tablespoon dry sherry or shao hsing wine *
1   teaspoon dark soy sauce *
1   teaspoon light soy sauce *
1   tablespoon peanut, vegetable, or corn oil
¾   cup shredded bamboo shoots *
1   quart Rich Chicken Broth (see recipe)
½   cup shredded Szechwan preserved vegetable *

* Available in Chinese markets and by mail order. For more information see Chapter XI.

1. Place the pork in a mixing bowl and add the cornstarch, wine, and soy sauces. Blend with your fingers.

2. Heat the oil in a saucepan and add the pork. Cook, stirring, over high heat about 2 minutes. Add the bamboo shoots and cook briefly, stirring.

3. Heat the chicken broth, and when it is simmering add the pork, bamboo shoots, and shredded Szechwan preserved vegetable. Bring to a boil and cook 1 minute. Serve.

YIELD: 4 to 6 servings

Dried shrimps, available in abundance in Chinese grocery stores, give an excellent flavor to this cucumber soup.

CUCUMBER AND DRIED SHRIMP SOUP ❖

5 cups water
⅛ cup small dried shrimps *
2 cups peeled, seeded cucumber, cut into "sticks" like French-fried potatoes (about 1 inch long)
¼ teaspoon monosodium glutamate
    Salt to taste

* Available in Chinese markets and by mail order. For more information see Chapter XI.

1. Bring the water to a boil and add the remaining ingredients.

2. Simmer 20 to 30 minutes, or until the shrimps are soft and the cucumber is tender.

YIELD: 6 to 8 servings

Whiting, one of the most delicate of fish in Western waters, is particularly well suited to numerous Chinese dishes. Here it is used with bean curd in soup.

WHITING AND BEAN CURD SOUP

2 whitings (about ½ pound each), cleaned, scaled, and head and tail removed
2 tablespoons rendered chicken fat (see Chapter XI)
1½ pads fresh white bean curd *
5 cups Rich Chicken Broth (see recipe)
¼ cup shredded bamboo shoots *
3 slices fresh ginger,* peeled
½ teaspoon monosodium glutamate (optional)
Salt to taste
1½ tablespoons cornstarch
¼ cup water
2 tablespoons dry sherry or shao hsing wine *
Freshly ground pepper to taste
1 egg white
3 tablespoons chopped fresh coriander * (optional)
¼ cup chopped scallions, green part included

* Available in Chinese markets and by mail order. For more information see Chapter XI.

1. Drop the whitings into boiling water to cover and simmer about 1 minute. Turn off the heat and let stand about 5 minutes, then drain.

2. When cool enough to handle, remove the skin and bones. Break the fillets into bite-size morsels. Pour the chicken fat over them and set aside.

3. Cut the bean curd into ½-inch cubes and set aside.

4. Put the chicken broth into a kettle and add the bean curd, bamboo shoots, and ginger. Bring to a boil, then add the monosodium glutamate and salt. Combine the cornstarch and water and stir in. Boil briskly and add the fish, wine, and pepper. Turn off the heat

and immediately but gradually add the egg white, while stirring in a circular motion with chopsticks or a fork. Pour the soup into a hot soup tureen and sprinkle with the chopped coriander, if desired, and the scallions.

YIELD: 6 to 8 servings

The bean curd soup below is a work of palatal art. The bean curd is blended until smooth with a fine puree of chicken, then the mixture is molded, decorated on top, and steamed. It is served in a rich broth with mushrooms and ham.

FLOWERY BEAN CURD SOUP

2   large and 3 small dried black mushrooms *
4   ¼-inch slices fresh ginger,* crushed
1   scallion, green part included, trimmed, crushed, and cut into
        pieces
     Water
¼   pound skinless, boneless chicken breast
1   egg white
1   tablespoon dry sherry or shao hsing wine *
¾   teaspoon ground white pepper
     Salt to taste
¼   teaspoon monosodium glutamate (optional)
2   pads fresh white bean curd *
2   fresh coriander * or watercress sprigs for decoration
     Shredded ham for decoration
1   quart Rich Chicken Broth (see recipe)
3   thin squares or rectangles of Smithfield ham
8   small snow peas *

* Available in Chinese markets and by mail order. For more information see Chapter XI.

1. Put the mushrooms into a mixing bowl and add boiling water to cover. Let stand 15 to 30 minutes.

2. Put the crushed ginger and scallion into a small bowl and add ¼ cup water. Let stand 30 minutes.

3. Cut the chicken breast into small cubes and put them into the container of an electric blender.

4. To the blender container add the egg white, wine, ¼ teaspoon of the ground pepper, salt, the monosodium glutamate, and 2 tablespoons of the ginger-scallion juice. (Discard the remaining ginger-scallion juice or reserve it for another use.) Blend the chicken mixture, stirring down as necessary to make a fine puree.

5. Crush the bean curd and add it to the chicken mixture. Blend, stirring down as necessary to make a fine, but not too thin puree. It may be necessary to add up to 1 tablespoon of water to make this blend properly.

6. Lightly grease an 8-inch pie plate with chicken fat or a little peanut, vegetable, or corn oil. Scoop out the blender mixture into the pie plate and smooth the top.

7. Squeeze the mushrooms to extract most of the moisture. Cut off and discard the tough stems. Set the 2 large mushrooms aside.

8. Shred the 3 small mushrooms and decorate the top of the bean curd mixture with the shredded mushroom, sprigs of coriander or watercress, and shreds of ham.

9. Place the pie plate in the top of a steamer, cover, and steam over simmering water 15 minutes.

10. Bring the chicken broth to a boil and add the 2 large mushrooms.

11. Sprinkle the bottom of a soup bowl with the remaining ½ teaspoon of ground white pepper and add the ham squares or rectangles and snow peas. Pour the broth with mushrooms into the bowl. Carefully remove the pie plate from the steamer and gently slip the bean curd "custard" into the soup without breaking it.

YIELD: 6 to 8 servings

The following dish is a far more elaborate and elegant dish than the name might imply. In addition to bean curd, it contains chicken, ham, bamboo shoots, mushrooms, and shrimp.

BEAN CURD CASSEROLE SOUP ❖

8   pads fresh white bean curd *
5 or 6   dried black mushrooms *
1   whole chicken (2½ to 3 pounds)
½   cup finely shredded ham, preferably Smithfield ham
¾   cup finely shredded bamboo shoots *
¾   cup small or medium raw shrimps, shelled, deveined, and cut in half
1   tablespoon cornstarch
1   cup peanut, vegetable, or corn oil
1½   quarts Rich Chicken Broth (see recipe)
    Salt to taste
¼   teaspoon monosodium glutamate (optional)

* Available in Chinese markets and by mail order. For more information see Chapter XI.

1. Rinse the bean curd pads and make 4 stacks of 2 each. Place the stacks in a suitable utensil in which the bean curd may be weighted down. Cover with a double fold of waxed paper and place one or more heavy weights on top, making sure that the weight is evenly distributed. (We use a round-bottomed pot filled with water and placed directly on the waxed paper-wrapped bean curd.) Let stand 24 hours or longer in a cool place.

2. When ready to cook, place the chicken in a saucepan and add cold water to cover. Cover the saucepan, bring to a boil, and simmer 15 minutes. Turn off the heat and let the chicken stand until lukewarm. Remove the breast meat from the chicken in whole pieces. Reserve the rest of the chicken and broth for another use.

3. Remove the weights from the bean curd pads and place the pads on a flat surface. Prepare them, one at a time, by slicing them horizontally, then cutting these slices into fine, even shreds. As

each bean curd is cut, drop the shreds into a basin of cold water. Drain and pour hot, almost boiling, water over them. Repeat this 3 times, ending by rinsing in cold water. Drain. There should be about 4 cups of bean curd. Arrange the bean curd in the bottom of a deep heatproof serving dish or casserole.

4. Place the mushrooms in a mixing bowl and add boiling water to cover. Let stand 15 to 30 minutes, then drain. Cut off and discard the tough stems and cut the caps into shreds. There should be about ½ cup. Arrange the shreds in a neat pile beside the bean curd in the soup bowl.

5. Cut the chicken breast into very neat shreds and arrange the shreds in a separate neat pile near the bean curd.

6. Similarly, arrange the ham and bamboo shoots around the bean curd.

7. Blend the shrimps with the cornstarch to coat evenly.

8. Heat the oil in a wok or skillet. Add the shrimps and cook, stirring, over high heat about 1 minute or less. If cooked longer, they will toughen. Set aside.

9. Slowly pour the broth into the casserole, bring to a boil, and add salt and the monosodium glutamate. Simmer 50 minutes. Arrange the shrimps beside the bean curd, then simmer 10 minutes longer.

YIELD: 8 to 12 servings

Note: This soup may be made with 1½ quarts of broth made from the same chicken. To do so, cook the whole chicken in 10 cups of water for 15 minutes as described in step 2. Remove the breast meat, then restore the rest of the chicken to the broth and simmer for about 2 hours, or until the broth is reduced to 6 cups. Let the chicken cool in the broth, then discard the chicken and strain the stock. Proceed with the recipe.

One of the rarities of the Chinese kitchen is a white fungus which, when cooked, has a delicate texture and flavor. It resembles, except for its color, tree ear mushrooms, which are common wherever Chinese staples are sold. One of the uses for the white fungus, when it is available, is in a highly refined steamed soup with squab.

STEAMED SQUAB SOUP ❖

2   whole squab, preferably with heads left on but carefully plucked and cleaned
5   cups Rich Chicken Broth (see recipe)
½   cup white fungus *
    Salt to taste
¼   teaspoon monosodium glutamate (optional)

* Available in Chinese markets and by mail order. For more information see Chapter XI.

1. Put the squab into a saucepan and cover with boiling water. Boil for 1 minute after the water returns to a boil. Drain and run the squab under cold water.
2. Select a soup dish large enough to contain the squab, broth, and fungus with some room to spare.
3. Place the dish in the top of a large steamer, such as a large bamboo steamer or a clam steamer (if the clam steamer is used, first add a cheesecloth sling to facilitate removing the dish when it is ready). Set the steamer top over a large quantity of boiling water.
4. Place the squab and broth in the dish and cover the steamer. Steam 2 hours.
5. Meanwhile, place the white fungus in a bowl and pour 3 cups or so of boiling water over it. Let stand 30 minutes and drain. Place the fungus in a saucepan and add more cold water to cover. Simmer about 5 minutes, then drain and set aside.
6. Add the salt and monosodium glutamate to the broth. Steam about 1 hour longer and add the fungus. Steam 1 hour longer. The meat of the squab should, by this time, be quite easy to remove

from the bones with chopsticks. Serve bits of squab, fungus, and the broth in soup bowls.

YIELD: 6 to 8 servings

There is a soup in the Chinese repertoire that is quite as handsome as it is edible, and it is called Three-Color Delicious Soup. The name derives from the white of a forcemeat of chicken dropped into the simmering broth, the green of peas, and the red of tomato.

THREE-COLOR DELICIOUS SOUP

½ large chicken breast (about ½ pound or less), skinned and boned
1 egg white
1 tablespoon milk
Salt to taste
1 medium tomato (about ⅓ pound)
5 cups Rich Chicken Broth (see recipe)
¼ teaspoon monosodium glutamate (optional)
¾ cup cooked fresh or frozen green peas
3 tablespoons cornstarch (optional)
¼ cup water (optional)
2 egg whites

1. Cut the chicken breast into cubes and drop it into the container of an electric blender. Add the egg white, milk, and salt. Blend, stirring down as necessary, to make a thick puree. There should be about ⅔ cup. Spoon the mixture into a pastry bag fitted with a No. 6 pastry tube.
2. Peel and seed the tomato. A simple way to do this is to drop the tomato into boiling water for approximately 12 seconds. Drain immediately and pull away the skin with a small knife. Remove the core of the tomato and slice it in half around the middle. Take one

half in the palm of your hand and squeeze it gently as you would an orange. Squeeze only enough to remove the seeds without bruising the flesh. Repeat with the other half.

3. Cut the tomato into small cubes and set aside. There should be about ¾ cup.

4. Bring the chicken broth to a boil and add salt and the monosodium glutamate. Add the peas and tomato cubes and turn off the heat.

5. Immediately start squeezing the chicken mixture through the tube into the broth, cutting off portions with a knife or spoon. The portions should be about ½ inch long or smaller.

6. Bring the broth to a boil again. The broth may be served at this point, or it may be slightly thickened. To do this, blend the cornstarch with the water and stir it into the simmering soup.

7. Put the soup into a serving bowl. Lightly beat the 2 egg whites and pour them into the soup in a thin stream, stirring constantly.

YIELD: 6 to 8 servings

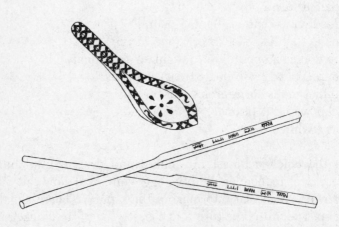

The following is a fascinating soup with what anyone will take to be made with an impressively rich stock. Actually the liquid is plain water, which, oddly enough, brings out the flavor of the other ingredients, the pork and bamboo shoots, but principally the Szechwan preserved vegetable.

SZECHWAN PRESERVED VEGETABLE SOUP

¼ pound pork
1 tablespoon light soy sauce *
1 teaspoon cornstarch
1 to 3 pieces Szechwan preserved vegetable *
1 tablespoon peanut, vegetable, or corn oil
5 cups water
Salt to taste
½ cup finely shredded bamboo shoots *

* Available in Chinese markets and by mail order. For more information see Chapter XI.

1. Place the pork on a flat surface and slice it against the grain into the thinnest possible slices. Carefully cut each slice into fine shreds. (This is easier to do if the meat is partially frozen before slicing and the slices stacked before shredding.) Put the shreds into a mixing bowl and add the soy sauce and cornstarch. Set aside.

2. Rinse the vegetable well under cold running water and pat dry. Slice it thin, then cut it into fine shreds. There should be about 1 cup.

3. Heat the oil and add the pork. Cook, stirring, about 1 minute.

4. Combine the pork and water and bring to a boil. Add salt to taste, the preserved vegetable, and the bamboo shoots. Boil for 2 minutes and serve.

YIELD: 6 to 8 servings

In Western culture rolled fish, meat, or poultry dishes are quite common in the kitchen repertory, specifically in such recipes as paupiettes of veal or turbans of sole or roulades. They exist, too, in the Chinese kitchen, as evidenced in the soup that follows. It consists of flounder fillets stuffed with an elegant mixture of chicken and pork and lightly seasoned with ginger and scallions. The fish rolls are served with cooked celery cabbage in a rich chicken broth.

FISH ROLL WITH CELERY CABBAGE SOUP

½   chicken breast, skinned, boned, and cut into cubes
3   tablespoons water
⅛   pound ground pork (about ⅓ cup)
1   teaspoon finely chopped fresh ginger *
2   teaspoons finely chopped scallions, green part included
½   teaspoon monosodium glutamate (optional)
½   teaspoon dry sherry or shao hsing wine *
¼   teaspoon finely ground pepper
½   beaten egg (beat 1 whole egg and divide in half)
     Salt to taste
¼   teaspoon sugar
½ to ¾   pound flounder fillets (1 or 2 fillets)
1   egg
2   tablespoons cornstarch
1   small head celery cabbage *
4¾   cups Rich Chicken Broth (see recipe)

* Available in Chinese markets and by mail order. For more information see Chapter XI.

1. Place the chicken breast in the container of an electric blender and add the water. Blend, stirring down as necessary, to make a fine puree. Empty the mixture into a mixing bowl.
2. Add the pork, ginger, scallions, half the monosodium glutamate, wine, pepper, the ½ beaten egg, salt, and sugar. Stir to blend well.
3. Place each flounder fillet on a flat surface. Hold a sharp slicing

knife at a close angle to the fish and very carefully cut the fillets into thin slices, the thinner the better. The pieces should measure approximately 1½ to 3½ inches or slightly larger. They will be irregular, of course.

4. Beat the egg with the cornstarch until well blended. Lay the slices of fish on a flat surface and brush the pieces one at a time with the cornstarch and egg mixture. As each piece is brushed add about 1 teaspoon of the chicken and pork mixture. Roll the slices jelly-roll fashion. Continue until all are filled and rolled.

5. Lightly oil a round dish, such as a dinner plate, that will fit into the top of a steamer. Arrange the fish rolls on it and steam the rolls, covered, over boiling water 8 minutes or less. Remove the plate and carefully pour off the accumulated liquid. Cover until ready to use.

6. Meanwhile, remove the large outer leaves from the cabbage to get at the more tender inner leaves. Trim off the tough base. Cut these leaves into 2-inch lengths, then split them in half or quarter them. There should be about 3½ cups. Drop the leaves into boiling water to cover and simmer 8 minutes. Drain and immediately run under cold water. Place them in a casserole and add about ¾ cup chicken broth. Bring just to a boil and set aside.

7. When ready to serve, bring the remaining 4 cups of chicken broth to a boil. Arrange the fish rolls over the bottom of a soup bowl. Drain the cabbage. Surround the fish rolls with the cabbage and pour the hot broth over all.

YIELD: 6 to 10 servings

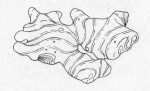

HOT POTS

In the world of food, one of the most extraordinary phenomena of recent years has been the incredible popularity of those dishes known—improperly, we think—as fondues. The name derives from the French word meaning "melted" and began with cheese fondue, which means "melted cheese." It is, of course, a "group-participation" dish, and the word came to mean any and all such dishes in which guests helped themselves to a common bubbling pot or casserole.

Interestingly enough, the original such dish may have come from China, and it is called Mongolian Hot Pot. It is said to have been introduced to China in the thirteenth century when the Mongol hordes invaded the nation, and it is certainly one of the most interesting and appetizing of those dishes where guests help themselves and create their own sauce.

The way it works is this: Guests are supplied with numerous plates on which are arranged thinly sliced meat such as lamb or beef. Using chopsticks or long forks, the guests spear or take up one or more pieces of meat at a time and dip them into a boiling liquid placed in the center of the table. The meat is cooked quickly—or to any desired degree of doneness—and while piping hot it is dipped into a special and savory sauce served in individual serving bowls. After the meat is eaten, other ingredients are cooked in the simmering liquid, and these, too, are dipped into the sauce before eating. Eventually the liquid is ladled into the individual bowls, onto the remaining sauce, and it is drunk as a sauce soup. In China, guests prepare their own sauce according to taste. For the Western public we offer a master sauce that guests may take and then improvise on.

The traditional hot pot is a round affair, a circular basin containing water that surrounds a chimney containing charcoal. As the charcoal ignites, the water boils. Any modern fondue pot or electric skillet that can sustain boiling when foods are dipped into it can be used for this dish.

MONGOLIAN HOT POT

The dipping materials:

    1   leg of lamb (6 or 7 pounds), boned, or 4 pounds boneless top round

3 or 4   quarts lamb broth (see Note) or lightly salted water

    ½   head of celery cabbage,* trimmed and cut into bite-size morsels

    ½   pound spinach, trimmed, rinsed well, and patted dry

    ½   pound cellophane noodles (bean thread, transparent noodles) *

    6   pads fresh white bean curd *

The master sauce:

    1   cup sesame oil *

    1   cup red wine vinegar

    ½   cup hot oil,* homemade or bottled

    1   cup fish sauce *

    1   cup red bean curd sauce *

¾ to 1   cup sesame paste *

  1¼ cups brewed tea

    ¾   cup sugar

    ½   cup light soy sauce *

        Salt to taste

Additions for the sauce to which guests may help themselves:

    ¼   cup finely chopped garlic

    ½   cup salted Chinese chives * or chopped fresh chives

    ½   cup light soy sauce *

    ½   cup fish sauce *

    ½   cup sugar

    ½   cup red wine vinegar

    ½   cup finely chopped scallions, green part included

    1   cup chopped fresh coriander *

    ¼   cup salt

        Sesame Seed Buns (see recipe; optional)

* Available in Chinese markets and by mail order. For more information see Chapter XI.

1. The leg of lamb or the beef should be sliced as thin as possible. To do this, it is recommended that the meat be frozen and partially thawed if it is to be sliced with a knife—or the butcher can slice it on a professional machine while the meat is frozen or partially so. Arrange a single layer of meat, about 2 to 4 ounces, on individual plates and chill. (Do not stack because the meat slices will stick together.)

2. Prepare the sesame seed buns. These are traditionally served with Mongolian hot pot and may be prepared in advance and reheated.

3. Prepare the water bath in which the meat and vegetables are to be dipped. If you use a traditional hot pot with chimney, begin by placing unfired charcoal in the chimney. Place the hot pot on a fireproof surface. Fifteen to 20 minutes before you are ready to eat, pour the broth or water into the ring basin that surrounds the chimney. (Do not ignite the charcoal until there is liquid in the ring, or the heat will melt the sealing parts of the utensil.) Ignite the charcoal to fiery hot, which will cause the water or stock to boil. Or you may put the liquid into a fondue pot or two or into an electric utensil and bring to a boil. Place the hot pot or fondue pot in the center of a table around which guests may sit or stand and circulate.

4. Arrange the cabbage and spinach in separate serving bowls and place around the hot pot.

5. Pour boiling water over the cellophane noodles and let stand until softened, about 5 to 10 minutes. Drain and put into a bowl. Place around the hot pot.

6. Cut the bean curd pads into smaller, bite-size squares, and put into a bowl around the hot pot.

7. Combine all the ingredients for the master sauce and stir to blend. Place the master sauce in one large bowl and put near the hot pot. Place the garlic, chives, soy sauce, fish sauce, sugar, vinegar, scallions, coriander leaves, and salt in smaller bowls around it.

8. Reheat the sesame seed buns in the oven, if necessary, and place around the hot pot.

9. Put several plates of the meat, depending on the size of the

table, around the hot pot. Replenish with fresh dishes of meat from the refrigerator as necessary.

10. Seat guests around the table or give each, buffet style, a dinner plate, chopsticks or a fondue fork, a soup spoon, and a small bowl, and let each guest serve himself with spoonfuls of the master sauce, putting it into the bowl. Let each help himself to additional flavorings for the sauce, such as garlic, chives, and so on.

11. Each guest, using chopsticks or a fondue fork, lifts up pieces of meat and dips them into the boiling liquid and then into the sauce before eating. After the guests have eaten enough meat, add the celery cabbage, spinach, cellophane noodles, and bean curd to the hot pot as desired. Cook only to heat through and eat—like the meat—by dipping first in the sauce. When all the meat and vegetables have been eaten, guests may spoon the hot pot liquid into the sauce remaining in their sauce bowls and drink it as a sauce soup.

YIELD: Serves 12 or more guests

Note: To make the lamb broth, add water to cover over the lamb bones and scraps left over from the leg. Do not add salt. Bring to a boil, then reduce the heat. Simmer 2 hours and skim.

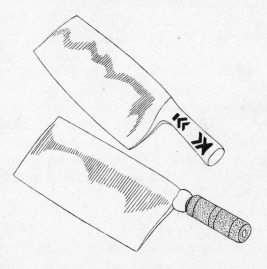

CHRYSANTHEMUM HOT POT

  2 raw chicken breasts, skinned and boned
  ½ cup dry sherry or shao hsing wine *
  ½ pound flank steak or other lean cut of beef, such as top round
 24 raw shrimps, peeled and deveined
  1 pound flounder or other white, non-oily fish fillets
  8 chicken livers, cleaned (optional)
  8 scallions, green part included, trimmed and cut into 2-inch lengths
 16 raw littleneck or cherrystone clams (optional)
  1 pound spinach, trimmed of tough stalks and rinsed well
  1 pound celery cabbage,* romaine lettuce, or other tender greens, cut into bite-size pieces
  4 ounces cellophane noodles (bean thread, transparent noodles)*
3 to 4 quarts boiling chicken broth or water
    Salt to taste
  1 large chrysanthemum flower (from the florist's)
6 to 8 raw eggs, one for each guest
  8 tablespoons soy sauce
    Sugar to taste
    Red wine vinegar to taste (optional)

* Available in Chinese markets and by mail order. For more information see Chapter XI.

1. Place the pieces of breast meat on a flat surface and, holding a sharp knife at an angle, slice thinly on the bias. (This is easier to do if the meat is partially frozen.) Arrange the slices on a plate.

2. Slice the beef against the grain into very thin slices. (Again, partial freezing of the meat makes this easier.) Arrange the slices on a plate.

3. "Butterfly" the shrimps by slicing almost but not quite in half lengthwise. Arrange on a plate.

4. Slice the fish fillets, like the chicken, on the bias. Arrange on a plate.

5. Slice the chicken livers, like the chicken, on the bias. Arrange on a plate.

6. Split the ends of each length of scallion and drop into cold water. Let stand until the ends curl, then drain well. Scatter the scallion "flowers" over the plates of chicken, beef, shrimp, fish, and chicken livers. Sprinkle the ½ cup wine over the meat and seafood.

7. Rinse the clams thoroughly and place them in a bowl.

8. Place the spinach in one bowl and the celery cabbage or other greens in another.

9. Pour boiling water over the cellophane noodles and let stand until softened. Drain and place in a bowl.

10. If a traditional hot pot is to be used, sit it on a fireproof surface. Place charcoal in the center section, but do not ignite it. Add the broth or water to the ring basin and then ignite the charcoal. Let the liquid come to a roaring boil. Or if an electric skillet or fondue pot is used, add the broth or water and let it come to a boil.

11. Surround the hot pot or cooking vessel with the plates and bowls of meat and vegetables. Separate the chrysanthemum flower into individual petals and place them in a bowl. Let guests help themselves to the petals.

12. Seat the guests or let them stand and circulate around the table within reach of the hot pot. Give them bowls for dipping. Break 1 egg into each bowl, and to each egg add 1 tablespoon of soy sauce and a small dash of sugar, wine, and vinegar. Beat lightly to blend. Serve with hot rice on the side, on a plate.

13. Using chopsticks or fondue forks, let the guests dip pieces of chicken, beef, shrimp, fish, chicken livers, and clams into the boiling broth. As soon as each piece is cooked, dip it immediately into the egg and soy sauce mixture. When the guests seem to have had enough of the meat and seafood, add to the boiling liquid the vegetables, a handful or so at a time, plus the cellophane noodles. Cook until wilted or thoroughly hot and dip the pieces in the sauce. When the foods have been eaten, you may add broth to each sauce and eat it as a soup.

YIELD: 6 to 8 servings

IX

Rice, Noodles, and Dumplings

The quality of rice varies, and we have found that the best rice commonly available in the United States for the Chinese kitchen is extra-long-grain rice. Specifically, we use Carolina brand.

Few Chinese cooks measure water for cooking rice by volume. Instead, they add water to a certain level above the rice and then test the depth by holding a finger in the water above the rice; it should come just to the first knuckle of the middle finger. Salt is almost never used in cooking rice in a Chinese kitchen.

HOW TO COOK RICE ❖

2   cups raw extra-long-grain rice
3   cups water

1. Pour the rice into a sieve and rinse it thoroughly under cold running water until the water runs clear. Drain.

2. Add the rice to a saucepan and add the water. (If softer rice is desired, up to an additional ½ cup water may be added.) Cook the rice, uncovered, over high heat about 10 minutes, or until "fish eyes" (tiny craters) form over the surface of the rice. Cover closely and cook over very low heat about 20 minutes longer.

YIELD: 4 or more servings

The best-known form of rice cake on Western menus is probably what is known as "sizzling rice." Rice cake probably came about by accident, like the roast pork in Charles Lamb's famed essay on the subject, although it didn't require the burning down of a house. Somebody—unintentionally, no doubt—left a rice pot over live heat for an hour or so longer than the normal cooking time. But to what must have been the cook's great pleasure, the result was altogether felicitous, and the Chinese have been doing it ever since. Rice cake is a firm, crisp mass that forms when ordinary rice is left over low heat for an hour or so after the top, separate, and perfectly cooked grains are eaten. The "overcooked" rice on the bottom takes on an admirable golden color and a nutty flavor. Nowadays the cake is deep-fried and served with a soup or a dish with a light sauce. The rice is often poured into the soup at the table, making it sizzle dramatically. A fried rice cake with sauce dish follows; rice cake can also be served with Egg Drop Soup (see recipe) or Fish Ball Soup (see recipe).

RICE CAKE ❖

2   cups raw extra-long-grain rice
3   cups water

1. This recipe for cooking rice starts out in the conventional manner. Place the rice in a sieve and rinse well under cold water. Or put it into a heavy casserole and rinse and drain several times until the water runs clear. Drain well.

2. Place the rice in a heatproof casserole and add the water. Do not add salt. Bring to a boil and cook, uncovered, about 10 minutes, until most of the liquid evaporates and "fish eyes" or tiny craters form on the surface of the rice. Cover tightly and cook over low heat at least 20 minutes.

3. Scoop the rice out neatly and carefully from the center of the pot with a spoon, and leave a border of about ½ inch around the sides and a bottom about ½ inch deep. Serve the scooped-out rice with a meal or reserve for later use.

4. Return the saucepan with the rice shell to the burner and cook over low heat, uncovered, for 1 hour, or until the rice pulls away from the sides and is easily removed. When ready the shell should be nicely dried and have a crusty brown look. Ideally, the rice can be turned out in one piece, a shell with a golden bottom. Let it cool. The rice cake can be broken into large pieces and placed in an airtight container. It will keep in this way for several weeks.

One of the simplest rice cake dishes is Fried Rice Cake with Shrimps. It includes not only shrimps but chicken served hot in a light tomato sauce. It is too light to serve as a meal in itself, but is very satisfying served with one or more other dishes.

FRIED RICE CAKE WITH SHRIMPS

½   pound raw shrimps (about 14 shrimps), shelled and deveined
½   chicken breast (about ½ pound), skinned and boned
   Cornstarch
1   egg white, lightly beaten
1   piece of bamboo shoot,* enough to yield about ⅓ cup when cut into thin slices
5   dried black mushrooms *
3   tablespoons water
   Peanut, vegetable, or corn oil
⅓   cup catsup
2   tablespoons tomato paste
1½   teaspoons sugar
   Salt to taste
2   cups chicken broth
3   scallions, green part included, trimmed, halved lengthwise, and cut into 2-inch pieces
   Rice Cake (see recipe), broken into pieces

* Available in Chinese markets and by mail order. For more information see Chapter XI.

1. Split each shrimp in half (lengthwise, as if butterflying) and put into a small bowl.

2. Place the chicken breast on a flat surface and, holding the knife at an angle to the breast, cut it into the thinnest possible slices. (This is easier to do if the meat is partially frozen.) Put the chicken into a small bowl.

3. Add 1 teaspoon cornstarch to the shrimp and ½ teaspoon to the chicken. Divide the egg white in half, and add one half to the shrimp and the other half to the chicken. Blend both mixtures and refrigerate for at least 30 minutes.

4. Slice the bamboo shoot and set aside.

5. Soak the mushrooms in boiling water to cover for 15 to 30 minutes. Squeeze dry, then cut off and discard the stems and cut the mushrooms into halves or quarters. Set aside.

6. Combine 1½ tablespoons cornstarch with the 3 tablespoons water and set aside.

7. Heat 1 cup of oil in a wok or skillet, and when it is warm add the chicken and turn off the heat. Cook, stirring, to separate the pieces. Remove the chicken with a slotted spoon and drain it in a sieve-lined bowl. Leave the oil in the pan.

8. Heat the oil again, and when it is warm add the shrimps, stirring. When they curl and turn pink, drain into the sieve-lined bowl holding the chicken.

9. Pour off all but 2 tablespoons of oil from the pan and add the mushrooms and bamboo shoot. Stir about 1 minute over high heat, then add the catsup, tomato paste, sugar, and salt. Cook briefly over medium heat, stirring constantly, until the sauce is slightly darker. Add the chicken broth and bring to a boil. Add the shrimps and chicken and cook, stirring, for a few seconds. Add the cornstarch mixture and cook till thickened, then add the scallions. Turn off the heat and leave the sauce in the pan while preparing the rice cake.

10. Put oil for deep frying in a wok or deep-fryer, and when it is very hot (about 450 degrees), add about half the amount of rice cake. To test the oil, you may add a small piece of rice cake; if the oil is ready, it should come to the surface quickly and puff lightly. When half the rice cake pieces are fried, drain and add the remainder. Cook until golden brown. Drain on paper toweling.

11. Arrange the rice cake on a hot platter and pour the sauce over all. Serve immediately. Part of the fried rice cake can be served on the side, if desired; it will stay crisper.

YIELD: 4 to 8 servings

As far as we know, dried mouth mushrooms are nowhere available in the United States. They are a highly prized delicacy in China and rare even there. They are somewhat grayish, with a distinctive perfume all their own. We are including this recipe in the hope that someday they may be made available here. In any event, the recipe is for the record.

FRIED RICE CAKE WITH MOUTH MUSHROOM SOUP

⅛   pound dried mouth mushrooms
6   cups boiling water
1   cup cold water, approximately
    Salt to taste
    Peanut, vegetable, or corn oil for deep frying
4   cups loosely packed Rice Cake (see recipe)

1. Place the mouth mushrooms in a bowl and add the boiling water. Let stand until cool.

2. Do not drain the mushrooms, because the liquid will be used later for the soup. Instead, remove them with a slotted spoon and, with your fingers, wash them well under cold running water.

3. Carefully pour the mushroom liquid from one container to another, leaving the sandy deposit in the bottom of the first bowl. Return the rinsed mushrooms to the liquid and let stand 6 hours or longer. Repeat once more, removing the mushrooms, pouring off and saving the liquid, and returning the mushrooms to the liquid.

4. As a final step, remove the mushrooms once more and rinse well. Pour off the clear mushroom liquid into a saucepan. There

should be about 4 cups. Add enough water to make 5 cups. Add the mushrooms and bring to a boil. Add salt to taste.

5. Heat the oil very hot for deep frying and add half the rice cake. Cook quickly about 15 seconds, then drain. Add the remaining rice cake, cook quickly, and drain. Serve the soup with the rice cake dropped in or serve the rice cake separately for dipping into the soup.

YIELD: 6 or more servings

Fried rice is, of course, one of the best-known of all Chinese dishes. If it is frowned upon as commonplace, it is because the run-of-the-mill fried rice served in most Chinese restaurants is precisely that. This fried rice is a bit of a masterpiece.

THE BEST FRIED RICE

5   cups cold cooked rice (cooked at least one day in advance; see recipe, page 347)
1   cup small raw shrimps, shelled, deveined, and split in half lengthwise
1   teaspoon baking soda
1   teaspoon salt
5   tablespoons peanut, vegetable, or corn oil
⅔   cup cubed Chinese sausages * (2 small) or cooked ham
3   eggs
½   cup cooked fresh or frozen green peas
1   tablespoon salt, approximately
2   tablespoons oyster sauce *
1   cup fresh bean sprouts * (see Note)
½   cup chopped scallions, green part included

* Available in Chinese markets and by mail order. For more information see Chapter XI.

1. Flake the rice so that the grains do not stick together. Set aside.

2. Combine the shrimps with the soda and salt and let stand 15 minutes or longer. Rinse thoroughly in cold water and pat dry on paper toweling.

3. Heat the oil in a wok or skillet until it is almost smoking and add the shrimps. Cook, stirring quickly and turning them in the oil until they turn pink, about 30 seconds. Remove them to a sieve fitted over a mixing bowl and let them drain well. Return the oil from the drained shrimps to the pan.

4. Add the sausages or ham to the pan and cook just to heat through, stirring. Add the rice, stirring rapidly, and cook until thoroughly heated without browning.

5. Do the following quickly: Make a well in the center of the rice and add the eggs, stirring constantly. When they have a soft-scrambled consistency, start incorporating the rice, stirring in a circular fashion.

6. When all the rice and eggs are blended, add the peas and the tablespoon of salt, stirring. Stir in the oyster sauce and the cooked shrimps, tossing the rice over and over to blend everything. Stir in the bean sprouts and cook, stirring and tossing, about 30 seconds. Add the scallions and serve immediately.

YIELD: 8 to 12 servings

Note: If you really want to be refined in this dish, pluck off and discard the head and threadlike "tail" of each bean sprout. But whether plucked over or left whole, there should be 1 cup to go into the dish.

One of the most remarkable dishes in the world is what is referred to in the Western world (by those who know it) as congee. The Chinese in this hemisphere also call it that, but the Chinese name is *tsook, jook,* or *chook,* depending on your pronunciation. The remarkable thing about congee is that it is not only delicious, but wildly inexpensive. Two cups of rice and a pound and a half of ground beef will amply serve twelve or more people. The important thing, however, is the garnish for the dish. The things that enliven the ultimate flavor of congee are such finally added oddments as slivered ginger, chopped scallions, chopped coriander, shredded lettuce, and ground white pepper—and, if desired, a few drops of sesame oil.

Congee is eaten for breakfast or supper or whenever a hot and filling snack is needed. It makes a delicious lunch served with one or more of the dumplings or pastries in this section, such as Spring Rolls, Jao-tze, or Roast Pork Steamed Buns (see recipes).

CANTONESE BEEF BALL CONGEE ❖

2   cups raw extra-long-grain rice
6   quarts water
      Salt
1   tablespoon peanut, vegetable, or corn oil
1½   pounds ground beef
      Preserved turnip * (or 1½ cups each finely chopped
          water chestnuts * or bamboo shoots *)
¼   teaspoon monosodium glutamate (optional)
2 to 4 cups shredded iceberg lettuce (optional)
½   cup finely slivered fresh ginger *
½   cup finely chopped scallion, green part included
½   cup finely chopped fresh coriander *
      Ground white pepper to taste
½   cup sesame oil *

* Available in Chinese markets and by mail order. For more information see Chapter XI.

1. Place the rice in a colander and rinse very well under cold running water.

2. Put the rice into a deep kettle and add 6 quarts water, 1 teaspoon salt, and the tablespoon of oil. Cover and bring to a boil. Do not stir the dish.

3. Reduce the heat to medium low and prop the lid of the kettle partially open, using a chopstick or similar device. Let simmer 3 hours without stirring.

4. When the rice is almost ready, place the beef in a mixing bowl.

5. If the turnip is used, rinse several pieces well, drain, and chop fine. There should be about 1½ cups. If not, add more.

6. Add the turnip or water chestnuts or bamboo shoots to the beef and start to stir, using one hand and stirring in one direction only. Gradually add ¾ cup cold water, always stirring in one direction. Shape the meat into 60 to 75 balls, each about 1 inch in diameter.

7. When the rice has cooked 3 hours, drop the balls into the simmering rice mixture. Add salt to taste, if needed, and the monosodium glutamate. Simmer 10 minutes.

8. Serve in soup bowls. If desired, use a few spoonfuls of shredded lettuce as a base for the soup. Serve the ginger, scallions, coriander, ground white pepper, and sesame oil on the side, letting each guest serve himself according to taste. Use only a drop or so of sesame oil, however, for each serving.

YIELD: 12 to 16 servings

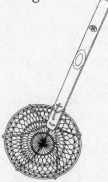

Given the rice, congee can be made with and accompanied by almost anything. Here is a congee made with chicken, and it is utterly delectable.

CHICKEN CONGEE

1   chicken (3 pounds), cut up, including gizzard, liver, and heart
1   cup raw extra-long-grain rice
3   quarts water
1   teaspoon salt
1   tablespoon peanut, vegetable, or corn oil
½   cup finely chopped scallion, green part included
½   cup finely chopped coriander *
½   cup finely shredded fresh ginger *
½   cup light soy sauce *
½   cup sesame oil *
     Ground white pepper to taste

* Available in Chinese markets and by mail order. For more information see Chapter XI.

1. Remove the gizzard, liver, and heart and discard or reserve for another use.

2. Drop the other chicken pieces into boiling water to cover and let simmer about 2 minutes. Drain immediately and run under cold running water, then drain again.

3. Rinse the rice well in cold water and drain. Put it into a kettle with the 3 quarts water. Bring to a boil and add salt and the table-spoon of oil. Add the blanched chicken pieces and return to a boil. Cover partially and simmer 1 hour.

4. Take out the legs, thighs, and breast of the chicken. Leave in the remaining pieces and let the congee continue to cook, partially covered, 1 to 1½ hours longer.

5. Meanwhile, finely shred the chicken breast and put the meat into a small serving bowl. Return the skin and bones to the kettle.

6. Remove the skin and bones from the legs and thighs and return the skin and bones to the kettle. Shred the meat and put this into another small serving bowl.

7. When the congee is ready to serve, remove and discard the skin and bones, and ladle the gruel into individual serving bowls. Serve with the shredded chicken, white and dark meat in the two bowls, and the scallions, coriander, ginger, soy sauce, sesame oil, and pepper on the side. Let each guest help himself. The soy sauce and sesame oil should be used sparingly.

YIELD: 6 to 10 servings

Lo mein, fresh Chinese noodles, are available in numerous shops where fresh noodles are made in the various Chinatowns of the Western world. They are also available in the refrigerator section of Chinese groceries and supermarkets. Like all fine noodles, these marry well with thousands of flavors and textures—including pork and bean sprouts.

LO MEIN WITH PORK AND BEAN SPROUTS

3	large or 6 small dried black mushrooms *
4 to 5	cups bean sprouts *
½	pound fresh Chinese noodles (lo mein) *
1	cup celery cabbage,* shredded crosswise
¼	pound lean pork
¼	teaspoon sugar
½	teaspoon monosodium glutamate (optional)
	Salt to taste
1	tablespoon dry sherry or shao hsing wine *
¼	cup peanut, vegetable, or corn oil
4	teaspoons dark soy sauce *
½	cup chicken broth
½	cup chives, preferably Chinese chives,* cut into 1-inch lengths
¼	cup red wine vinegar (optional)
1	teaspoon or more hot oil * (optional)

* Available in Chinese markets and by mail order. For more information see Chapter XI.

1. Place the mushrooms in a mixing bowl and add boiling water to cover. Let stand 15 to 30 minutes, then drain and squeeze to extract most of the moisture. Cut off and discard the tough stems.

2. Rinse the bean sprouts and drain well, then set aside.

3. Drop the noodles into a large quantity of boiling water—at least 2 quarts—and cook 3½ to 5 minutes, until tender. Do not overcook. Drain and rinse under cold water. Set aside.

4. Shred the mushrooms. There should be about ¼ cup.

5. Add the cabbage to the mushrooms.

6. Cut the pork across the grain into the thinnest possible slices, then cut the slices into fine shreds. (This is easier to do if the meat is partially frozen before slicing and the slices stacked before shredding.) There should be about ½ cup or slightly more.

7. Combine the sugar, monosodium glutamate, salt, and wine and set aside.

8. In a wok or skillet heat 2 tablespoons of the oil. When hot, add the pork, stirring to separate the pieces. When it loses color, add 1 teaspoon of the soy sauce and cook, stirring, about 30 seconds. Drain.

9. To the pan add the remaining oil, then add the cabbage and mushrooms. Cook, stirring, for about 1 minute. Add the pork and the noodles and cook over high heat, tossing the ingredients together. Cook about another minute, stirring, then add the wine mixture. Add the chicken broth and cook, stirring, about 30 seconds. Add the remaining 3 teaspoons of soy sauce and cook, stirring, about 3 minutes. Add the bean sprouts and chives and toss to blend.

10. Serve hot with a sauce made of the red wine vinegar and hot oil. The sauce is optional.

YIELD: 4 to 8 servings

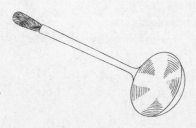

The word *mein* means noodles, and *lo* has been translated as "mixed." These noodles are mixed with beef and cabbage.

LO MEIN WITH BEEF

½ pound fresh Chinese noodles (lo mein) *
3 large dried black mushrooms *
¼ pound flank steak
1 to 2 tablespoons oyster sauce *
¼ teaspoon pepper
2½ teaspoons sesame oil *
1 cup peanut, vegetable, or corn oil
½ cup shredded bamboo shoots *
½ cup any kind of cabbage—celery,* Chinese,* or plain— cut into crosswise shreds
½ teaspoon sugar (optional)
  Salt to taste
1 tablespoon light soy sauce *
½ cup chicken broth
1½ teaspoons dark soy sauce *
½ cup chives (preferably Chinese chives *), cut into 2- inch lengths (optional)
3 cups bean sprouts,* rinsed and drained

* Available in Chinese markets and by mail order. For more information see Chapter XI.

1. Drop the noodles into a large quantity of boiling water—at least 2 quarts—and cook 3½ to 5 minutes, until tender. Do not overcook. Drain and rinse well under cold water. Set aside.

2. Place the mushrooms in a bowl and add boiling water to cover. Let stand 15 to 30 minutes or longer, then drain and squeeze them to extract most of their moisture. Cut off and discard the tough stems.

3. Place the meat on a flat surface and cut it across the grain into the thinnest possible slices. (It is easier to do this if the meat is par-

tially frozen.) Place the slices in a bowl and add the oyster sauce, pepper, and 1 teaspoon of the sesame oil.

4. In a wok or skillet, heat the 1 cup oil, and when it is warm, not hot, add the beef and cook, stirring constantly, about 1 minute. (If the oil is hot, the meat will stick together in a lump.) Drain the beef in a sieve-lined bowl to catch the drippings and drain off all but 2 tablespoons of the oil in the pan.

5. Heat the oil remaining in the pan to almost smoking, then add the bamboo shoots and mushrooms and cook, stirring, over high heat about 15 seconds. Add the cabbage, sugar, and salt. Cook, stirring, about 1 minute, then scoop out and reserve the solids.

6. Add the drippings and oil from the beef to the pan. There should be about 3 tablespoons of oil; add some if necessary. Turn the heat to high, and when hot add the noodles. Cook, stirring, about 20 seconds. Add the light soy sauce, bamboo shoots, and mushrooms. Cook about 15 seconds, stirring, and add the chicken broth and dark soy sauce. Cook, stirring, about 8 minutes, then add the chives, if used, bean sprouts, and beef. Cook, stirring, about 2 minutes.

7. Add the remaining sesame oil, toss to blend, and serve hot.

YIELD: 4 to 8 servings

TWO-SIDES-BROWN NOODLES

½   pound medium raw shrimps, shelled and deveined
1   teaspoon baking soda
1   teaspoon salt
½   pound fresh Chinese noodles (lo mein) *
½   pound flank steak
      Cornstarch
2   teaspoons dark soy sauce *
      Peanut, vegetable, or corn oil
½   egg white (beat the egg white lightly, then divide in half)
10   dried black mushrooms *
1   pound Chinese cabbage *

½ cup thinly sliced bamboo shoots * (about 1 x 2 inches)
3 teaspoons salt, or to taste
1 teaspoon sugar
1 cup chicken broth

* Available in Chinese markets and by mail order. For more information see Chapter XI.

1. "Butterfly" the shrimps by cutting them open from the back. Put into a bowl and mix with the soda and salt. Let stand for at least 15 minutes.

2. Drop the noodles into a large quantity of boiling water—at least 2 quarts—and cook 3½ to 5 minutes until tender. Do not overcook. Drain and rinse under cold water, then set aside.

3. Cut the piece of flank steak into half lengthwise, then slice across the grain into the thinnest possible slices. (This is easier to do if the meat is partially frozen.) Put the slices into a bowl and mix well with 2 teaspoons cornstarch, the soy sauce, and 1 tablespoon oil. Set aside.

4. Wash the soda and salt off the shrimps and pat them dry on paper toweling. Add 2 teaspoons cornstarch and the half egg white and mix well. Refrigerate for at least 30 minutes.

5. Soak the mushrooms in boiling water to cover for 15 to 30 minutes, then squeeze the mushrooms dry. Cut off and discard the tough stems, and cut in half. Set aside.

6. Cut off the withered leaves of the cabbage and peel off the tough parts of the coarser stalks with a sharp knife. Cut the remaining leaves and stalks into 3-inch lengths. Slice the stalks further diagonally along their length into pieces about ¼ inch thick and 2 inches long. Set aside.

7. Heat 1 cup of oil in a wok or skillet over a medium high flame until it is almost smoking—it must be very hot or else the noodles will stick to the bottom of the pan. Lower the noodles into the hot fat in a cake and let cook without stirring until the bottom is brown, about 15 to 20 minutes. Turn the cake over and brown the other side.

8. When the noodle cake is a nice golden brown on both sides, remove from the oil and drain on paper toweling. Put onto a large serving platter and keep warm.

9. Let the oil in the pan cool until it is just warm. Add the shrimps and stir about in the oil until the shrimps are pink. Remove to a sieve-lined bowl to drain.

10. To the same oil add the sliced beef and cook until most of the pink has disappeared. If the oil has become too cool, turn on the heat again, but it may not be necessary. Do not overcook the beef. Remove and add to the shrimps in the strainer.

11. Drain off all but about ¼ cup of oil in the bottom of the pan. Heat the oil over a high fire until almost smoking. Add the mushrooms and bamboo shoots, stir, then add the cabbage and cook until tender. Add the salt, sugar, and chicken broth, stirring all the time. Add the beef and shrimp, then stir in 1 tablespoon cornstarch mixed with 2 tablespoons cold water. Cook briefly until the contents of the pan are warmed through.

12. Pour the sauce over the noodle cake and serve immediately. At the table each person cuts a piece of noodle cake and spoons the sauce over it.

YIELD: 6 to 12 servings

THREE-SHREDS SOUP NOODLES

1   cup chicken broth, fresh or canned
½   chicken breast
¼   pound Smithfield ham
10   dried black mushrooms *
½   teaspoon monosodium glutamate
1   teaspoon salt, or to taste
1   scallion, green part included
½   pound fresh Chinese noodles (lo mein),* cooked in 2
       quarts boiling water for 3½ minutes
1½ quarts Rich Chicken Broth (see recipe)

* Available in Chinese markets and by mail order. For more information see Chapter XI.

1. Bring the cup of chicken broth to a boil in a large saucepan and simmer the chicken breast in it 15 to 20 minutes. Turn off the heat, remove the breast, and discard the skin and bones. Shred the meat and set aside. Leave the broth in the saucepan.

2. Slice the ham into the thinnest possible slices, then shred into matchstick slivers. Set aside.

3. Place the mushrooms in a bowl and add boiling water to cover. Let stand 15 to 30 minutes, then drain and squeeze dry. Cut off the tough stems. Place the caps in a saucepan, cover with water, bring to a boil, and simmer for 10 minutes. Cool, then shred the caps into matchstick slivers. Set aside.

4. Shred the scallion diagonally into matchstick slivers. Set aside.

5. Bring the cup of broth in the saucepan to a boil again and heat the noodles in it until the broth comes back to a boil.

6. In another saucepan heat the 1½ quarts rich broth and add the monosodium glutamate and salt. Drain the noodles, discarding the first boiling broth, and put them into a serving bowl. Pour the boiling rich broth over them. Put the ham, chicken, and mushrooms into separate piles on top of the noodles and sprinkle with the scallions. Serve immediately. At the table mix the topping into the noodles and serve the mixture in individual serving bowls.

YIELD: 4 to 8 servings

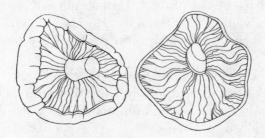

There is elsewhere in this book a recipe for Pon Pon Chicken, a spicy cold dish flavored with sesame paste and sesame oil. This is a variation of that dish.

COLD NOODLES WITH SPICY SAUCE ❖

1 whole chicken breast
4 ounces fine egg noodles
1 teaspoon plus 1 tablespoon sesame oil *
¼ cup sesame paste *
3 tablespoons brewed tea or water
2 tablespoons hot oil * (optional)
3 tablespoons light soy sauce *
3 tablespoons red wine vinegar
2 teaspoons sugar
   Salt to taste
¼ teaspoon monosodium glutamate (optional)
¼ cup peanut, vegetable, or corn oil
2 tablespoons chopped garlic

* Available in Chinese markets and by mail order. For more information see Chapter XI.

1. In a kettle or large saucepan, bring about 6 cups of water to a boil and add the chicken breast. Do not add salt. Return to a boil and simmer about 10 to 15 minutes. Do not overcook, or the meat will be dry. Remove the chicken breast, but leave the water in the kettle.

2. Bring the water to a boil again. Do not add salt. Add the noodles and cook, stirring occasionally, until they are tender, 7 minutes or less. Drain in a colander and run under cold water until they are thoroughly chilled and the strands are separated. Drain. Sprinkle with the teaspoon of sesame oil and toss to coat. Set aside.

3. To make the sauce, spoon the sesame paste into a mixing bowl and add the tea or water gradually, stirring with chopsticks or a fork. Stir in the remaining ingredients and the 1 tablespoon sesame oil.

4. Arrange the noodles on a serving dish. Cut the chicken into uniform shreds and arrange neatly over the noodles. Spoon the sauce over all and serve cold.

YIELD: 2 to 4 servings

The following is a famous Peking dish, traditional for birthday celebrations. It is a minced pork and bean sauce dish with noodles as its base. The sauce itself is somewhat spicy and a bit on the salty side, which admirably complements the noodles. Note that it is made and served with what may seem to some Western minds as a large amount of oil, but the oil may be reduced according to conscience. The sauce, incidentally, keeps well in the refrigerator up to two weeks.

TSA CHIANG MIEN
(Noodles with Minced Pork and Bean Sauce)

1	pound ground pork
½	cup bean sauce *
¾	cup peanut, vegetable, or corn oil
3 to 4	teaspoons sugar
¼	teaspoon monosodium glutamate
2	scallions, green part included, finely chopped
½	pound fresh Chinese noodles (lo mein)* or one 8-ounce box thin egg noodles

* Available in Chinese markets and by mail order. For more information see Chapter XI.

1. Measure out the pork and bean sauce in separate bowls and have ready.
2. Heat the oil in a wok or skillet, add the pork, and cook about 3 minutes, stirring to separate the pieces. Add the bean sauce and cook, stirring, over high heat about 2 minutes.

3. Add the sugar and cook, stirring, over high heat until the oil loses its cloudy look and becomes clear, about 3 minutes or longer. Add the monosodium glutamate and scallions and stir to blend. Spoon out, oil and all, into a serving dish and keep warm. Or, if desired, pour off as much of the oil as you wish.

4. Prepare the noodles. If Chinese noodles are used, bring a large quantity of water—at least 2 quarts—to a boil. Add the noodles and cook 3½ to 5 minutes. Or cook the thin egg noodles according to package directions. In either case, drain and put the noodles into a large serving bowl.

5. At the table, serve the noodles in individual bowls and pass the bowl of pork and bean sauce. Each individual tops his noodles with a spoonful or two of the sauce and oil to taste, and mixes it thoroughly with chopsticks.

YIELD: 4 to 8 servings

There is a dish of pure delight in Chinese cookery, a marvelously elegant thing called Spring Rolls. The spring roll is, in truth, a relative of the egg roll, but the relation ends with the fact that both are deep-fried filled pastries. Egg rolls, at least those that most people recognize from Chinatown restaurants, are an abomination. Spring rolls are a delicacy to be prized. Cut into halves or thirds, they are an excellent cocktail appetizer. Spring roll skins, ready to fill, are available in Chinese markets where raw pastries are sold and in many grocery stores.

SPRING ROLLS

The filling:

    ½   pound fresh bean sprouts *
    6 or 8 dried black mushrooms *
    ½   pound ground or shredded pork
    4   teaspoons cornstarch

1 teaspoon dark soy sauce *
⅓ cup chopped raw shrimp
1 teaspoon dry sherry or shao hsing wine *
2 tablespoons peanut, vegetable, or corn oil
½ cup shredded bamboo shoots *
Salt to taste
½ cup chicken broth
2 cups coarsely chopped chives (preferably Chinese chives; * optional)

The spring roll skins:

20 square Shanghai spring roll skins *
Beaten egg for sealing
Peanut, vegetable, or corn oil for deep frying

The sauce:

3 tablespoons finely minced fresh ginger *
3 tablespoons minced garlic
½ cup light soy sauce *
2 tablespoons vinegar
1 tablespoon sugar
½ teaspoon salt
2 teaspoons hot oil *

---

* Available in Chinese markets and by mail order. For more information see Chapter XI.

1. The bean sprouts in this recipe do not have to be picked over, but, as we have said before, it is more elegant if they are. To do this, pluck off the threadlike root and the top small curlicue, leaving only the body. Whether plucked or not, there should be 2 cups measured for the recipe.

2. Place the mushrooms in a bowl and add boiling water to cover. Let stand 15 to 30 minutes. Save the mushroom liquid, if desired. It may be used to replace part of the chicken broth in the recipe. Otherwise, discard it.

3. Squeeze the mushrooms to extract much of their liquid, then cut off and discard the stems. Shred the mushrooms and set aside.

4. Combine the pork with 1 teaspoon of the cornstarch and the soy sauce. Set aside.

5. Combine the chopped shrimp with the wine and 1 teaspoon of the cornstarch. Set aside.

6. Heat the oil in a wok or skillet and cook the pork mixture, stirring, until the pork loses its raw color. Add the bamboo shoots and shredded mushrooms and salt to taste. Add half the chicken broth, stirring and cooking quickly.

7. Blend the remaining 2 teaspoons of cornstarch with the remaining ¼ cup of chicken broth and stir it into the filling. Add the shrimp and bean sprouts and cook, stirring, briefly. Immediately remove the filling from the heat. Let the filling cool, then stir in the chives.

8. Meanwhile, prepare the sauce by combining all the ingredients and stirring to blend well.

9. Leave the spring roll skins in one stack and keep them covered with a damp cloth as you work. Take one spring roll skin and lay it shiny side down on a flat surface, one corner pointing toward you. Spoon 2 level tablespoons or so of filling onto the lower corner of the spring roll skin in a sausage shape.

Fold the corner of the skin pointing at you over the filling until just covered.

Give it another turn to enclose the filling, open cylinder fashion.

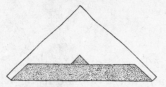

Moisten the left and right corners of the triangle with beaten egg, fold over the corners, and press down firmly to seal, making a kind of envelope.

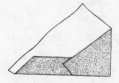

Moisten the flap of the envelope with egg and give one more turn, rolling it into a cylinder and sealing it firmly.

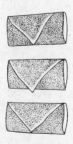

Set aside and repeat until all the filling has been used.

10. Heat the oil for deep frying in a wok or deep-fryer, and when it is almost smoking cook the spring rolls until crisp and golden brown. Drain on several layers of paper toweling. Serve with the sauce as a dip.

YIELD: 20 spring rolls, approximately

WON TON ❖

1   pound lean pork, ground
1   bunch watercress
1   egg
2   tablespoons light soy sauce *
1   tablespoon dry sherry or shao hsing wine *
½   pound raw shrimps, peeled, deveined, and finely chopped
½   teaspoon monosodium glutamate (optional)
1   tablespoon cornstarch
2   tablespoons water
    Salt and pepper to taste
1   package won ton skins *
    Chicken broth (1 cup per serving)

* Available in Chinese markets and by mail order. For more information see Chapter XI.

1. Place the pork in a bowl.
2. Pick over the watercress to remove any very tough stems. Drop the watercress into boiling water and let stand about 30 seconds. Drain immediately and run under cold water. When cold, press to extract excess water. Chop the watercress until fine, then add to the pork.
3. Add all the remaining ingredients except the won ton skins, chicken broth, and pepper and stir to blend well.
4. If very thin won tons are desired, roll each skin with a rolling pin or put through a home noodle machine. Or they may be stuffed just as they come from the store. Fill the skins, one at a time, with about a teaspoon of filling. As you work, keep the stack of won ton skins covered with a damp cloth so that they do not dry out.

To fold, bring up two sides of the won ton skin and pinch it all around to seal in the filling. Dampen the edges with a little water if necessary to make them stick.

Pull the two bottom edges together and pinch firmly to seal, using a little water if necessary.

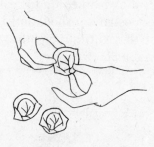

5. Continue until all the filling is used up. As you work, cover the finished won tons with a damp cloth to prevent their drying out.

6. Bring several quarts of water to a boil in a large kettle and add the won ton. When the water returns to a boil, add half a cup of cold water and let the water come to a boil again. The won ton are done when they float to the top.

7. Meanwhile, heat the chicken broth. To serve, put a little salt and pepper into the bottom of individual serving bowls and pour the hot broth over it. Ladle a few cooked won ton into each bowl, and serve immediately.

YIELD: About 90 to 100 won ton

Note: Allow about 5 to 10 won ton per person, depending upon whether the dish is to be served as a soup or as a light meal. The balance can be frozen for 2 weeks or more. Wrap individual servings in foil and seal well. When ready to serve, cook without defrosting.

SWEET AND SOUR FRIED WON TON

32   fresh, ready-to-cook Won Ton (follow preceding recipe
         through Step 5)
2   tablespoons tree ear mushrooms *
2¼   cups water
1   cup sugar
⅔   cup red wine vinegar
      Salt to taste
1   tablespoon light soy sauce *
      Peanut, vegetable, or corn oil
1   green pepper, cored, seeded, and chopped (or use a sweet
         red pepper if available; it adds color)
2   cloves garlic, peeled, crushed, and left whole
1   onion, peeled and cut into eighths
3   tablespoons cornstarch
12   drops red food coloring

* Available in Chinese markets and by mail order. For more information see Chapter XI.

1. Keep the uncooked won ton covered with a damp cloth.

2. Place the tree ears in a bowl and add very hot water to cover. (Remember that tree ears expand considerably.) Soak 15 to 30 minutes, then drain and squeeze dry. Pick off any hard parts.

3. Meanwhile, put 2 cups of the water into a saucepan and add the sugar, vinegar, salt, and soy sauce. Bring to a boil and stir until the sugar dissolves.

4. Heat oil for deep frying in a wok or deep-fryer, and when very hot add the won ton, one at a time. Cook until golden brown, about 5 minutes. Drain.

5. Heat ¼ cup of oil in a wok or skillet and add the green or red pepper, garlic, onion, and tree ears. Cook, stirring, 4 to 5 minutes.

6. Blend the cornstarch with the remaining ¼ cup of water and stir into the simmering sauce. Stir in the food coloring. Pour the sauce over the vegetables and bring to a boil.

7. Transfer the won ton to a serving dish. Customarily in America the sauce and vegetables are poured over the won ton before serving. We prefer to serve the won ton on one platter and the sauce

with vegetables separately, so that each guest may help himself to sauce.

YIELD: 32 won ton

The dumplings here were traditional fare sold on the streets of Chungking. The vendors would sell ten or twelve to a customer to be eaten on the spot or taken home. They are invariably served with a spicy sauce made with hot oil and garlic.

SZECHWAN SPICY CHICKEN DUMPLINGS

The dumplings:

½ pound skinned, boneless chicken breast, cut into 1-inch cubes
2 egg whites
1 tablespoon cornstarch
¼ teaspoon sugar
Salt to taste
¼ teaspoon monosodium glutamate (optional)
1 tablespoon dry sherry or shao hsing wine *
3 tablespoons water
1 package won ton skins *

The sauce (for 1 person; to be increased as necessary):

1 tablespoon finely chopped garlic
1 tablespoon finely minced Szechwan preserved vegetable *
1 scallion, green part included, trimmed and finely chopped
1 tablespoon hot oil,* more or less to taste
¼ teaspoon monosodium glutamate (optional)
¼ teaspoon sugar
1 tablespoon light soy sauce *
1 teaspoon red wine vinegar

The garnish:

1 tablespoon chopped fresh coriander *
1 teaspoon minced Tientsin preserved vegetable * (optional)

* Available in Chinese markets and by mail order. For more information see Chapter XI.

1. To make the dumplings, put the chicken cubes, egg whites, cornstarch, sugar, salt, monosodium glutamate, wine, and water into the container of an electric blender. Blend, stirring down as necessary, to make a fine paste. Spoon the mixture into a mixing bowl.

2. Neatly stack the won ton skins on a flat surface, one or a few at a time, and use a biscuit cutter 2 to 2½ inches in diameter to cut out rounds. (Leftover bits of pastry can be dried and used in soups.)

3. Spoon a teaspoon or so of the filling into the center of each round, fold the round over to enclose the filling, and seal the edges completely, using a little water and pressing the edges together to make a filled crescent. Continue until all the filling is used.

4. To make the sauce, simply combine all the ingredients listed and stir to blend.

5. To cook the dumplings, bring a large quantity of water to a boil. Do not add salt. When the water is boiling furiously, add the dumplings and ½ cup of cold water and cook until they come to the surface. Cook a few seconds longer until they are piping hot inside, then drain. Place on a platter and sprinkle with the minced coriander and Tientsin vegetable. Serve hot, with the sauce on the side.

YIELD: About 68 dumplings

Cantonese dumplings are distinctive in that the pork filling is flavored with oyster sauce, among other things, and the dough for the pastry is made with wheat starch and rice powder, both of which are available in Chinese groceries in one-pound paper packages. When the dumplings are steamed, they have a somewhat translucent look. To cook this dish, it helps to have a many-layered Chinese bamboo steamer so that all the dumplings may be steamed at once, but it is not essential.

CANTONESE DUMPLINGS ❖

The filling:

6 to 10	dried black mushrooms *
¼	pound raw pork
1	tablespoon cornstarch
½	cup finely diced raw shrimp (about ¼ pound)
¼	cup lard
¾	cup finely diced bamboo shoots *
½	cup finely diced roast pork
	Salt to taste
1	tablespoon dry sherry or shao hsing wine *
½	teaspoon sugar
1	tablespoon light soy sauce *
1	teaspoon sesame oil *
¼	teaspoon ground white pepper
80 to 120	fresh coriander leaves,* approximately, leaf part only

The dough:

2	cups wheat starch *
8	tablespoons rice powder *
¼	cup cornstarch
2⅔	cups boiling water
1	tablespoon lard, preferably rendered leaf lard (see Chapter XI)

The dip:

3	tablespoons oyster sauce *
1	teaspoon sesame oil *

* Available in Chinese markets and by mail order. For more information see Chapter XI.

1. Place the mushrooms in a bowl and add boiling water to cover. Let stand 15 to 30 minutes, then drain and squeeze them to extract most of their moisture. Cut off and discard the tough stems. Slice the mushrooms, then dice them finely. There should be about ½ cup.

2. Cut the raw pork into small dice and mix well with half the cornstarch. Set aside.

3. Place the shrimp in another mixing bowl and add the other half of the cornstarch. Mix well and set aside.

4. Heat the lard in a wok or skillet, and when it is hot add the raw pork, stirring to break up the lumps. When the pork has lost its red color and is cooked through, add the bamboo shoots, roast pork, mushrooms, shrimp, salt, wine, sugar, and soy sauce. Cook, stirring, until piping hot, then add the sesame oil and pepper. Mix well, then spoon the mixture into a bowl. There should be about 4 cups. Let stand until thoroughly cool. The mixture may be chilled until ready to use.

5. Prepare the dough by combining the wheat starch, rice powder, and cornstarch in a mixing bowl. Gradually add the boiling water while stirring rapidly with chopsticks. As soon as you can handle it, knead the dough for a short while until it becomes quite glutinous, starchy, and stiff. Immediately add the tablespoon of lard or leaf lard. Turn the dough out onto a clean board and knead while still hot, about 5 minutes. Shape the dough into a ball and put it into a clean mixing bowl. Cover with a towel and let stand for 3 or 4 minutes.

6. With your fingers, lightly oil a plate that will fit into the top of a steamer.

7. Divide the dough into 4 equal pieces. Roll each piece with your hands into a sausage shape about 16 inches long. Pinch one sausage into about twenty 1½-inch pieces, rolling each into a ball. Roll each ball out into a circle 3 to 3½ inches in diameter. Place the circles side by side (do not stack or overlap; they will stick to each other) on a flat surface, and keep them covered with a cloth to keep them moist.

8. When one sausage has been completely rolled out, fill with 2 level teaspoons of filling. Place a coriander leaf or two on top of the filling. Bring up the other side of the skin and pinch the edges together all around to make a filled crescent. Place the filled dumpling on the oiled plate, the side with the coriander facing up.

9. Continue until all the circles are filled, keeping the finished dumplings covered with a cloth so they won't dry out. Repeat the process with the remaining sausages of dough until either the filling

or the pastry has been used up, arranging the dumplings on oiled plates.

10. Place each dish of dumplings in the top of a steamer over boiling water. Cover closely and steam from 5 to 8 minutes, until thoroughly done. Serve hot on the plates they were steamed on, with a dipping sauce made of the oyster sauce and sesame oil blended together.

YIELD: 75 to 80 dumplings

Note: The raw filled dumplings may be frozen for up to a month, after sealing them securely, plate and all, in foil or plastic wrap. When ready to use, the dish should be steamed without defrosting but the steaming time should be increased to 15 to 20 minutes.

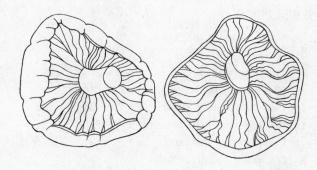

There are many ways to cook one of the most delectable of all northern Chinese dishes, the dumplings known as *jao-tze* or *jow-tse*. They may be fried or steamed or boiled, and they are generally served as an appetizer or as part of an assortment of foods known as *dim seum* or *dem sem* or *deem seem* or any of numerous other spellings to indicate the same thing. Jao-tze are generally served with a combination of light sauces, the commonest of which is vinegar and soy sauce plus, if desired, shredded ginger and, for those who wish it, hot oil. Some addicts (and it is easy to become one) eat twenty dumplings at one sitting. This is the amount yielded by this recipe, which for ordinary purposes serves three to six, depending upon appetite and circumstance.

FRIED JAO-TZE

The dumpling dough:

> 1   cup all-purpose flour
> 6   tablespoons cold water

The dumpling filling:

> 4 to 6   dried black mushrooms *
> ¼   pound ground pork (about ½ cup)
> ⅓   cup finely chopped bamboo shoots *
> ¼   cup shredded fresh crab or chopped shrimp
> 1   tablespoon dry sherry or shao hsing wine *
> 1   tablespoon light soy sauce *
> 2   teaspoons cornstarch
> ½   teaspoon sugar
>   Salt to taste
> ¼   teaspoon monosodium glutamate (optional)
> ½   beaten egg (beat 1 egg and divide in half)

To fry:

> ¼   cup peanut, vegetable, or corn oil
> ¾   cup water

* Available in Chinese markets and by mail order. For more information see Chapter XI.

1. Place the flour in a mixing bowl and add the water, stirring with chopsticks until blended. Knead with your hands and shape with your hands into a ball. Put the ball into a clean bowl and cover closely. Let stand at least 30 minutes.

2. Place the mushrooms in a bowl and add boiling water to cover. Let stand 15 to 30 minutes, then drain and squeeze to extract most of the moisture. Cut off and discard the tough stems. Chop the mushrooms. There should be about ⅓ cup.

3. In a mixing bowl mix the pork and bamboo shoots and add the remaining ingredients for the filling. Put the mixture into the freezer for about 5 minutes—do not allow it to freeze. The chilling makes the filling easier to handle. (It may also be chilled overnight in the refrigerator.)

4. Lightly flour a working surface and pour out the dough. Knead it about 5 minutes, until smooth and elastic, then stretch it into a sausage shape.

5. Using floured fingers, pull off about 20 equal-weight pieces. Roll each piece into marble-shaped balls, then flatten into "biscuits." Roll each biscuit into 3- or 3½-inch circles. Keep the circles covered with a cloth as you work to prevent them from drying out. Fill them as follows:

Place about 1½ to 2 level teaspoons of filling in the center of the dough in a slightly oval shape.

Bring up the edges of the dough and pinch together firmly in the center, forming a filled crescent, using a little water to seal if necessary. Leave each end open.

Make a pleat on the side facing you.

Gather up the balance of the dough on the side away from you, pleating toward the center in 3 or 4 pleats.

Do the same with the other end, pleating toward the center. This method of sealing the dumpling gives it a broad bottom.

As each dumpling is finished, place it on a lightly floured board and cover with a cloth to prevent drying out.

6. When ready to cook, heat the oil in a 10- or 11-inch lidded skillet, and when it is hot add the dumplings, bottom side down. Cook about 2 minutes, or until golden brown on the bottom. Pour the water all around the dumplings and cover as tightly as possible with the lid. Cook over high heat until the water almost boils away, about 5 minutes, then turn the heat to low. After about 10 or 12 minutes' total cooking time, turn the heat to high briefly to brown

the dumplings well on the bottom. Watch them closely, however; do not let them burn.

7. Transfer the dumplings from the skillet and serve them bottom side up, with Jao-Tze Sauce I or II (see recipes).

YIELD: About 18 to 20 dumplings

BOILED JAO-TZE

The dumpling dough:

2	cups all-purpose flour
10	tablespoons cold water

The filling:

6 to 10	leaves Chinese cabbage *
½	pound ground beef or pork
2	teaspoons cornstarch
1	tablespoon sesame oil *
	Salt to taste
1	tablespoon dry sherry or shao hsing wine *
½	teaspoon monosodium glutamate (optional)
1	tablespoon dark soy sauce *
¼	teaspoon sugar
1	cup chopped scallions, green part included
3 to 4	tablespoons chicken broth

* Available in Chinese markets and by mail order. For more information see Chapter XI.

1. Put the flour into a mixing bowl and stir in the water gradually, using chopsticks or a fork in the beginning, then using your hands. Knead the dough in the bowl or on a lightly floured surface about 5 minutes. Shape into a ball and place in a clean bowl, covered with a cloth wrung out in cold water.

2. Drop the cabbage leaves (the number will depend on size; the object is to wind up with 1 cup of chopped cabbage after cooking it) into boiling water to cover. Cook 10 to 12 minutes, until crisp tender, and drain well. Immediately run under cold water and squeeze to extract as much excess liquid as possible.

3. Chop the cabbage, squeeze again, and measure 1 cup.

4. Put the ground meat into a mixing bowl and add all the other filling ingredients except the cabbage and chicken broth. Stir in the chopped cabbage and broth (the amount will depend on the residual wetness of the cabbage). Set aside.

5. Remove the dough from the bowl onto a lightly floured board. Roll it with palms and fingers into a sausage shape about 13 to 14 inches long. Tear off bits of dough and shape each bit into a ball about 1 inch in diameter. Flatten on a lightly floured board, then roll with a rolling pin into a circle about 3 to 3½ inches in diameter. Put about 2 level teaspoons of the filling into the center of the circle. Bring up the edges and seal as shown in the steps on p. 379. Arrange on a lightly floured baking sheet, covered with a damp cloth to prevent drying out.

6. Bring about 6 quarts of water to a vigorous boil and add the dumplings quickly, one at a time. Let boil again, uncovered.

7. Immediately add ½ cup of cold water and return to a boil once more.

8. Boil about 1 minute; the dumplings will float up when cooked. Skim out and serve hot, with Jao-Tze Sauce I or II (see recipes).

YIELD: About 40 jao-tze

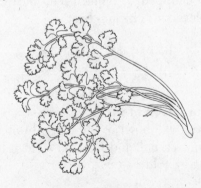

Here is an excellent way to serve leftover boiled jao-tze.

FRIED JAO-TZE MADE FROM
COOKED, BOILED JAO-TZE

Boiled Jao-Tze (see preceding recipe)
Peanut, vegetable, or corn oil for shallow frying (¼ cup of oil
   to a skillet)

1. Transfer the Boiled Jao-Tze to a lightly oiled platter to cool.
2. Heat one-quarter inch of oil in one or two skillets large enough to hold the quantity of jao-tze desired. Place the dumplings bottom side down in the oil and cook until appetizingly brown on the bottom. Turn and cook on another side until brown. Serve with Jao-Tze Sauce I or II (see recipes).

YIELD: About 40 jao-tze

A third version of Chinese dumplings is Steamed Jao-Tze, and they are a joy to eat.

STEAMED JAO-TZE ❖

The dumpling dough:

      2   cups all-purpose flour
10 to 12   tablespoons hot water

The filling:

  1   pound ground pork (about 2 cups)
  1   egg, lightly beaten
     Salt to taste
  ½   teaspoon sugar
1½   tablespoons cornstarch
  ½   teaspoon monosodium glutamate (optional)
1½   tablespoons dry sherry or shao hsing wine *
  1   tablespoon dark soy sauce *
  ½   cup chopped scallions, green part included
  ½   cup plus 2 tablespoons Rich Chicken Broth (see recipe)

* Available in Chinese markets and by mail order. For more information see Chapter XI.

1. Place the flour in a mixing bowl and add the water gradually, kneading constantly. When all the water is added, continue kneading about 5 minutes, then shape the dough into a ball. Put the ball into a clean bowl and cover closely. Let stand 30 minutes.

2. Meanwhile, place the pork in a mixing bowl and add all the remaining ingredients except the chicken broth. Stir the mixture with your hands, using a circular motion, and always stirring in the same direction. While stirring, gradually add the chicken broth. Place it in the freezer for about 15 minutes. It must be very, very cold but not frozen.

3. When ready to make the dumplings, lightly flour a working surface and pour out the dough. Knead it about 5 minutes, then roll it with palms and fingers into a sausage shape. Cut the sausage in half and keep one half covered. Shape the other half into another sausage shape and, using floured fingers, pull off about 20 equal-weight pieces. Roll each piece between the palms into marble-shaped balls, then flatten into "biscuits." Using a floured rolling pin, roll each biscuit into 3- or 3½-inch circles. Fill the center of each circle with about 2 level teaspoons of the cold pork mixture. Bring up the edges of the dough and seal by pinching the edges together as shown in the steps on page 379. As each dumpling is finished, place it on a lightly floured board (see Note below). Cover with a cloth to prevent drying out.

4. Repeat, using the other half of the dough.

5. When ready to cook, line the top of a steamer with cheesecloth wrung out in cold water. Arrange the dumplings over it and steam, covered, over boiling water about 15 minutes. Serve piping hot with Jao-Tze Sauce I or II (see recipes).

YIELD: About 40 jao-tze

Note: Before steaming, these jao-tze freeze to advantage. To freeze them after they are made, arrange them on a wire rack that will fit in the freezer. Do not cover, but place the rack in the freezer. When the dumplings are frozen, transfer them to one or two plastic bags and seal. Steam as indicated, but lengthen the steaming time to 20 minutes.

JAO-TZE SAUCE I
(For 2 persons)

¼　cup dark soy sauce *
¼　cup white vinegar
1　tablespoon sesame oil *
2　tablespoons minced fresh ginger *
1　tablespoon minced garlic
½　teaspoon sugar
2　tablespoons hot oil * (optional)

* Available in Chinese markets and by mail order. For more information see Chapter XI.

Stir the ingredients in a mixing bowl to blend well.

YIELD: Slightly less than ¾ cup

JAO-TZE SAUCE II
(For 6 persons)

2　tablespoons chopped garlic
4　tablespoons light soy sauce *
8　tablespoons red wine vinegar
1　teaspoon sugar
½　teaspoon monosodium glutamate (optional)

* Available in Chinese markets and by mail order. For more information see Chapter XI.

Combine all the ingredients and serve.

YIELD: About ¾ cup

Legend has it that all forms of pasta—ravioli, spaghetti, tortellini, vermicelli, fettucini, and so on—were unknown in Italy until Marco Polo visited the Orient four or five hundred years ago. Such dishes have been known and enjoyed in China, it is said, more than a thousand years. This is one version of Chinese pasta that Marco Polo may very well have sampled.

SHIU MAY

12 to 14   round won ton skins *

The filling:

½   pound ground pork
1   tablespoon light soy sauce *
1   teaspoon cornstarch
1   tablespoon dry sherry or shao hsing wine *
¼   teaspoon salt
½   pound shelled, deveined, raw shrimps, each shrimp
　　　split in half and each half cut into thirds
3   tablespoons chicken broth
2   teaspoons sesame oil *
½   teaspoon sugar
¼   teaspoon monosodium glutamate (optional)
¼   cup finely chopped scallions, green part included
　　　(optional)

The garnish:

1 to 2   tablespoons finely minced ham
2 to 3   water chestnuts,* finely minced
2 to 3   dried black mushrooms,* soaked in hot water 15 to 30
　　　minutes and drained, squeezed dry, and finely
　　　minced
½   package frozen peas, partly thawed

* Available in Chinese markets and by mail order. For more information see Chapter XI.

1. Combine all the ingredients for the filling in a mixing bowl and mix well.

2. Take the won ton skins, one at a time, and put one rounded tablespoon of filling, more or less, in the middle of each skin.

3. With your fingers gather up and pinch and pleat the skin around the filling, forming an open-topped pouch. Pinch the pouch gently in the middle to give it a "waist." Decorate the sections of the open top with a pinch of ham, a pinch of water chestnut, and a pinch of mushroom. Fill in the remaining space with a pea or two.

4. Bring water in the bottom of a steamer to a boil. Line the top of the steamer with cheesecloth wrung out in cold water. Place the shiu may in the top of the steamer, cover, and steam for 15 to 20 minutes. Serve immediately.

YIELD: About 12 to 14 shiu may, serving 4 to 8 persons

Chinese chefs are ingenious in their techniques for filled breads. The following easily made recipe is for individual buns filled with marvelously seasoned roast pork and then steamed.

ROAST PORK STEAMED BUNS

The dough:

    3½   cups all-purpose flour
    1   tablespoon chilled lard
    ¼   cup sugar
    1   teaspoon active dry yeast
    1   cup warm water

The filling:

½ pound Chinese roast pork,* purchased or home cooked (see recipe for Cantonese Roast Pork)
2 tablespoons chopped scallions, green part included
2 tablespoons chopped garlic
3 tablespoons oyster sauce *
3 tablespoons sugar
2 tablespoons light soy sauce *
1 tablespoon sesame oil *
2 teaspoons all-purpose flour
2 teaspoons cornstarch
⅓ cup water
2 tablespoons lard

* Available in Chinese markets and by mail order. For more information see Chapter XI.

1. To make the dough, place 3 cups of the flour in a mixing bowl and add the lard. Work it with your fingers to blend well. Add half the sugar and blend well.

2. In another, smaller bowl combine the yeast with the remaining sugar and 6 tablespoons of the warm water, stirring to blend. Add the remaining ½ cup of flour and stir to blend.

3. Add the yeast mixture to the contents of the larger bowl. Work the dough with your hands while adding the rest of the warm water. When blended, the dough should be fairly stiff. Knead the dough until smooth, about 5 minutes. Shape it into a ball and place it in a clean bowl. Cover with a damp cloth, but do not let the cloth touch the dough. Place in a warm place for 1½ to 2 hours, until doubled in bulk.

4. Meanwhile, prepare the filling. Cut the pork into ⅜-inch cubes or slightly smaller. There should be about 2 cups. Set aside.

5. Chop the scallions and garlic together and set aside.

6. Blend the oyster sauce, sugar, soy sauce, and sesame oil and set aside.

7. Blend the flour, cornstarch, and water and set aside.

8. Heat the lard and add the pork. Cook, stirring, to heat thor-

oughly, about 40 seconds. Add the garlic-scallion mixture. Toss and stir about 15 seconds. Add the oyster sauce mixture. Cook, stirring, about 45 seconds.

9. Stir the flour, cornstarch, and water mixture briefly and add it, stirring. Cook about 30 seconds and remove from the heat. Let cool, then chill thoroughly.

10. When the dough has risen, punch it down and turn it out onto a lightly floured board. Using your hands, roll and shape it into a thick sausage shape about 18 inches long.

11. Slice the "sausage" in half and keep one half covered with a cloth to prevent drying out.

12. Roll the other half into a smaller sausage shape and break off pieces of dough that can be rolled into small balls, each about 2 inches in diameter.

13. On a lightly floured board press each ball into a biscuit shape, then use a rolling pin to roll the edges out to make a circle about 3½ inches in diameter. Roll it so that the centers of each circle are thicker than the edges.

14. Put about 1½ tablespoons of the pork filling into the center of each circle, then gather up the edges of the dough, pulling them together and pressing to seal the top. The top of the dough should have a puckered look.

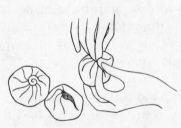

15. As the pastries are filled, arrange them on a lightly floured surface. Cover with a dry cloth and let rise 15 or 20 minutes.

16. Line the top of a steamer with cheesecloth wrung out in cold water and arrange the buns on it, about 2 inches apart. Steam over boiling water 15 minutes. Serve hot.

YIELD: 20 to 22 buns

Sesame seed buns (or biscuits, really) have a nutty flavor that comes both from the sesame seed topping and from the sesame oil filling in the center. The breads are easy to make, and the only difficult part is getting the sesame oil in the center. With a little practice it is a technique easily mastered. The buns are served with Mongolian Hot Pot (see recipe).

SESAME SEED BUNS

2	cups lukewarm water
2½	teaspoons active dry yeast
2	teaspoons sugar
5	cups all-purpose flour
¼	cup sesame oil,* approximately
1	tablespoon corn syrup or honey
¼	cup water
1	cup sesame seeds,* approximately

* Available in Chinese markets and by mail order. For more information see Chapter XI.

1. Have the lukewarm water ready to be added as necessary.
2. Place the yeast in a large, warm mixing bowl (rinsed in hot water, drained, and wiped dry). Add ½ cup of the lukewarm water and stir to dissolve the yeast. Add the sugar and flour and start stirring with your hands. Add the remaining lukewarm water, stirring and kneading constantly with your hands to incorporate all the flour. Knead the dough well, and when smooth shape it into a ball. Place in a mixing bowl and cover closely with a towel. Let stand about one hour or until it rises, then turn it out onto a lightly floured board. Knead again.
3. Preheat the oven to 450 degrees.
4. Pinch off enough dough (about 2 ounces, if you have a scale) to make a biscuit measuring about 2 inches in diameter and just less than ½ inch thick. Press down to flatten it, then shape with your fingers to make it cup shaped. Always keep the unused dough covered as you work.

5. Have the sesame oil near in a small bowl. Break off a small piece of dough about the size of a large marble to be used as a "brush" for the oil. Dip the bottom of this dough into the sesame oil and rub the oil inside the cup of the biscuit that you shaped. Gather the outer edges of the biscuit together and pinch together to enclose the oil. The edges must be completely sealed, or the oil will escape. Now flatten the biscuit once more, sealed side down. Continue until the dough is used up.

6. Combine the syrup or honey and water in a small saucepan and warm, stirring to blend.

7. Brush the top of the biscuit with the syrup mixture and dip the top into the sesame seeds until generously coated. Place, seeded side up, on a lightly oiled baking sheet. Continue making biscuits until 1 baking sheet is filled. Do not let stand, but bake immediately in the oven 15 to 20 minutes, or until golden brown.

YIELD: About 2 dozen buns

Steamed loaf breads for the table are all but unheard of in the Western world outside of private Chinese kitchens, yet such breads are a staple food in the North, where rice is not grown. The bread has an excellent texture, and is very good served with Spicy Fresh Pork Casserole, Red-Cooked Pork, or Casserole Duck with Onions (see recipes), where it can be used to sop up the sauce. It can also be sliced thin and used instead of pancakes with Peking Duck I or II (see recipes). Sliced and deep-fried, it is quite phenomenally good.

STEAMED CHINESE BREADS

Follow the instructions for making the dough in the recipe for Roast Pork Steamed Buns. But after the dough has doubled in bulk, punch it down and turn it out onto a lightly floured board. Divide it in half and knead each half about 10 times. Shape into oval loaves each about 7 inches long. Allow to rise again for 10 to 15 minutes, until the loaves are plump. Line the top of a steamer with dampened cheesecloth and add the breads. Cover and steam over boiling water 30 minutes. Serve hot, cut into thirds, or, when cold, slice and deep-fry as indicated below.

DEEP-FRIED CHINESE BREAD

Heat oil for deep frying in a large saucepan, wok, or skillet, and when it is hot add ⅜-inch-thick slices of steamed bread (see preceding recipe). Cook, turning as necessary, until golden brown on both sides. Drain on paper toweling and serve hot. In Chinese homes the fried bread rounds are often served sprinkled with sugar as a snack; they are also good served (without the sugar) with Stir-Fry Crab Meat with Shrimp (see recipe).

Here is a recipe for the pancakes to be served with Peking Duck I and II and Mo-Shu-Ro (see recipes).

CHINESE PANCAKES ❖

2　cups unsifted all-purpose flour, or more as needed
¾　cup water, approximately
　　Sesame oil *

* Available in Chinese markets and by mail order. For more information see Chapter XI.

1. Place the flour in a mixing bowl and make a well in the center. Bring a little more than ¾ cup water to a boil. Start adding the boiling water to the flour, stirring rapidly with chopsticks or a fork. Add almost all the water, but reserve 2 or 3 tablespoons, unless it seems necessary to make a not too sticky dough. Turn the dough out onto a lightly floured surface and knead well until smooth and firm, about 5 minutes, using a little more flour as necessary to make a proper, smooth, not too sticky dough. On the other hand, you must

not use too much flour, or the dough will be tough. Put the dough into a mixing bowl and cover. Let stand 30 minutes to 1 hour.

2. Turn the dough out onto a lightly floured surface and knead briefly once more. Using your hands, roll it into a sausage shape about 1½ inches in diameter. With your fingers, divide the dough into 16 pieces of more or less equal size. Roll each piece between your hands to make a smooth ball.

3. Moisten your fingers and palms with a little sesame oil. Flatten one ball lightly with your palms to make a round "biscuit." Place it on a flat surface and brush the top with sesame oil.

4. Flatten another ball lightly with the palms to make another biscuit, and place this atop the first biscuit. They should be carefully matched in size. Using a rolling pin, roll out the biscuits, one atop the other, into a circle, turning the dough this way and that as necessary to keep the circle as uniform as possible. Roll first one side, then the other. The paired, sealed-together pancakes should measure about 5 to 7 inches in diameter.

5. Place a skillet on the stove and brush the bottom with sesame oil. Add one of the double pancakes and cook briefly, about half a minute or less. Turn and cook on the other side about half a minute longer. If brown spots appear, the pancake is overcooked. While still hot, use your fingers to pull the pancakes apart into 2 single pancakes. Continue cooking and separating the pancakes until all are cooked and separated. Lay out a length of aluminum foil and make a stack of pancakes in the center. Fold over the side of the foil to completely enclose the pancakes. Place the foil-wrapped pancakes in a steamer, cover, and steam 20 to 30 minutes.

YIELD: 16 to 20 pancakes

Note: Leftover pancakes may be frozen, wrapped in foil. They may be defrosted and steamed again, still in their foil wrapping, for 20 to 30 minutes.

Chinese cooks are masters of filled pastries, and one of the best of these is a northern Chinese delicacy that is similar in concept to American turnovers or French rissoles. This pastry is not found in Chinese restaurants because the ample meat and shrimp filling is too expensive for a commercial establishment.

PORK AND SHRIMP PASTRIES

The dough:

- 2 cups all-purpose flour
- ¾ cup cold water, approximately

The stuffing:

- 3 large leaves of celery cabbage *
- 1 tablespoon salt
- ½ pound raw shrimps, shelled and deveined
- ¾ pound ground pork
- 1 tablespoon cornstarch
- 2 tablespoons peanut, vegetable, or corn oil
- 1 tablespoon light soy sauce *
- 1 tablespoon dry sherry or shao hsing wine *
- 2 tablespoons water
- 1 tablespoon sesame oil *
- ½ teaspoon sugar
- 2 teaspoons salt, or to taste
- 3 tablespoons chopped scallions, green part included

Peanut, vegetable, or corn oil for pan frying

* Available in Chinese markets and by mail order. For more information see Chapter XI.

1. To make the dough, put the flour into a mixing bowl and gradually add the ¾ cup water, stirring with chopsticks to make a stiff dough. Gather the dough into your hands and shape it into a ball. If it won't hold together, add more water by the tablespoon.

Place in a bowl, cover with a cloth, and let stand at least 1 hour.

2. While the dough rests, prepare the stuffing. Pile the cabbage leaves on top of one another and cut into large dice, then chop until finely minced. Put into a bowl, add the salt, and mix in well. Set aside and let stand at least 10 minutes.

3. Chop the shrimps into small pieces, ½ inch or smaller. Add to the ground pork mix, then add the cornstarch and mix in well. Add 2 tablespoons oil, the soy sauce, the wine, the 2 tablespoons water, sesame oil, sugar, and salt and mix in thoroughly. Set aside.

4. Put the cabbage into a colander and discard the yielded liquid. Rinse the cabbage under running water, then squeeze dry with your hands. You should have about 1 cup, but a little more or less won't matter.

5. Add the cabbage to the meat mixture. Add the chopped scallions and mix thoroughly.

6. Turn the dough out onto a lightly floured board, and with floured fingers start rolling and kneading the dough until it is smooth in texture and malleable—about 5 to 10 minutes. Form into a sausage shape and divide the dough into 12 equal portions. Shape each portion into a ball, then with a rolling pin roll the ball out into a round about 4 inches in diameter. Keep both the balls and the round covered with a cloth as you work to prevent them from drying out.

7. Holding a circle of dough in your palm, put ¼ cup of filling in the center of the dough. With your other hand gather up the edges of the dough to enclose the filling, pleating and pinching the edges together into a little pouch similar to that for Roast Pork Steamed Buns (see p. 390). Pinch the top together and twist it to seal more firmly, twisting off and discarding a nugget of dough. Put the pastry on a floured board, pinched side down, and pat it gently into a biscuit about 3½ to 4 inches in diameter and ½ inch thick. As each piece is finished, transfer to a lightly floured baking sheet. Continue until all the dough is filled and ready.

8. In one or two skillets heat enough oil to amply cover the bottom of the pan. Cook the pastries over medium heat on one side until golden brown, then turn and cook the other side until browned, about ten minutes in all. Add a little more oil to the pan as necessary. Drain on paper toweling and serve hot.

YIELD: 12 pastries

These dumplings, as appetizers or as an entree, are as dainty as a lotus blossom and splendid to the taste. They are made with a spinach dough and a fresh pumpkin and dried shrimp filling. This is a family recipe from Virginia Lee, not available elsewhere.

PUMPKIN DUMPLINGS WITH SPINACH CASINGS

The dough:

    3   cups all-purpose flour, approximately
    6   spinach leaves
    1¼ cups boiling water

The filling:

    1   cup dried shrimps *
    3   tablespoons peanut, vegetable, or corn oil
    3   cups finely diced fresh pumpkin
    ¼   cup hot water
    ½   teaspoon sugar
    ½   teaspoon monosodium glutamate (optional)
        Salt to taste
    1   cup finely chopped scallions, green part included
    3   tablespoons sesame oil *

* Available in Chinese markets and by mail order. For more information see Chapter XI.

1. To make the dough, place the flour in a mixing bowl.
2. Drop the spinach leaves into boiling water and let stand about 1 minute. Drain well, squeeze dry, and measure out 1 rounded tablespoon. Discard the remainder.
3. Put the spinach into the container of an electric blender and add the 1¼ cups boiling water. Blend quickly.
4. While the water is still piping hot, start adding it to the flour, stirring with chopsticks or a fork. When the dough is cool enough to handle, start kneading it. If necessary, add 2 to 4 more table-spoons flour to make a soft but workable dough. Knead about 10

minutes, roll into a ball, and place in a lightly floured mixing bowl. Cover with a clean cloth and let rest about 30 minutes.

5. Meanwhile, prepare the filling. Put the shrimps into a mixing bowl and add boiling water to cover. Let stand 15 minutes. Drain and chop fine.

6. Heat the oil in a wok or skillet and add the shrimps. Cook over high heat, stirring, about 1 minute. Add the pumpkin and cook, stirring, about 2 minutes. Add the hot water and cook about 2 minutes, stirring, until soft. Add the sugar, monosodium glutamate, and salt and turn off the heat. Add the scallions and sesame oil and stir just to blend. Transfer to a mixing bowl and let stand until cool.

7. To make the dumplings, pull off pieces of dough to shape into balls about 1 inch in diameter for regular dumplings; about ¾ inch in diameter for cocktail-size dumplings. Roll out thin and spoon about 2 teaspoons of filling into the larger rounds of dough, 1 teaspoon for the smaller rounds. Fill and fold like jao-tze (see step 5 of Fried Jao-Tze recipe). Arrange the dumplings on plates that will fit in the top of a steamer. Cover and steam one or two plates at a time (depending on the size of plates and number of racks or layers in the steamer) over boiling water for 12 to 15 minutes.

YIELD: 18 dumplings (regular)

This is an incredible fermented dish that serves both as a dessert eaten plain (it is, by the way, slightly intoxicating) or with preserved fruit and as an ingredient in numerous Chinese dishes, including Szechwan shrimp. It is called *junya* or *chu yao*, pronounced vaguely "june yow."

FERMENTED RICE OR WINE RICE ❖

  1½ pounds glutinous rice *
  1   wine ball or wine cube *
  1   tablespoon all-purpose flour

* Available in Chinese markets and by mail order. For more information see Chapter XI.

1. Soak the rice overnight in cold water to cover, then drain.

2. Line a steamer top or a colander with cheesecloth and add the drained rice. Cover and steam 1 hour.

3. Crush the wine ball or cube on a flat surface, using a mallet or rolling pin. When it is crushed fine like a powder, blend well with the flour. Set aside.

4. Rinse the rice delicately in lukewarm water, working gently with your hands to separate the grains. The rice should be at about body temperature when it is ready. If it is too warm at this time, it will ferment too quickly. If it is too cold, it will not ferment.

5. When the rice is right, drain it well. Sprinkle with the wine ball or cube mixture and work gently with your fingers to mix thoroughly. Spoon the rice into a thin bowl and smooth the top with the fingers.

6. Using your fingers, make a hole or well in the center, about 1 inch in diameter. Pat the top of the rice with wet fingers to smooth it. But do not disturb the hole or well. You will see later when you uncover the rice that the hole or well accumulates liquid as the rice stands.

7. Cover the bowl well and then carefully wrap it in blankets. Set the blanket-covered bowl in a warm (but not too warm) place and let it stand for 24 hours. If properly made and all the elements are right, liquid will have accumulated in the hole or well.

8. Spoon the rice and liquid into mason jars and seal loosely. Let stand to room temperature, then refrigerate. The wine rice keeps for weeks in the refrigerator, but you should loosen the tops occasionally to make sure too much gas is not accumulating inside the jars.

YIELD: 3 pints

Note: If you wish to make a fresh batch, save about ½ cup of the old batch and add it to each quart of the new batch before storing. This will make the new batch sweeter and give it more kick.

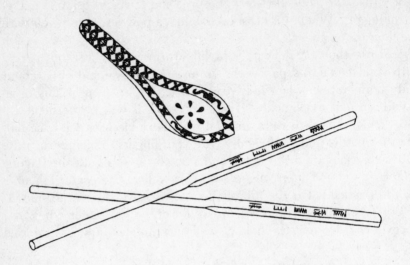

X

Desserts

Soup, in China, is one of the commonest forms of dessert, and one of the most agreeable is a smooth, delicate, and lightly sugared coconut soup made from the milk extracted from freshly grated coconut.

COCONUT SOUP

2   fresh coconuts in the shell
3   cups water
2   cups milk
7   tablespoons sugar

1. Preheat the oven to 325 degrees.
2. Place the coconuts on an oven rack and bake about 10 or 15 minutes. This will facilitate removing the coconut meat from the shells when they are cracked.
3. Remove the coconuts, and when they are cool enough to handle puncture the "eyes" at the top of each coconut with an ice pick. Drain and discard the white liquid from the center. Using a hammer or other heavy instrument, crack the coconuts. Pare away the dark outer coating of the snow-white coconut meat with a swivel-bladed paring knife. Rinse and drain the coconut meat and then cut it into cubes, 1 inch or smaller.

4. Put half the coconut cubes (or fewer depending on the capacity of the blender) into the container of an electric blender.

5. Bring the water and milk almost but not quite to a boil and add about half of it to the blender. Cover the container and blend the coconut as fine as possible.

6. Line a large mixing bowl with a double layer of cheesecloth and pour in the first batch of coconut. Repeat with the second batch. Gather up the edges of cheesecloth and squeeze quite gently to extract only the liquid without the pulp. There should be about 4½ cups of liquid, which is, in cooking terms, coconut milk.

7. Pour the coconut milk into a saucepan and add the sugar. Bring to a boil, stirring, and serve hot.

YIELD: 6 or more servings

This dessert soup is one of the most intriguing soups of any national kitchen. It has the subtle sweetness of Chinese dried dates, plus the odd and unusual goodness of fresh walnuts.

WALNUT DATE SOUP

¼   pound dried Chinese dates * (about 40 dates)
4   cups plus 2 tablespoons water
1½   cups walnut meats
¼   cup sugar
½   tablespoon cornstarch

* Available in Chinese markets and by mail order. For more information see Chapter XI.

1. Put the dates into a saucepan and soak them in about 2½ cups of cold water for about 4 hours. Drain. Put on to boil in the 4 cups of water, and when the water boils cover and simmer about 1½ to 2 hours. Let cool. Drain but reserve the cooking liquid.

2. Peel and remove the seeds of the dates. There should be about ¾ cup of pulp. Set aside.

3. Bring enough water to a boil to cover the walnut meats. Add them and simmer about 6 minutes. Drain.

4. Put the date pulp into the container of an electric blender and add 1 cup of the reserved date water. Add the drained walnuts and blend until the mixture is smooth. Pour this into a saucepan and add 1 more cup of date liquid to the blender. Add 2 cups of cold water and blend to rinse out the blender. Add this to the saucepan. Stir in the sugar and bring to a boil.

5. Blend the cornstarch and the remaining 2 tablespoons of water and stir into the simmering soup. Serve piping hot.

YIELD: 6 to 8 servings

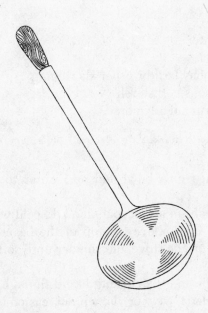

Perhaps the most traditional and best-known Chinese "banquet" dessert in the Western world is what is called Eight Precious Jewel Pudding or, sometimes, simply "Eight Precious Pudding." The name comes about because of the colors used to garnish the outside of the dish—the red of cut-out cherries, the brown of dates, and so on. The basis for the dish is glutinous rice filled with bean paste.

EIGHT PRECIOUS JEWEL PUDDING

The pudding:

> 2　cups glutinous rice *
> 1　cup dried red beans * (about ½ pound)
> ½　cup sugar
> ¼　cup peanut, vegetable, or corn oil
> 　　Lard or other shortening
> 　　Assorted dried and candied fruits, such as cherries, angelica, figs, dates, for decoration

The sauce:

> 2¼　cups water
> ½　cup sugar
> 2　tablespoons lard or other shortening
> 2　tablespoons cornstarch
> 　　Grated rind of 1 lemon

* Available in Chinese markets and by mail order. For more information see Chapter XI.

1. Place the rice in a bowl and add water to cover. Let stand overnight.

2. Place the beans in a saucepan and add cold water to cover to a depth of about 1 inch above the top of the beans. Let stand overnight, then place on the stove and simmer until soft, about 1½ hours. Do not drain.

3. Put the beans and the cooking liquid through a sieve. Pour the mixture into a clean wok or flameproof casserole and cook over

high heat about 30 minutes, stirring frequently. Add the sugar and continue cooking, stirring almost constantly, 10 to 15 minutes, until the mixture has the consistency and look of black bean soup.

4. Dribble the oil around the edges of the beans in a fine stream, stirring all the while to incorporate it into the beans. Continue cooking and stirring until the beans have the consistency of refried beans or mashed potatoes. Spoon and scrape the mixture into a mixing bowl with a rubber spatula.

5. Drain the rice. Line the top of a steamer with cheesecloth and spread the rice over it. Cover and steam over boiling water for 1 hour. Cool.

6. Select a mold. (A soufflé dish that measures 3 by 7 inches will do.) Lightly grease the inside of the mold, sides and bottom, with lard. Put into the freezer briefly to harden the lard so the decorations will stick. Use cut-out pieces of thinly sliced dried and candied fruits to garnish the bottom and sides of the mold. Press down a layer of glutinous rice over the bottom of the mold, then press a layer uniformly around the sides. Leave a neat well in the center for the bean paste. Spoon the paste in the center and mold it to fit the rice. Cover with a layer of rice to totally enclose the bean paste. Place the mold, uncovered, in the top of a steamer and steam 1 hour. Unmold and serve hot.

7. For the sauce, combine 2 cups of the water, the sugar, and lard in a saucepan. Bring to a boil. Blend the cornstarch with the ¼ cup water and stir in. Add the grated lemon rind and cook, stirring, until thickened. Pour over the unmolded pudding.

YIELD: 8 to 10 servings

Although to Westerners Eight Precious Jewel Pudding is probably the best-known dessert in the Chinese repertoire, there is one that could match it in flavor and texture. An interesting dish, it too is made with glutinous rice and a paste of Chinese red beans. They are rolled together and served with a powder of toasted ground sesame seeds and sugar.

RED SAND RICE ROLL ❖

    1½ cups glutinous rice *
    1½ cups dried red beans *
    ½   cup plus ⅔ cup sugar
    ⅓   cup peanut, vegetable, or corn oil
    2   4-ounce packages black sesame seeds *

* Available in Chinese markets and by mail order. For more information see Chapter XI.

1. Soak the glutinous rice in cold water to cover for 6 hours or overnight.

2. Place the beans in a mixing bowl and add water to cover to a depth of 1 inch above the top of the beans. Let stand overnight.

3. Pour the beans and water into a saucepan and bring to a boil. Cook 1 hour, or until the beans are soft. Do not drain.

4. Meanwhile, drain the glutinous rice. Line the top of a steamer with cheesecloth and add the glutinous rice, distributing it evenly over the cheesecloth. Place a lid on the steamer and steam 1 hour. Let cool.

5. Put the cooked beans and the cooking liquid through a sieve. Pour the mixture into a clean wok or flameproof casserole and cook over high heat about 30 minutes, stirring frequently. Add the ½ cup sugar and continue cooking, stirring almost constantly, 10 to 15 minutes, until the mixture has the consistency and look of black bean soup.

6. Dribble the oil around the edges of the beans in a fine stream, stirring all the while to incorporate it into the beans. Continue cooking and stirring until the beans have the consistency of refried beans

or mashed potatoes. With a rubber spatula, spoon and scrape the mixture into a mixing bowl.

7. Lay out a clean wet dish towel on a flat surface and spoon the glutinous rice in a mound in the center of the cloth. Using your hands, shape the rice into a smooth rectangle measuring more or less 7 x 14 inches.

8. Spoon 2 cups of the red bean paste onto the bottom third of the rectangle. The bean paste will be the filling, and the object is to wrap the glutinous rice around the bean paste uniformly.

9. Shape the bean paste into a sausage shape with your hands. Bring up that end of the towel and lift so that the rice rolls over and over itself to enclose the paste. Shape the rice, bean paste enclosed, into a fat oval. Lift this onto a plate.

10. Empty the sesame seeds into a saucepan and toast over medium low heat, shaking the pan and stirring the seeds, until they have a nice nutty odor. Do not let them burn. Once they are toasted, remove them from the heat and continue shaking the pan and stirring because they keep cooking briefly from retained heat. Let cool.

11. When the seeds are at room temperature, empty them into the container of an electric blender and blend fine.

12. Blend ¾ cup of the powdered sesame seeds with the ⅔ cup sugar and sprinkle over the rice roll. Slice and serve cold.

YIELD: 10 to 12 servings

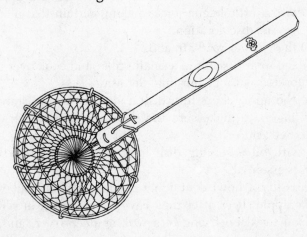

Among the great and most interesting desserts of the Chinese kitchen are fried apple slices bathed in candy syrup with black sesame seeds, which are eaten piping hot after a quick dip in cold water to harden the syrup. The technique is basically simple, although it does require a judicious eye in knowing the precise moment when the syrup is ready—at the hard-crack stage.

CANDIED APPLE SLICES

3   firm, sweet, unblemished apples (about 1½ to 1¾ pounds)
     Lemon juice
1   teaspoon red wine vinegar
2   tablespoons black sesame seeds °
1   cup cornstarch
     Peanut, vegetable, or corn oil
2½   cups cold water, approximately
1½   cups sugar

° Available in Chinese markets and by mail order. For more information see Chapter XI.

1. Peel the apples and core them, using a melon ball cutter. Cut the apples into sixths. Cut each slice into thirds and sprinkle immediately with a little lemon juice, making certain that all slices are coated to prevent discoloration.

2. Have the vinegar ready to add.

3. Place the sesame seeds in a small skillet and cook over moderate heat until toasted without burning. Set aside.

4. Place the apple slices in a dish and add the cornstarch. Work with your fingers to make sure the slices are liberally coated with cornstarch. Set aside.

5. Rub with oil a serving dish large enough to hold the apple slices. This is essential.

6. Have ready a bowl containing 2 cups of very cold water for dipping the apple slices after they have been dipped in syrup.

7. Heat oil for deep frying in a wok or deep-fryer, and when it

is very hot add the apple slices. Cook about 10 minutes, or until golden brown, without being mushy. Drain.

8. In another wok or saucepan add the ½ cup water and the sugar. Cook, stirring, until the sugar spins a thread. Watch carefully and spoon the syrup a few drops at a time into a basin of cold water to test. When the sugar come to the hard-crack stage and hardens in the water and starts to caramelize, add the vinegar, stirring, and immediately add the apples. Turn the apples in the syrup to coat, then add the sesame seeds. Add the slices to the prepared dish and serve with the bowl of cold water. Each slice is dipped in the cold water before it is eaten.

YIELD: 6 to 8 servings

The Chinese delight at times in novel desserts, those with surprise fillings and three different textures and flavors from outside in. This is one of those desserts, a fantasy with a toasted black sesame seed center, a rice powder shell, and an outer coating of white sesame seeds. After it is cooked, the dessert is served with a final "dust" of more toasted black sesame seeds and sugar.

SESAME SEED BALLS

1   pound solid leaf fat * (this is not commercially packaged rendered lard)
2   4-ounce packages black sesame seeds * (2 cups)
1½ cups sugar
2½ cups glutinous rice powder *
1¼ cups warm water, approximately
½   cup white sesame seeds *
    Peanut, vegetable, or corn oil for deep frying

* Available in Chinese markets and by mail order. For more information see Chapter XI.

1. Place the leaf fat on a flat surface and scrape it across the top with a knife to remove the fine, smooth, buttery, soft-textured fat. If any traces of fiber or membrane are scraped off with the fat, remove with your fingers and discard. Continue scraping off smooth fat to make 6 level tablespoons, and set aside. Save the rest of the piece of lard for another use.

2. Empty the black sesame seeds into a saucepan and toast over moderate heat, shaking the pan constantly, until they give off a nutlike fragrance. Do not let them burn or they will become bitter. Let cool, then empty the seeds into the container of an electric blender. Blend to a powder, stirring down as necessary.

3. Empty out one cup of the powdered seeds and set aside. Pour the remainder into a mixing bowl.

4. To the seeds in the bowl add ½ cup of the sugar (more to taste if desired) and the 6 tablespoons leaf fat. Blend together well with your fingers. Shape into 18 to 20 balls.

5. Put the rice powder into a bowl and add the warm water a little at a time while kneading. Knead to make a soft but firm dough; you may need a little more or a little less than 1¼ cups water.

6. Using the palms of your hands, shape the dough into 2-inch round, smooth balls.

7. With thumb and fingers, form each ball into a cup shape large enough to go around a sesame seed ball. Fill the center of each cup with one ball. Gather the edges of each cup together to enclose the ball, pinch the ends to seal, and roll once more between your palms to make a round, smooth ball. That amount of dough should cover approximately 18 to 20 balls, but if you have some sesame seed balls left over they may be frozen indefinitely.

8. Pour the white sesame seeds into a pie plate or some other rimmed container. Roll each ball liberally in the seeds. If they don't stick, moisten the surface of each ball with wet fingers and roll it in the seeds again.

9. Heat the oil in a wok or deep-fryer to moderately hot. The oil must not be too hot, for the balls must cook through to the center. Let the balls simmer gently in the oil while spooning oil over and turning the balls over as they cook, 8 to 10 minutes. Drain on paper toweling.

10. Mix the cup of reserved powdered black sesame seeds with the remaining cup of sugar. Arrange the balls on a platter and cover with the sugar and seed mixture. Serve warm or hot.

YIELD: 18 to 20 balls, 6 to 10 servings

The following dish is quite similar to the crepe desserts found in French cooking. It is made with Chinese pancakes stuffed with an apricot filling plus peanuts.

CHINESE PANCAKES WITH APRICOT FILLING AND PEANUTS

The pancakes:

    1   cup all-purpose flour
    1½ tablespoons sugar
    1   egg
    1   egg white
    1   cup minus 3 tablespoons water
    1   tablespoon peanut, vegetable, or corn oil

The filling:

    2   1-pound cans whole apricots
    3   tablespoons peanut, vegetable, or corn oil
    2   tablespoons cornstarch
    ¼   cup water

The assembly and garnish:

        Peanut, vegetable, or corn oil
    2   cups raw shelled and hulled unsalted peanuts *
    1   cup sugar

* Available in Chinese markets and by mail order. For more information see Chapter XI.

1. Measure the flour into a mixing bowl and add the sugar, egg, and egg white. Mix well to blend and add the water gradually, stirring constantly. Strain through a sieve to remove any lumps, then stir in the oil. A 2-cup glass measuring cup is good for pouring the batter.

2. Follow any standard procedure for making French crepes; that is to say, use a standard 6- or 7-inch crepe pan or a small skillet. It must be brushed lightly with oil and wiped out to remove excess oil before using. Heat the pan, and when it is hot add a tablespoon or so of batter, swirling it around as the pan is tilted this way and that to distribute the batter as evenly as possible over the bottom of the pan. Cook briefly without browning—just until the pancake sets on one side—then turn the pancake, using a spatula or pancake turner. Cook briefly on that side, but just enough to dry the pancake without browning. Continue making pancakes until all the batter is used, wiping the pan with oil as necessary.

3. To make the filling, drain the apricots but reserve ½ cup of liquid. Remove and discard the pits from the apricots and put the apricots into a saucepan. Add the ½ cup of liquid and cook, stirring and mashing down to thicken the fruit, about 3 minutes. Add the oil and continue cooking and stirring to make a paste, about 4 or 5 minutes. Blend the cornstarch with the water and stir it in. Spoon out. There should be about 1¼ cups.

4. Before finishing the dish, heat about 2 cups of oil for deep frying in a saucepan, and when it is quite hot add the peanuts. You may test the heat of the oil by dropping one peanut in to see the time it takes to brown. Add the peanuts and stir, cooking just until they are golden. Take care, because they can become overdone or burned quickly. Drain immediately, then spread on paper toweling to remove excess oil.

5. Grind the peanuts in a grinder or blend them coarsely. Mix with the sugar.

6. To assemble the dish, spoon equal amounts of filling into each of the pancakes and fold over, envelope fashion, to enclose.

7. Heat about ⅛ inch of oil in one or two skillets and add the pancakes. Cook, turning gently to heat through, then drain on paper

toweling. Serve on individual plates. Sprinkle with the peanut and sugar mixture before serving.

YIELD: 16 pancakes

FLUFFY DATE PASTRY

The filling:

    1 pound dried Chinese dates,* soaked in cold water to cover overnight
    ¼ cup peanut, vegetable, or corn oil
    ¼ cup sugar or more to taste

The pastry:

    3 cups all-purpose flour
    1 cup melted lard (preferably rendered leaf lard; see Chapter XI)
      Peanut, vegetable, or corn oil
    ½ cup water

    Peanut, vegetable, or corn oil for deep frying, at least 6 cups

---

* Available in Chinese markets and by mail order. For more information see Chapter XI.

---

1. Place the drained dates in a kettle and add 3 quarts cold water. Bring to a boil, cover, and cook over medium heat until soft, about 1½ hours or more.

2. Cool the dates in the liquid until they can be handled. Remove them and reserve the liquid. With your fingers press out the pulp from each date, discarding the skin and pit.

3. Heat the ¼ cup oil in a wok or skillet and add the date paste. Measure out 1 cup of the reserved liquid and stir into the dates. Cook over medium heat, stirring and pressing the dates against

the sides of the pan, for about 2 minutes. Add the sugar, stirring and mashing the mixture briskly and constantly until the liquid has cooked off. The mixture should become quite "volcanic" and thick, but be careful not to let it burn. When it is ready it should stand in peaks and have the consistency of mashed potatoes, or just a bit thinner. Pour the filling into a bowl to cool and refrigerate overnight if desired.

4. To make the pastry, put half the flour into a mixing bowl that will fit in the top of a steamer. Steam, covered, over boiling water for at least 30 minutes. Let cool, overnight is desired.

5. To this flour gradually add ½ cup of melted lard. Stir with chopsticks, adding just enough oil to make the flour hold together. Knead to make a dough. (This oil dough will be called dough A to simplify matters.)

6. Put the remaining flour into a mixing bowl. Blend the remaining melted lard with the ½ cup of water. Add this gradually to the flour in the bowl, stirring the liquid before each addition to mix the oil and water, and kneading thoroughly into the flour with your hands until the dough is soft and malleable. You may need only half of the oil and water mixture; the amount required will depend on the absorbency of the flour. Knead with your hands for about 5 minutes, then cover and let stand for 15 minutes. (This dough will henceforth be referred to as dough B.)

7. Roll dough A between your palms into a thick sausage and pinch it off into 24 pieces. Roll each piece between your palms into a ball.

8. Roll dough B into a sausage and divide into about 20 pieces. Roll each piece into a ball, then form into a cup with your fingers. Wrap each cup around a ball of dough A, making sure that dough A is completely covered. Continue until all of dough B is used up and discard the remainder of dough A.

9. Roll each ball between your palms into a tube the size of a fat cigar.

10. With a rolling pin roll each tube into a long oval. Roll up the oval into a cylinder.

11. Cut each cylinder in half. Stand each cylinder, coiled side up, and press down and roll out into a 2½-inch circle. Continue until all the dough has been prepared.

12. To fill, take one of the circles and put about 1 level tablespoon of filling in its center. Top with another circle and pinch the edges together firmly to seal, making a ¼-inch border all around. If the edges are very uneven, trim into a circle with scissors.

13. Pinch and crimp the edges with your fingers as illustrated.

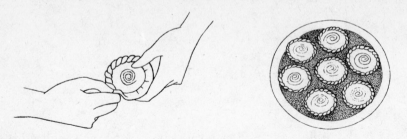

Continue until the filling or pastry has been used up. (The pastries may be refrigerated at this point until you are ready to cook. They may also be frozen in a tightly sealed container. If frozen, defrost before proceeding with the recipe.)

14. In a wok or deep-fryer, heat oil until hot, about 200 degrees. Use as much oil as possible; the deeper the oil, the fluffier the pastry. Add the pastries, one at a time, and fry until the pastry puffs up on both sides, which means it is done. Watch the heat of the oil carefully, turning the fire off if the pastries start to turn brown. They should remain a very pale gold, almost white. It may or may not be necessary to turn the pastries over in the oil; if one side doesn't puff, or looks raw, turn it over.

15. The first pastries should be almost cooked by the time the last pastry is added if you are using a large pan; if the pan is small, cook the pastries in batches. Drain on paper toweling and serve hot or warm.

YIELD: About 20 pastries

XI

Chinese Ingredients– Where and How to Obtain Them

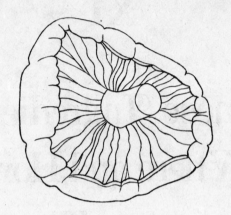

For convenience this list is arranged alphabetically with the name of the ingredient given exactly as it appears in the recipe. For instance, information about various kinds of mushrooms will be listed individually under "Dried Black Mushrooms," "Straw Mushrooms," and "Tree Ear Mushrooms" rather than under "Mushrooms."

Many Chinese markets package ingredients under their own brand names, and in general Chinese markets and manufacturers are somewhat casual about translating the names of their wares into English. Sometimes the name of a product is not given in English on the label at all; at other times it may be vague or inaccurate. The Chinese name of any ingredient, on the other hand, is usually specific and unambiguous. A reader buying an ingredient for the first time would be well advised to trace the Chinese name of the food he wants so that he can show it to the storekeeper, or to bring this book with him when he shops.

A list of Chinese markets and mail-order sources appears at the end of the chapter.

Abalone 鮑魚

The flesh of this deep-sea shellfish comes in cans weighing approximately 1 pound. Once opened, the abalone can be stored in the refrigerator for 4 to 6 days if it is put into a jar with a tight lid and covered with its own liquid.

Bamboo Shoots 冬筍

The most common variety of this basic ingredient is the size of an egg or larger and comes in various-sized cans weighing from 6 ounces upward. Smaller bamboo shoots—sometimes labeled "Bamboo Shoot Tips"—which resemble large white asparagus are also available. Both kinds of bamboo shoot can be used interchangeably in recipes. All parts of the canned bamboo are usable, since the shoots have been cleaned and trimmed before canning. Once opened, bamboo shoots may be covered with water and stored in the refrigerator in a lidded container for about a month if the water is changed every few days. To freshen the taste of canned bamboo, drain and rinse the shoots and put them into a saucepan with cold water to cover. Bring the water to a boil and simmer the shoots for 15 to 30 minutes. This is a desirable but not essential step.

Banshu Somen 掛麵

Sometimes called "Alimentary paste noodles," these are thin dried Japanese noodles made from wheat flour. They are widely available in Japanese markets as well as in Chinese stores. Each 1-pound package contains 5 packets of noodles.

Bean Sauce 豆辦醬

Also called "Whole Bean Sauce" or "Yellow Bean Sauce," this thick sauce is made from yellow beans, flour, and water and is sold in round or oblong 1-pound tins. Once opened, it will keep for several months in the refrigerator if transferred into a clean screw-top jar.

Bean Sprouts 綠豆芽

Mung bean sprouts are sold fresh, by the pound, in Chinese groceries. The best bean sprouts are plump and very white. The entire sprout is edible, but in fine Chinese cooking it is customary to pluck off and discard both the small yellow nubbin at the top and the fine threadlike root at the bottom. This is a tedious task—it takes about an hour to prepare a pound—and in most run-of-the-mill Chinese restaurants in America it is a refinement that is seldom bothered with. In the home, of course, it is an optional matter. However, if the sprouts are not to be plucked, they should be dropped into a basin of cold water and rinsed and picked over. Only the firm, whitest bean sprouts should be used; bruised ones should be discarded. The measurements for bean sprouts are given by volume in this book: when the recipe calls for a cup of bean sprouts, it means one cup of plucked or whole sprouts. Like any other vegetable, bean sprouts are at their best when they are bought fresh and used the same day. They do keep very well, however, for two or three days if they are placed in a closed plastic bag and stored in the refrigerator.

Bitter Melon 苦瓜(凉瓜)

These vegetables resemble cucumbers in size and shape. They are generally available from April to September. They are cooked and served with the skin left on; the seeds and pulp in the center should be scraped off and discarded. The melons are usually blanched to remove some of the bitter taste.

Caul or Lace Fat 網油

Caul fat comes in large, webby sheets which look like delicate lace. Sold by the pound, it can be purchased in butcher shops in German and Italian neighborhoods as well as in Chinese markets. The fat will keep in the refrigerator for 2 or 3 days or in the freezer for 1 or 2 months. Caul fat melts away to nothing when it is cooked.

Celery Cabbage   天津白菜

This is often called Tientsin cabbage by Northern Chinese. The kind usually available in Chinese markets is rounder and fatter than a long, thin variety often found in supermarkets. Both varieties taste the same and can be used interchangeably in all recipes. Celery cabbage will retain its crispness for about a week if it is wrapped tightly in plastic wrap and stored in the vegetable compartment of the refrigerator. Many recipes for this cabbage call for use of the stalks only, since the tender leafy part cooks very quickly and makes the dish mushy. The discarded leaves can be saved for soup.

Cellophane Noodles   粉絲

Also labeled "bean thread," "transparent noodles," or "vermicelli," these noodles are made from mung bean flour. They really do look as if they have been made from cellophane. They are sold by the package in quantities ranging from 2 to 8 ounces. The noodles can also be purchased in Japanese groceries.

Chili Paste with Garlic   香豉辣醬

Sometimes called "Szechwan Paste," this is made from hot peppers, salt, and garlic and is sold in 8-ounce bottles. It will keep indefinitely in the refrigerator.

Chinese Cabbage   白菜（中國）

A dark green leafy vegetable with a yellow flower, this is called "*bak choy*" by the Cantonese. (The term is not used in this book because Northerners refer to celery cabbage by this name, which makes things confusing.) The cabbage is available in Chinese groceries all year round. It will keep for a week in the vegetable compartment of the refrigerator if it is wrapped in a plastic bag or plastic wrap.

Chinese Chives   中國韭菜

This seasonal vegetable is available in spring and early summer, when it is sold by the bunch in Chinese markets. Garden-variety American chives are not a satisfactory substitute for these chives, which have a different and more pungent taste. The chives will last for a week in the vegetable compartment of the refrigerator if wrapped in plastic wrap.

Chinese Dates   中國紅棗

These dried red prunelike objects are about the size of a marble. They are sold in 4-, 8-, and 16-ounce plastic packages. The dates must be soaked in cold water overnight before use. In their dried state, they will keep for a month or even years.

Chinese Mustard   芥末粉

To make hot Chinese mustard, put a small quantity of any brand of dried mustard powder (the kind sold on the spice shelves of American markets) into a small bowl and slowly pour over it a little boiling water, stirring constantly until it has the consistency of a thin puree. Do not make the mustard too thin, but remember it will thicken slightly as it stands. Season to taste with salt, then let stand for at least 20 minutes. Do not serve immediately because it will be bitter.

Chinese Mustard Greens   芥菜

Called "*gai choy*" in Cantonese, this leafy vegetable has somewhat the same shape as a head of escarole. Its green stems are deeply grooved in a handsome swirling pattern. Mustard greens will keep for a week in the vegetable compartment of the refrigerator, tightly wrapped in plastic wrap.

Chinese Roast Pork   义燒肉

Almost every Chinese grocery barbecues its own strips of roast pork, displayed on hooks in the meat section. The dark brown meat is completely cooked and can be sliced and eaten as it comes or used in a recipe. The pork strips should be stored like any other cooked meat.

Chinese Sausage   臘腸

Chinese sausage is made either from liver or from pork; the liver sausage is a somewhat darker reddish-brown than the pork sausage. Pork sausage is scarce or unavailable during the hottest summer months of July and August. The sausage can be stored without refrigeration for a week or ten days and for a month or so in the refrigerator in a plastic bag.

Chinese sausage is cooked by steaming. Place the whole sausage on a dish in a steamer, cover it, and steam it over boiling water for at least 20 minutes. Serve it cut diagonally into slices about ¼ inch thick. A traditional way of cooking sausage is to place the sausage (after cutting the string) on rice while it is cooking, once the rice has absorbed all the water in the pot. The oil from the sausage seeps down into the rice and flavors it.

Chinese Winter-Cured Pork   臘肉

A form of Chinese bacon made from pork belly, this is sold in strips in Chinese markets by weight. The strips will keep for a month or so if hung in a cool place.

Chrysanthemum Leaves   塘蒿

These leaves are not from the kind of chrysanthemum that grows in American gardens, although the leaves of both plants resemble each other. The vegetable, available only in the spring and summer, is sold by the bunch. The leaves will keep for about a week in the vegetable compartment of the refrigerator, wrapped in plastic wrap.

Dried Bean Curd Sheets   大腐皮

These paper-thin light brown half-circles are very fragile and are often broken; they can be repaired by wetting and overlapping the broken edges. They are sold in packages of 10 and will keep without refrigeration for 3 to 4 months or longer. Eventually the sheets will turn rancid, since oil is used in making them.

Dried Black Mushrooms 冬菇

These mushrooms are sold in 4- and 8-ounce plastic bags and will keep in their dried state for months or even years. They are always soaked in boiling water to cover for at least 15 to 30 minutes before they are used.

Dried Brown Bean Curd 豆腐乾

These are tan (or darker) pressed squares about 2½ inches across, which are sold by the piece. They will keep in the refrigerator for about a week if they are carefully sealed in plastic wrap to prevent them from drying out.

Dried Chestnuts 乾粟子

These are available in some supermarkets as well as in Chinese markets. Sold already peeled in 12-ounce plastic bags, they must be soaked in water overnight before they are used in a recipe.

Dried Jellyfish 海蜇皮

Sometimes found in the refrigerator section of a store, this comes in 1-pound tan slabs sealed in a plastic bag. Sometimes it is labeled "Salted Jelly Fish." It will keep in the refrigerator for several weeks.

Dried Lotus Seeds 蓮子

These starchy "seeds" are the color and shape of an oversized raw peanut. They come from the giant lotus pods which resemble a shower head. They are sold in 8- and 16-ounce plastic bags. Like most dried ingredients, they will keep indefinitely in their dried form.

Dried Red Beans 紅豆

These beans are sold in 1-pound plastic bags. They will keep without refrigeration for months if stored in a covered jar.

Dried Sea Slug 海參

The size of a sea slug varies, but it averages about 2 inches in diameter and 8 inches in length. Sold by the piece, it will keep indefinitely without refrigeration.

Dried Shrimps 蝦米

These are highly salted and have a pungent taste which many Westerners never manage to acquire. They are sold in 2- to 8-ounce plastic packages. They will keep indefinitely in a covered container without refrigeration.

Dried Squid 魷魚

Pieces of squid are sold in plastic bags weighing 8 to 16 ounces. They will keep indefinitely without refrigeration.

Fermented Salted Black Beans 豆豉

An ingredient of Cantonese cooking but virtually unknown elsewhere in China, these black beans, sometimes simply called "Salted Black Bean," are sold in 1-pound cans or in 8- and 16-ounce plastic bags. They will keep for months if stored in the refrigerator in a covered jar.

Fish Sauce 魚露

A sauce made with fish extract, water, and salt, this is sold in 12- and 24-ounce bottles.

Five Spices Powder 五香粉

This is commercially available in 4-ounce plastic bags. A homemade powder can be made by combining 60 peppercorns, 4 whole star anise (or the equivalent in broken bits and pieces), 2 teaspoons fennel seeds, 4 1-inch pieces cinnamon bark, and 12 whole cloves in the container of an electric blender and blending until everything is powdered. This will yield about 1½ tablespoons of powder; the quantities may be doubled or tripled. Five spices powder should be tightly wrapped in a plastic bag or piece of plastic wrap and stored in a screw-top jar. It will stay fresh for up to 6 months.

Fresh Bacon 五花肉

Often called pork belly, the fresh bacon sold in Chinese markets comes with the rind left on and the bone in as a matter of course. You should remember to specify this when ordering the meat from a non-Chinese butcher, since the recipes in this book require the rind.

Fresh Chinese Noodles 麵

These noodles are sold in 1-pound plastic bags. They may be refrigerated for 3 or 4 days and will keep for several months in the freezer if the bag is wrapped tightly in heavy foil.

Fresh Coriander 香菜

An essential in any well-run Chinese kitchen, this green is grown from ordinary coriander seeds such as those found on supermarket spice shelves. It is available almost all year round in Chinese groceries, and occasionally during the spring and summer in Italian greengrocers, where it is called *cilantro,* and in Spanish markets, where it is called *culantro.* To store, put the root ends into a tall jar and fill the jar with water. The leaves should be covered with a plastic bag which fits over the mouth of the jar. Secure the bag with a rubber band and put the whole thing into the refrigerator. The coriander will stay fresh for about a week.

Fresh Ginger 薑

Knotty knobs of fresh ginger root are sold by the piece, by weight. It will keep for a month in the refrigerator if it is tightly wrapped in plastic wrap. For appearance' sake, a piece of ginger should be peeled before it is added to a dish, although this is not necessary if the ginger is to be discarded before serving. Powdered or candied ginger is not a satisfactory substitute for fresh ginger.

Fresh Red or Green Long Hot Peppers 新鮮的紅與青辣椒

Available in Chinese, Italian, and Spanish groceries all year round in a spotty fashion, these peppers may be available for two weeks, then disappear for another two. They will keep in the vegetable compartment of the refrigerator for a week or two in a plastic bag.

Fresh White Bean Curd 豆腐

Pads of this type of bean curd are sold by the piece. They are rather fragile and should be handled carefully. They can be stored in the refrigerator for 2 to 3 days, covered with water—a day or two longer if the water is changed.

Gingko Nuts 白菓

Gingko nuts are sold in 10½-ounce cans. Once opened, they should be covered with water. They will keep for 3 to 4 days in the refrigerator—up to two weeks if the covering water is changed every 3 or 4 days.

Glutinous Rice 糯米

Glutinous rice has smaller grains than ordinary rice. It is sold in 1-, 2-, and 3-pound packages. Like any other cereal, it can be stored indefinitely in a covered canister.

Glutinous Rice Powder 糯米粉

This is glutinous rice milled to a fine powder. It is sold in 1-pound paper packages. It should be stored like ordinary flour and will keep as long.

Ground Bean Sauce 磨原豉

This sauce contains the same ingredients as Bean Sauce, except that the whole beans have been ground to a paste. It is sold in oblong 1-pound cans. Once opened, it will keep for months in the refrigerator if transferred to a clean jar.

Hoi Sin Sauce 海鮮醬

Made from pumpkin, this sweetish sauce comes in 1-pound oblong cans identical to those for Bean Sauce and Ground Bean Sauce. Once opened, it will keep for months in the refrigerator if transferred to a clean screw-top jar.

Hot Dried Red Peppers 乾紅辣椒

These papery dried whole pods of red peppers are sold in 2-ounce or larger plastic bags and are widely available in specialty food stores as well as in Chinese markets. They are also sold in powdered form for use in making homemade Hot Oil.

Hot Oil 辣油

This is commercially available in various-sized bottles. To make your own hot oil, heat 1 cup of peanut, vegetable, or corn oil in a small saucepan just until it starts to smoke. Turn off the heat and wait 30 seconds. Add 6 tablespoons powdered red pepper all at once and stir, then let stand until cool. Pour the oil and residue into a bottle with a tight stopper.

Kao Liang Liqueur 高粱酒

A liqueur made from sorghum, this is not available outside of Chinese wine shops.

Leaf Fat or Leaf Lard 豬板油

The solid fat from the chest of a pig, this can be bought in pork stores and probably from your local butcher if you order it specially. It can be stored for about a week in the refrigerator, and for 2 to 3 months in the freezer. To render leaf fat, cut two pounds of the fat into 1½-inch pieces and put them into a saucepan. Add 1 cup of cold water and bring to a boil. Boil uncovered over medium heat about 30 minutes, or until the oil comes out and the solids are reduced to brown cracklings. (The water boils off.) Watch the fat closely toward the end of the cooking time to be sure it doesn't burn, and press the solids with a spatula to get all the oil out. Spoon out the oil into a jar and discard the solids; the yield is about 3 cups. The hardened rendered fat will keep in the refrigerator for several months.

Licorice Root 乾草

This dried spice solid is sold in Chinese pharmacies by the ounce.

Long Beans 長江豆

A foot-long thin bean which, when cut up and cooked, resembles string beans, this is a seasonal vegetable available in the fall. It will keep in the refrigerator for about a week, wrapped in plastic wrap.

Miniature Ears of Baby Corn 玉筍

These tiny ears of baby corn, 2 to 3 inches in length, are sold in 8- to 19-ounce cans labeled "Young Corn" or "Young Sweet Corn." Once opened, the corn may be stored in the refrigerator covered with its own liquid in a clean covered jar for 4 to 6 days. It will keep an additional 4 to 6 days if the corn is boiled in its own liquid for 30 seconds.

Oyster Sauce 蠔油

A thick sauce made from oysters, this is sold in 8-ounce bottles. It will keep indefinitely in the refrigerator.

Pickled Scallions 甜酸喬頭

These pickles, made with the white bulbs of scallions, are sold in jars. They will keep in the refrigerator almost indefinitely.

Preserved Turnip 冲菜

Sometimes labeled Tai Tau Tsoi or Tsung Tsoi, this moist cured turnip is sold in 8-ounce plastic bags and in 1-pound cans. It is heavily salted, and each piece should be rinsed under running water to rid it of excess salt before proceeding with the recipe.

Raw Shelled and Hulled Fresh Unsalted Peanuts 生花生仁

Sold in 12-ounce plastic bags, these peanuts may be stored for a month or more but will eventually turn rancid. Peanuts should be watched vigilantly while they are being fried, since they burn easily.

Red Bean Curd Sauce 紅荳腐乳

A thick sauce made from soy beans, red rice, and salt water, this is available in 11-ounce oblong cans and also in 12-ounce round cans labeled "Bean Curd."

Red Rice 紅米

A red-dyed raw rice used as food coloring, this is sold loose by the ounce, and is rather expensive. Like ordinary rice, it keeps indefinitely.

Red Wine Rice Paste 紅糟

This sauce is difficult to find in Chinese markets but may be ordered by mail from The Oriental Country Store (see end of chapter for address).

Rendered Chicken Fat 熟鷄油

To melt chicken fat, pull the solid raw fat from the inside of a chicken or purchase it from the butcher. Place it in a mixing bowl and set it in the top of a steamer over boiling water. Cover the steamer and cook until all the oil is rendered—about an hour, depending on the quantity of fat. Strain and discard the solids and refrigerate to harden. Stored in a covered jar, it will last indefinitely under refrigeration.

Rice Powder 粘米粉

A flour made from raw rice, this is sold in 1-pound paper packages. It will keep indefinitely.

Rock Sugar   冰糖

This is sometimes called rock candy. The kind sold in 8- and 16-ounce packages in Chinatown groceries is pale brown in color and is less refined than the white rock sugar sold in candy stores and groceries. It is also considerably cheaper. The candy-store type is a satisfactory substitute, although its use may be complicated by the string on which the rock candy is often threaded.

Rose Wine Spirits   烏梅酒

This liqueur, made from roses, is available in Chinese wine stores.

Salted Duck Eggs   鹹鴨蛋

These eggs are sold individually and will keep without refrigeration for about two weeks. Hard-boiled salted duck eggs make a good accompaniment to congee or soup noodles. Bring one or more of the eggs to a boil in a small saucepan in water to cover and simmer for 1 hour. Cool until the eggs can be handled, then cut into quarters lengthwise, shell and all, and serve on a small dish.

Sesame Oil   蔴油

This reddish-brown oil is sold in 6-ounce bottles and large (almost 2-quart) cans. The more refined light yellow sesame oil sold in Middle Eastern groceries has less flavor and does not make a satisfactory substitute. The oil will keep for a few months without refrigeration but eventually turns rancid.

Sesame Paste   芝蔴醬

Sometimes labeled "Sesame Seed Paste," this is also found in Middle Eastern groceries, where it is called "*taheeni*" or "*tahini*." However, the variety found in 8-ounce jars in Chinese groceries should be used where possible, since it has a stronger flavor. The paste can be kept for several months in the refrigerator.

Sesame Seeds 芝蔴(黑芝蔴白芝蔴)

There are two varieties of these seeds, black and white. Both are sold loose by weight or in 4- or 8-ounce packages.

Shao Hsing Wine 紹興酒

This wine is made from rice and is available in Chinese wine stores. Dry cocktail sherry is an acceptable substitute.

Shark's Fin 魚翅

Two kinds of whole dried shark's fin are sold in Chinese groceries: an unprocessed fin which still has its skin and bone, and a boned and skinned fin that has also been washed. Buy the latter, since the unprocessed fin is too difficult for an amateur to prepare. In buying shark's fin, pick the pieces that are palest in color and clean in appearance. The fin will keep for several months.

Shark's Fin Needles 散魚翅

Packaged shark's fin needles have been cleaned and processed and are somewhat easier to prepare than whole shark's fin. They are sold in ½- and 1-pound packages or boxes.

Shrimp Eggs 蝦子(蝦卵)

Sold by the ounce by Chinese groceries, these are used to add a delicate shrimp flavor to dishes. They are stronger tasting than fresh shrimp but lighter in flavor than dried shrimp.

Snow Peas 雪荳

These peas are prepared and eaten pod and all. When buying them, pick thin pods—the plump ones have matured and will be tough. Snow peas are available all year round, although they are scarcer and more expensive in the winter.

Soy Sauce 醬油

Soy sauce ranges from light to very dark, depending on the brand; the difference lies more in the color than in the flavor. It is sold in bottles ranging from 12 to 21 ounces. The soy sauce generally sold in American supermarkets is light soy sauce—it is most suitable used as a dip or in some stir-fry dishes but in general is too light to lend an appetizing color to a dish. Dark soy sauce, usually found only in Chinese markets, is sometimes labeled "Black Soy." Soy sauce will keep for months and sometimes years without refrigeration.

Spring Roll Skins 春卷皮

These are made by a different process from that used for egg roll skins and produce different results; however, they are sometimes confusingly labeled "Egg Roll Skins." To be sure of getting what you want, ask the shopkeeper in a Chinese grocery for Shanghai spring roll skins. The skins come in both round or square shapes, about 10 to 25 skins to a package. They will keep from three days to a week in the refrigerator if they are securely sealed and wrapped in plastic wrap and then in foil to prevent them from drying out. Once they have dried out, they are very hard to handle.

Star Anise 八角

This spice is generally sold loose or in 4-ounce plastic packages. It will stay fresh indefinitely if it is stored in a tightly sealed container.

Straw Mushrooms 草菇

These mushrooms come in 8-ounce cans. They will keep for 3 days if transferred to a clean lidded container and covered with water—an additional 2 or 3 days if the water is changed.

Szechwan Peppercorns 花椒

These reddish-brown crushed peppercorns are sold loose or in 1-ounce plastic bags. They will keep indefinitely in a tightly sealed container. To make seasoned salt, heat ¼ cup Szechwan peppercorns in a dry skillet. Cook, shaking the skillet, until the peppercorns start to smoke. Put them into the container of an electric blender, add 2 or 3 tablespoons of salt, and blend thoroughly.

Szechwan Preserved Vegetable 榨菜

This canned pickled cabbage is sometimes labeled Chinese Preserved Vegetable, Preserved Szechwan Cabbage, or Jar Choi. Once opened, it will keep for several months if transferred to a clean lidded jar. It is heavily salted, and the excess salt should be rinsed off before the vegetable is used in a recipe.

Tientsin Preserved Vegetable 冬菜

This is cured celery cabbage, sold in plastic bags or in crocks. It will keep for several months without refrigeration, since it is heavily salted. The excess salt should be rinsed off before the vegetable is used in a recipe.

Tiger Lily Stems 黄花

These dried shoots faintly resemble pieces of dry brown noodle. They are sold in 8-ounce plastic bags. Like most dried vegetables, they will keep indefinitely without refrigeration.

Tree Ear Mushrooms 木耳

These delicate black mushrooms are dried and sold in 2-ounce plastic bags. They are not to be confused with cloud ear mushrooms, which look similar, but are bigger and thicker. The dried mushrooms will keep indefinitely without refrigeration.

Water Chestnut Powder 馬蹄粉

This is a flour made from water chestnuts, which is sold in 1-pound boxes. Like any flour, it will keep indefinitely.

Water Chestnuts 馬蹄

Fresh water chestnuts resemble a large brown chestnut; they are sold by the pound in Chinese markets, and are available all year round. Peeled fresh water chestnuts should immediately be placed in cold water to cover; otherwise, they will discolor. They will keep in the refrigerator or outdoors for about a week.

Canned peeled whole water chestnuts are an acceptable substitute for the fresh ones.

Wheat Starch   太白粉

This is sold in 1-pound paper packages. It will keep indefinitely.

White Chinese Turnips   白蘿蔔

These are sausage-shaped root vegetables, large, long, and white with green tops. They are sold individually, by the pound. White turnip will keep for a week in the refrigerator.

White Fungus   銀耳

Sometimes called "silver ears" or "white jelly fungus," this is a dried form of a fungus which grows on trees in Szechwan province. Formerly an expensive delicacy, white fungus is sold in 1-ounce boxes for under two dollars.

Wine Ball or Wine Cube   酒麴

This is sold individually in Chinese groceries. It will keep indefinitely in a dry place.

Winter Melon   冬瓜

This is a pumpkin-size squash with a light green rind, white meat, and a center core of seeds which should be discarded before the melon is cooked. It is sold whole or in slices by the pound. It will keep for up to a week in the refrigerator if it is closely wrapped in plastic film.

Won Ton Skins   雲吞皮

These skins vary from store to store in thickness and also in shape

—they can be round or square. They generally come in 1-pound packages. The thinnest skins obtainable should be used for Won Ton; rolling them through a noodle-making machine, if you have one, improves the finished dish. The thick skins should be used for Shiu May.

SOURCES FOR CHINESE INGREDIENTS

Below is a list of representative stores throughout the country which carry Chinese foodstuffs. The list is only a sampling, and you will find that many specialty and foreign (particularly Middle Eastern and Japanese) food stores in urban areas carry a good assortment of ingredients used in Chinese cooking. Many of these stores also carry Chinese cooking utensils.

California

*Kwong On Lung Company, 686 North Spring Street, Los Angeles, Calif. 90012

Wing Chong Lung Company, 922 South San Pedro Street, Los Angeles, Calif. 90015

Manley Produce, 1101 Grant Avenue, San Francisco, Calif. 94133

Shing Chong and Company, 800 Grant Avenue, San Francisco, Calif. 94108

Illinois

Kam Shing Company, 2246 South Wentworth Avenue, Chicago, Ill. 60616

Shiroma, 1058 West Argyle Street, Chicago, Ill. 60640

Star Market, 3349 North Clark Street, Chicago, Ill. 60657

Massachusetts

Legal Sea Foods Market, 237 Hampshire Street, Cambridge, Mass. 02139

Wing Wing Imported Groceries, 79 Harrison Avenue, Boston, Mass. 02111

Minnesota

Kwong Tung Noodle Manufacturing Company, 326 Cedar Avenue,
Minneapolis, Minn. 55404

New York

Eastern Trading Company, 2801 Broadway, New York, N.Y. 10025
United Supermarket, 84 Mulberry Street, New York, N.Y. 10013
* Wing Fat Company, 35 Mott Street, New York, N.Y. 10013
Wo Fat Company, 16 Bowery, New York, N.Y. 10013
Yuet Hing Market, Inc., 23 Pell Street, New York, N.Y. 10013
* Delicacies Shop, Bloomingdale's, Lexington Avenue and 59th
Street, New York, N.Y. 10022

Ohio

Crestview Food Town, 200 Crestview Street, Columbus, Ohio 43202
International House of Foods, 712 Washington Avenue S.E., Columbus, Ohio 43206

Pennsylvania

Wing On, 1005 Race Street, Philadelphia, Pa. 19107

Texas

Oriental Import-Export Company, 2009 Polk Street, Houston, Texas
77003

The starred (*) stores will fill mail orders. The Oriental Country
Store, 12 Mott Street, New York, N.Y. 10013, sells Chinese cooking
utensils. It will also fill orders for Chinese ingredients by mail only.
A catalog is available on request, and it will also undertake to fill
orders for nonperishable items not presently listed in the catalog.

Index